Samuel Colcord Bartlett

Life and Death Eternal

A Refutation of the Theory of Annihilation

Samuel Colcord Bartlett

Life and Death Eternal
A Refutation of the Theory of Annihilation

ISBN/EAN: 9783337389130

Printed in Europe, USA, Canada, Australia, Japan

Cover: Foto ©Lupo / pixelio.de

More available books at **www.hansebooks.com**

LIFE AND DEATH ETERNAL:

A REFUTATION

OF THE

THEORY OF ANNIHILATION.

BY SAMUEL C. BARTLETT, D.D.,

PROFESSOR IN CHICAGO THEOLOGICAL SEMINARY.

PUBLISHED BY THE
AMERICAN TRACT SOCIETY,
28 CORNHILL, BOSTON.

Entered, according to Act of Congress, in the year 1866, by
THE AMERICAN TRACT SOCIETY,
In the Clerk's Office of the District Court of the District of Massachusetts.

BOSTON:
Geo. C. Rand & Avery, Stereotypers and Printers.

PREFACE.

This volume was prepared at the earnest solicitation of many persons who found no full and satisfactory reply to the specious arguments of annihilationists, and who were greatly troubled at their industrious efforts to diffuse the system. It was nearly completed more than two years since, and only lacked a final revision preparatory to publication. But a sudden and long-continued pressure of other duties has prevented that revision until the present time. Meanwhile, no considerable change has taken place in the aspect of the case, and no new treatise of any account has appeared. But the heresy has been laboriously disseminating itself. Its ablest advocate in this country travels about, selling his own books, and boasting of a larger number of adherents among educated men than we suppose the facts will warrant. But we do receive information from various quarters, that many simple-minded persons are led astray by the sophistry. Among our Baptist brethren, we hear of some very considerable movements, as in Gratiot County, Mich., where the sect has gained strength enough to attempt the building of a church. And, in the denomination to which the writer belongs, we have not forgotten the development at a recent council held in Portland, Me.

The spread of this error differs somewhat from that of Universalism. The latter has never, in this country, made any considerable progress among devout persons. Individual cases may perhaps be mentioned of seemingly pious and spiritual men who have accepted the belief of universal salvation. But the great mass of its advocates have been those who have manifested no religious life whatever. It is otherwise with the present system. We are told that it has, in many instances, ensnared men of unquestioned piety.

The chief plausibility of the argument for annihilation lies upon the surface; and its greatest force is felt by those who have never analyzed language so much as to reflect upon the idioms that constantly flow from their own lips, and that run through the word of God. To this class of men there is presented a set of phrases, carefully detached from all other subjects and all other similar uses, and they are startled, as it were, into an entire misapprehension of the forms of speech familiar from their childhood; just as a man, who for the first time looks through a powerful microscope, is confounded by the appearance of the insect that has been buzzing round him all day long. To this class of men, most of the arguments for annihilation are addressed; and from them largely, we believe, are its adherents drawn. There are others, however, of more reading and mental culture; and arguments have been written for them also, — arguments presented with much parade of learning, yet making no scruple to deny some of the plainest facts in the history of opinion, and to accumulate the most heterogeneous monstrosities and incompatible fallacies in interpreting the word of God.

It has been found necessary, in the present discussion, to attempt the somewhat difficult task of meeting the wants of two quite different classes, — to frame an argument intelligible to "plain people," and satisfactory to the more scholarly and critical. It is hoped that each class will be indulgent to the other. The writer would have preferred to retain the work still longer in his hands, for improvement in various respects. But the friends who have called for it are impatient of delay, and the want is thought to be pressing. His own labors are meanwhile imperatively demanded in other directions. He is willing, therefore, to issue the work as it is, for the purpose of doing good, rather than to retain it for the sake of higher elaboration. Should any portions of the discussion seem to require further confirmation, modification, expansion, or abridgment, it may be done hereafter as experience shall dictate.

In the general correctness of his statements, and the entire soundness of his main positions, the writer has absolute confidence. In the multiplicity of topics considered, however, he can not hope to have escaped some minor oversights not affecting the validity of the argument. Any such blemishes will be cheerfully corrected on being pointed out.

This volume is not written in reply to any one writer. As matter of fact, more allusions will be found to the writings of Mr. C. F. Hudson than of any other author; for the reason that Mr. Hudson, having devoted the labor of years to the subject, has presented by far the most respectable work in advocacy of the doctrine of annihilation. His chief treatise, "Debt and Grace," unquestionably combines a great amount of labor, and a very high degree of dexterity in the presentation. It has been customary for some evangelical writers to praise the fairness and candor of his discussion; commendations which we can account for only on the supposition that the writers have never followed him, as we have done, through any considerable number of his quotations and interpretations. We have made no attempt at a review and criticism of his procedures, except in a few instances where it lay very directly in our way. To do so would require a larger volume than his own, and would change the character of the discussion.

We have commonly employed the term "annihilation" to designate the cessation of existence which these writers advocate. We are aware that many of them object to the term as not being fully expressive of *their* mode of stating and arguing the case. We would only say that we can not be debarred the use of a convenient, indeed an indispensable, term, out of deference to their preferences. We state their views and arguments fairly and fully; and it will be found, we trust, that the validity of our reasoning does not at all hinge upon the name by which we characterize the system.

It will be observed that we do not devote any of our discussion to the natural evidence of immortality. The argument seemed to us sufficient without it. We have shown that the Scriptures actually and historically involve the doctrine. We might, like others, have taken the ground that the Scriptures could assume it as the belief of the race. *For, as matter of fact, the race have believed it.* We certainly have testimony showing that the expectation of another life existed throughout the tribes of the Western Continent, from Greenland to Patagonia. African tribes, New-Zealanders, Feejees, Sandwich-Islanders, Kamtschadales, Philippine-Islanders, Papuans, Borneans, Chinese, have held the belief in all parts of the world. It was the doctrine of the ancient Vedas and of the Egyptian monuments; it lies embedded in the Greek and Roman mythologies; it was held by Persian, Etruscan, Celt, Gaul, and Scandinavian. In modified forms, it is received by five hundred million Brahminists and Buddhists to-day. The exceptions are apparently limited to two classes: First, *perhaps*, certain tribes too degraded to have developed the full functions of humanity; secondly, certain individuals and sects in very advanced states of society, who have deliberately trained themselves as doubters, as the Epicureans of Greece and Rome, the Sadducees of Judea, the Revolutionists of France, and the Annihilationists of England and America.

How the human race have so universally attained this belief, thus shown to be natural, it is not important here to indicate. We believe it to be not so much the result of speculative reasonings as of a pressure on the moral nature. Just as God's own existence is revealed *practically* to every man in that inner authority, that irrepressible law of right which saith, "Thou shalt, and thou shalt not;" so he intimates a future state *practically*, by the irresistible apprehensions of a guilty conscience, by the yearnings for immortality which are restrained only by those fears, and which throb again in the holy, and by the natural sense of the necessity of another state to rectify the inequalities of this. These intuitive impressions, no doubt, are subsequently re-enforced by arguments drawn from various sources. But the conviction is older than the arguments.

CHICAGO, June, 1866.

CONTENTS.

PART I.

REFUTATION OF THE ARGUMENTS ADVANCED IN SUPPORT OF THE ANNIHILATION OF THE WICKED.

CHAPTER I.

THE DOCTRINE OF ANNIHILATION STATED.

The doctrine of eternal punishment generally admitted to be in the Bible. A few deniers, who are in threefold conflict with each other,— Universalists, Restorationists, Annihilationists. The latter differ. The whole question one of fact and testimony. God the only witness, and the Scriptures his testimony. Annihilation appeals only subordinately to Scripture, and with a narrow range. It depends on a few perverted phrases...... 15

CHAPTER II.

THE FUNDAMENTAL VICE OF THE SCRIPTURE ARGUMENT FOR ANNIHILATION.

The Bible speaks in the idioms of the common people: figurative on all subjects. On one subject, annihilationism *materializes*. Jacob Blain. The process of human speech: first, outward and physical. Spiritual phenomena symbolized by material. Examples from common life. Material interpretation contradicts the real meaning. Examples of Scripture phraseology; never misunderstood by common readers; fully recognized on all other subjects; wrenched out of all analogy on this. The same process would find a material God, and did find an earthly Messianic kingdom in the Bible... 23

CHAPTER III.

THE SCRIPTURE ARGUMENT FOR ANNIHILATION EXAMINED.— DEATH AND LIFE.

The words "death" and "life" comprehensively describe the two destinies; therefore are frequently, but not exclusively employed. Every such instance is quoted by annihilationists to prove extinction of the sinner. 1. But they do not even literally, and in the lower sense, signify the continuance or cessation of existence. 2. They also have in all languages a higher or pregnant sense. Instances from common life, classical usage, and the Scriptures. All involve a common element of meaning; only the Scriptures propose a higher aim of *living.* 3. In the Scriptures, the terms denote spiritual conditions, with their adjuncts and issues. The terms singularly appropriate and natural. Philo Judæus. The origin of the usage found in Gen. iii. The passage interprets itself. This mode of utterance runs through the Bible; life, eternal life, death, the second death. Indisputable instances considered: Luke xv. 24, 32; 1 Tim. v. 6; Matt. viii. 22; Rev. iii, 1; Eph. ii. 1-6; Col. ii. 13 (modified use of Eph. iii. 3; Rom. vi. 1, 11); John v. 24; 1 John iii. 14, 15; John vi. 47; Gal. ii. 19, 20; John xi. 25, 26; viii. 51; 1 Tim. vi. 19; John iii. 36. Life begins at regeneration (Rom. vi. 4, 14; Eph. v. 14). Consists in the true knowledge of God (John xvii. 3). Scholarly commentators of all classes accept this interpretation. Life may be viewed in its beginning or its consummation, therefore under variant aspects. The whole usage sustained by the phrase "kingdom of heaven," in all respects. Analagous representations of a present sonship — a union to Christ or separation from him — health and disease — liberty and slavery. This usage of life and death abundant in the Bible. The states are very often viewed in their consummation, as states of pre-eminent blessedness or woe. No objection that the words are used also in the lower sense of physical life and death. Sarcasms of Blain and Hudson superfluous. Their evasive assumptions, that "life" is made merely synonymous with happiness, and "death" merely the punishment of sin by sin. Chief method of evasion, *prolepsis.* Alleged instances examined, and the argument refuted. Hudson involves himself in contradictions, and virtually yields the point. The case summed up.. 36

CHAPTER IV.

THE SCRIPTURE ARGUMENT EXAMINED. — "DESTRUCTION" AND OTHER TERMS.

Annihilationists attempt to press several other words and phrases to their support. The attempt refuted in the following instances: destroy and destruction; perish and perdition; lose and lost; consume and devour; tear in pieces, break in pieces; grind to powder; cut off; blot out; not be; be as nothing; be nought; end; burn; burn up; put under his feet. The futility of the annihilationist argument shown by numerous quotations from the mouth of Job, who, while uttering them, should have been extinct more than twenty times over................................... 92

CHAPTER V.

THE SCRIPTURE ARGUMENT EXAMINED.— THE RESURRECTION AND THE SECOND DEATH.

Promises of a blessed resurrection perverted into promises of a "resurrection state" (John vi. 39, 40; Luke xx. 35; Phil. iii. 11). The fallacy refuted, and the tables turned. The fact of any resurrection for the wicked an ominous difficulty to annihilationists. Confession of Mr. Hudson. Confusion among the advocates: some deny the fact. Hudson reduces it to a minimum. An unsuccessful attempt to rise. The second death. Alleged *literal* sense. Hudson resorts to the Rabbins of later date, with no clear usage nor definite result. The New Testament capable of explaining itself. The phrase occurs four times, in one of which (Rev. xxi. 8), it is explained as "having their part" in the lake of fire; elsewhere described as a place of perpetual torment. This view sustained by Rev. xx. 14, 15. The latter passage discussed. 117

CHAPTER VI.

THE RATIONAL ARGUMENT EXAMINED.

The chief reliance of the system. Quotations from Hudson and Hastings. Arguments from the nature of evil, and the nature of God. Evil alleged to be (1) not necessary in God's universe, (2) frail in its own nature. Fallaciousness of the positions. The argument from God's attributes answered negatively from our incompetency to decide for him; and positively from existing facts: sin is and has been here from the creation. Its eternal continuance involves no different principle. Common misapprehension refuted by Dr. Whately, — not the amount of evil, but its existence, constitutes the difficulty. Its continuance for a time proves its continuance for eternity to be compatible with God's perfections, if sufficient reasons exist. Will the reasons cease? What are they? The present aspect of the case an overwhelming refutation. The triumph over sin. John Foster quoted, and refuted by himself..................... 129

PART II.

POSITIVE DISPROOF OF THE DOCTRINE OF ANNIHILATION.

CHAPTER I.

BELIEF OF A FUTURE EXISTENCE AMONG THE EARLIER JEWS.

The inquiry important. Belief of another state of existence familiar to the Jews from ancient times. 1. Their residence in Egypt must have made them conversant with it. It existed in Egypt. Proof not alone from historic testimony, but from the surviving records,— papyrus-rolls, mummy-cases, tombs. Wilkinson, Bunsen, Lepsius, Röth. 2. The Hebrew doctrine of the soul lays a foundation for it. The animating spirit everywhere distinguished from the earthly body. Quotations. 3. Another sphere of existence early indicated in the translation of Enoch; the testimony repeated in the case of Elijah. 4. The patriarchs are gathered to their fathers. The meaning of the statement proved by incontrovertible cases. Admitted by scholars of all schools. Baumgarten, Gerlach, Knobel, Delitzsch. 5. The present life was reckoned a pilgrimage. 6. The practice of invoking the dead required to be forbidden by law. A monarch violates the law of his kingdom. 7. Distinct references are made to the other world as a scene of retribution. Clear instances.— Ps. xvi., xvii., lxviii., xlix.; Eccl. xii. 13, 14; Dan. xii. 2, 3, and others. 143

CHAPTER II.

BELIEF OF A FUTURE EXISTENCE AMONG THE JEWS AT CHRIST'S COMING.

The fact susceptible of clear proof by secular and sacred writers. Josephus on the Pharisees, Essenes, and Sadducees. His own remonstrance with his comrades, and other passages. The attempt to impeach the testimony of Josephus refuted at large. The testimony of Tacitus imperfectly given by Hudson. The testimony of Philo, very full and explicit. Paul's allusion to the Jewish doctrine (Acts xxiv. 15). Other implications in the New Testament of the general admission of a future existence for all (Luke xx. 27-33; Acts xxiii. 5-8; Matt. xxii. 23; John xi. 24). John the Baptist "risen" (Matt. xiv. 2).................................. 168

CHAPTER III.

NEW TESTAMENT TEACHINGS. — IMMORTALITY. — IMMEDIATE DESTINY.

The Saviour and his apostles, finding the doctrine of twofold retribution, were not called upon to announce the fact as a new teaching. Naturally dwelt on the characters to which these retributions should be assigned. Had no occasion to dilate on an abstract immortality, but only on a concrete retribution. "The immortal soul:" cavil of Hastings and Hudson answered. The Scripture view and mode of speech; deals with the actual fate of men hereafter. The Scriptures affirm the conscious existence of both classes after death, and prior to the resurrection. 1. The righteous (1) might enjoy celestial glories without the body (2 Cor. xii. 3); (2) would enjoy them if separated from the body (Phil. i. 21-24; 2 Cor. v. 1-9); (3) and do enter on them at once after death (Luke xxiii. 42, 43). Perversions refuted (Acts vii. 55-60); (4) spirits of departed believers are with God (Heb. xii. 23; vi. 12; Rev. xiv. 13; vi. 9-11). 2. The wicked pass immediately to their doom. Analogy from the fate of fallen angels. Specific indications (Acts i. 25; 1 Pet. iii. 18-20; Luke xvi. 19-31). Objections and evasions. Hudson, Hastings, Blain, Burnham, Storrs, Whately. 2 Pet. ii. 9..... 189

CHAPTER IV.

A RESURRECTION AND A JUDGMENT FOR THE WICKED.

Death leaves both classes of men in a state of existence and of consciousness. The Scriptures follow them further, to the judgment and the final retribution. The doctrine of a general judgment. Hinted at in the Old Testament; revealed in the New. The last day universal; the wicked will be present. The judgment preceded by the resurrection of the wicked as well as the good. Proofs. Cavils. The momentous significance of the resurrection. Embarrasses the annihilationists. Hastings admits the difficulty. Others deny the fact. Some evade. Hudson's resurrection. 231

CHAPTER V.

NEW TESTAMENT TEACHINGS. — SHARING THE DOOM OF SATAN.

Companions in the doom of the wicked; the fallen angels. Scriptures decisive. The doom of fallen angels is suffering, incessant and endless. Proof-texts. Replies of Dobney, Blain, Ellis and Read, Hudson. Marvelous interpretations, — "dramatic" annihilation. Satan's doom. Bruising the serpent's head. The utterances of the Apocalypse sustained by the gospels. The abyss; deep; bottomless-pit; lake of fire. Result. 249

CHAPTER VI.

NEW TESTAMENT TEACHINGS. — DIRECT DECLARATIONS. — FUTURE PUNISHMENT CONSISTS IN SUFFERING.

The question is not left to inference. The Scriptures unfold in detail the meaning of their own threats. Degrees of punishment involve the fact of conscious suffering. The difficulty felt. Reply of Dobney, Hastings, and others. Its insufficiency and inconsistency. The sufferings of the wicked vary like the joys of the righteous. The direct statements of the New Testament lay the whole emphasis of the punishment on the suffering involved. Instances. Whatever the figure, the suffering is the main feature. "Outer darkness" attended with "gnashing of teeth." The "furnace of fire;" the "portion with hypocrites;" exclusion from the kingdom; all coupled with the same description. "Torment" in the lake of fire. Evasions. The unquenchable fire. Various evasions considered. Everlasting punishment. The words vacated of their proper meaning by annihilationists. Their devices examined. Other passages........ 264

CHAPTER VII.

NEW TESTAMENT TEACHINGS. — SUFFERINGS PROTRACTED AND ENDLESS.

The Scriptures teach not only suffering in the future, but that suffering protracted and endless. In various modes, 1. Passages which involve the representation without using the words "everlasting," etc. (Matt. v. 25; xviii. 34, 35; xii. 31, 32). 2. Passages which employ the terms "eternal," etc. (Matt. iii. 12; Mark ix. 43–48; Matt. xxv. 41, 46; xviii. 8; Jude 7; 2 Thes. i. 9; Jude 6; Mark iii. 29; Heb. vi. 1, 2; Jude 13; 2 Pet. ii. 17; Rev. xiv. 11; xix. 3; xx. 10). The terms discussed, and evasions refuted at length. Limited duration, eternity of effect, or finality, alleged instances of "finality" (Heb. v. 9; vi. 2; ix. 12; xiii. 20; Philem. 15; Rev. xiv. 6). 3. The suffering of the wicked coeval and co-eternal with the happiness of the righteous. Simultaneous with it (Luke xiii. 24–30; Matt. viii. 11, 12; Rev. xxii. 14, 15; and other passages). Co-eternal (Matt. xxv. 34–41, 46; 2 Thess. i. 7–11)......................... 298

CHAPTER VIII.

TENDENCIES AND AFFINITIES OF THE SYSTEM OF ANNIHILATION.

Theories show their character in their influences and affinities. Time is requisite, and freedom from outer restraint. This system too young to have a history. But its tendencies already betray themselves. 1. Rationalism: a disposition to disparage and over-ride God's Word. Quotations from Hudson, Ellis and Read, Blain, Hastings, Burnham. 2. Sympathy with the Universalist and infidel, and concessions to them. Employing their modes of argument. Conceding the validity of their positions as against orthodoxy. Quotations. 3. Materialism: the denial of the spirit's existence. Storrs, Blain, Ellis and Read, openly renounce the belief of any soul distinct from the body and its functions. Quotations. The fact deprecated by Hudson. 4. Gross sensualism. Conclusion......... 334

APPENDIX.

NOTE A.	Extracts on Life and Death............................	359
NOTE B.	The meaning of Phil. i. 21–24.........................	361
NOTE C.	Hades..	364
NOTE D.	Misinterpretation of Dan. xii. 2.......................	366
NOTE E.	Perversion of Rev. xx. 10..............................	368
NOTE F.	Unquenchable Fire......................................	374
NOTE G.	The meaning of κόλασις................................	377
NOTE H.	Gehenna..	381
NOTE I.	The Book of Enoch on future punishment............	385

LIFE AND DEATH ETERNAL.

ERRATA.

Page 201, line 4, for "Bergel," read *Bengel*.
" 232, " 15, for "ever," read *even*.
" 247, " 1, strike out the semi-colon, and for "though," read *through*.
" 253, " 5, for "weariness," read *mariners*.
" 276, " 25, for "simply," read *simple*.
" 312, " 15, for "applied," read *supplied*.
" 356, " 18, for "documents," read *doctrines*
" 376, " 40, for "Fonteio," read *Fonteia*.

CHAPTER VII.

NEW TESTAMENT TEACHINGS. — SUFFERINGS PROTRACTED AND ENDLESS.

The Scriptures teach not only suffering in the future, but that suffering protracted and endless. In various modes, 1. Passages which involve the representation without using the words "everlasting," etc. (Matt. v. 25; xviii. 34, 35; xii. 31, 32). 2. Passages which employ the terms "eternal," etc. (Matt. iii. 12; Mark ix. 43–48; Matt. xxv. 41, 46; xviii. 8; Jude 7; 2 Thes. i. 9; Jude 6; Mark iii. 29; Heb. vi. 1, 2; Jude 13; 2 Pet. ii. 17; Rev. xiv. 11; xix. 3; xx. 10). The terms discussed, and evasions refuted at length. Limited duration, eternity of effect, or finality, alleged instances of "finality" (Heb. v. 9; vi. 2; ix. 12; xiii. 20; Philem. 15; Rev. xiv. 6). 3. The suffering of the wicked coeval and co-eternal with the happiness of the righteous. Simultaneous with it (Luke xiii. 24–30; Matt. viii. 11, 12; Rev. xxii. 14, 15; and other passages). Co-eternal (Matt. xxv. 34–41, 46; 2 Thess. i. 7–11)............................ 298

CHAPTER VIII.

TENDENCIES AND AFFINITIES OF THE SYSTEM OF ANNIHILATION.

Theories show their character in their influences and affinities. Time is

LIFE AND DEATH ETERNAL.

LIFE AND DEATH ETERNAL.

PART I.

CHAPTER I.

THE DOCTRINE OF ANNIHILATION STATED.

THE great mass of believers in the divine inspiration and authority of the Bible, in all ages, have understood that book plainly to assert the endless misery of the wicked. Open rejecters of the divine authority of the volume, men of scholarship and ability, priding themselves upon accepting no man's statement at second hand, have also declared that doctrine to be among the things that "Jesus taught."*

By the general admission of friend and foe, that doctrine is in the Scriptures. It is there, not as the central doctrine of the scheme of grace, nor as the vital truth on which depends the soul's regeneration and sanctification, but as the dark back-ground of that scheme of grace, — a solemn feature of God's government, and a fact of momentous import to the human

---

* "I believe that Jesus Christ taught eternal torment: . . . I do not accept it on his authority." — THEODORE PARKER'S "Two Sermons," p. 14.

race. Its aspect is confessedly terrific. The thought of it is appalling, and sometimes confounding, even to those who are safe from its power; while those who claim no such protection can not fail to look upon it with dread and aversion. If the fact could be set aside from God's government by the vote of his sinning subjects, it would at once be stricken out by an overwhelming majority. It is not surprising that the doctrine should be resisted; that some should reject the volume that contains it; and that others, constrained to receive the book, should labor hard to clear it of the doctrine. Accordingly, in the midst of this general agreement, there have arisen from time to time individuals and bodies of men who have denied that the doctrine of endless misery is in the word of God.

But here appears a singular phenomenon: the opposers can not agree among themselves. They are at irreconcilable odds. They say, "The Bible does not teach that the destiny of the wicked is endless suffering." We ask them, "What, then, does it declare to be their future destiny?" And the first and largest body of them answer, "Suffering, we know not how protracted and severe, but final restoration to holiness and happiness." Another portion boldly say, "No punishment at all hereafter; but all men at death enter on a state of happiness." And here comes a third section, who, with equal boldness and positiveness, aver that God's word teaches neither the future suffering and recovery, nor the immediate blessedness, of the wicked, but their complete extinction. Antagonism could not be more total than it is between the advocates of final

Restoration, of extreme Universalism, and of Annihilation. The fact is significant; the great body of interpreters, friend and foe, agreeing as to the clear teaching of the Bible on this subject; a minority denying, but propounding instead three separate doctrines, as contradictory to each other as to that which they deny!

The present discussion concerns only the third of these three errors, — the theory which teaches the annihilation of the impenitent wicked. The fundamental doctrine common to the advocates of the theory is this: The death with which God threatened sin, and which actually became the doom of the sinful race, was absolute extinction of being. Only believers in Christ are delivered from this doom; and immortality is the "eternal life" which was promised to his followers.

In the subordinate doctrines, the advocates of annihilation are not agreed. Most of their writers hold that this extinction of being takes place when the body dies; the soul or spirit being nothing more than the *life* of the man. Thus says Jacob Blain, "The Bible plainly tells us that men and beasts are made of the same material, 'dust;' and that both have the 'same breath;' and that they both die alike, — but, mark, a resurrection is not told for both." Again: "The existence of a soul or spirit as an entity within us is only inferred from a few uncertain texts, which can be explained another way; while numerous plain texts and the sense of the Bible are against it."* Thomas Read lays down as one of his main positions,

---

* Death, not Life, pp. 30, 42.

"The corporeal being and mortality of the soul, and the nature of the spirit of man; which spirit, not being a living entity, is neither mortal nor immortal;" and affirms, that "no conscious spirit or soul survives the death of man."* George Storrs, in discussing the question, "Does the Bible teach that the creature, man, which the Lord God formed of the dust of the ground, has a superadded entity called the soul?" says, "*We take the negative;*" † and again: "I regard the phrase 'immaterial,' as one which properly belongs to the things which *are not;* a sound without sense or meaning; a mere cloak to hide the nakedness of the theory of an immortal soul in man." ‡ Zenas Campbell declares that "no Scripture or philosophy has ever yet been shown to prove the mind any thing more than an attribute of the living, organized dust; and if so, it must cease with the life of the body." § Thus the whole being becomes extinct at death. At the resurrection, God re-organizes the body, and endows it with its former active and thinking powers: the righteous then live on for ever; and the wicked are again blotted out of existence,—which is the second death. Some of the writers speak doubtfully about the resurrection of the wicked, or even deny it.

H. L. Hastings not only holds to the resurrection of the wicked, but intimates that their complete extinction may occupy a protracted and unknown period thereafter. ||

---

* Bible *vs.* Tradition, pp. 13, 121.
† Discussion between Prof. H. Mattison and George Storrs, p. 4.
‡ Six Sermons, by George Storrs, p. 29.
§ The Age of Gospel Light.
|| Retribution, or The Doom of the Ungodly, pp. 77, 153.

C. F. Hudson teaches that the sentence is executed in two installments,— the dissolution of the body first, then the extinction of the soul at the time of resurrection. Rejecting the extreme materialism of his coadjutors, he holds that the soul may require the body as the necessary means of its activity. An intermediate state or "detention" receives all souls on parting from the body,— a state of inaction, which, at its close, may seem to have been but momentary, and to which, in the case of the righteous, he applies the phrase "fallen asleep" in Christ; from which at the resurrection, the just are called forth to be clothed with a glorified body, and to enter on immortal activity; and from which, like a damaged seed that exhausts its vitality and perishes in the act of germination, the unjust start up at the voice of God to become extinct in the very act.*

The whole question thus at issue is a question of fact. The only valid testimony concerning it must be the declaration of Him who holds the destiny of the soul in his hands. For as no being on earth can pretend to have witnessed events that lie still in the future, so none can testify what they shall be, except Him on whose sole decision they depend. Nor can any man, from his general estimate of God's character, affirm what definite thing God will do. It would require a knowledge of God's whole being, resources, views, intentions, of his entire plan of government, with all its necessities and peculiarities, more thoroughly exhaustive than one man ever yet possessed concerning a fellow-man, his equal. To declare con-

---

* Debt and Grace, pp. 263-4.

fidently what God will do with the finally impenitent, aside from his own declaration, is to put ourselves in the place of God. In the absence of all communications from him, the judgments of our reason and the anticipations of our moral nature would be entitled to some respect, more or less. Reason has expressed her *apprehensions* of a coming retribution. But to give positive testimony as to the facts or methods of the case is beyond her province; much more, to speak in opposition to God's testimony.

We repeat it, God is the only competent witness on this subject. If therefore we accept the Scriptures as the word of God, and if the Scriptures have spoken on this subject, it is in the highest degree reprehensible to draw our decisive views on this subject from any other source, or to override their fair testimony by any other considerations. Against sound testimony mere speculations are never of any account: against the testimony of God they are preposterous.

Our appeal, then, is to the Scriptures. The advocates of annihilation profess to make this appeal, but often in such a way as to show that the decisive consideration lies elsewhere. Thus Mr. Hudson, who has written far the most elaborate treatise in defense of the doctrine, in a volume of four hundred and seventy pages devotes but sixty-seven to the scriptural argument, which lies embedded in a great mass of other matter, and seems to form but a limited part of his reliance. Stimulated, however, by the remark of a reviewer who called attention to this circumstance, the same writer subsequently published a separate volume of Scripture arguments "*to meet the convenience of* *those who rely, for their views of future life, upon their reading and interpretation of the Scriptures.*" In the preface, from which we quote, he also adds, that he " doubts if an exclusively scriptural argument will prove satisfactory to very many, however clearly it may appear to be made out."* This is a confession indeed. The treatises of Blain and others, though in form more scriptural, are sprinkled with remarks which indicate that certain rational considerations are allowed great weight in determining the question. These considerations will receive some attention in the course of this discussion. But the first business is to examine the testimony of the Scriptures.

Now, all the plausibility there is in the scriptural argument for annihilation consists of two main features: first, the constant restriction of the phrase " eternal life," with its opposite, " death," to denote simply continued existence and cessation of existence respectively, in violation alike of the common use and the clear Scripture use of the words ; and, secondly, the attempt to confine certain other expressions, setting forth the punitive anger of God in vivid and terrific material imagery, down to the lowest *sensual* aspect of those figurative expressions. Among these phrases are the following: to be destroyed or lost, to perish, to be devoured, to be consumed, slain, cut off, torn in pieces, broken to pieces, dashed in pieces, crushed, ground to powder, burned, or burned up, cut in sunder, to be as nothing, to be as ashes, to be put away as dross ; perdition, end, corruption. All these diverse, and, if literally taken, conflicting modes of representation are

---

* Christ our Life, preface, p. 3.

cited as conveying the one meaning of annihilation. These several modes of expression will be examined in due time. Meanwhile it becomes necessary to say something concerning the genuine methods of representation employed in the Scriptures, and concerning the radical fallacy with which those representations are treated by the advocates of annihilation.

CHAPTER II.

THE FUNDAMENTAL VICE OF THE SCRIPTURE ARGUMENT FOR ANNIHILATION.

THE Scriptures everywhere speak in the language of the people. They never employ metaphysical terms, but constantly set forth the most thoroughly spiritual facts by means of such sense images as the common people always use and understand. It is a book not for the metaphysicians, but for the millions. Its language and idioms throughout are conformed to those of the multitude. As it is the universal custom to speak of men as elevated, cast down, sunk, overthrown, wounded, stung, cut to the heart, broken, broken down, broken up, devoured, consumed, eaten up, shattered, crushed, and the like, to denote purely spiritual phenomena, which leave the entire being of the man unimpaired; precisely so the Scriptures speak in the language of men. Abundant expressions of this general nature are found extending through the Old and New Testaments. Indeed, it is mostly by such figurative expressions, — and that too, as will presently be shown, from the necessity of the case, — that all the leading truths concerning God's dealings and man's destiny are communicated. They are employed, not alone respecting the destiny of the wicked, but concerning the enjoyments of the righteous, and all the other themes of the word of God.

Now, the grand mistake of the system under discussion is, that its advocates single out one topic from the whole mass of themes, and violate here the whole usage of the Bible to maintain their tenet. Men who see in a moment the folly of understanding literally the statement that David's soul "thirsteth," "panteth," "melteth," and is "poured out," or that the righteous are to attend a literal wedding-feast, where they shall eat and drink, and recline in Abraham's bosom, lay aside all the settled laws of speech when they reach this one subject, — the future destiny of the wicked. Terms that are plainly metaphorical, or terms that are used in a secondary or pregnant sense, they insist on forcing down to a narrow and sensuous meaning, which is inconsistent alike with the general tenor of Scripture phraseology, *and with the use of these very phrases* in other passages. On this one subject, the future destiny of the wicked, they persistently degrade all phraseology to a gross, material meaning. If a term has both a lower and a higher signification, in this connection they insist upon the lower. If a term significant of spiritual facts had a sensuous origin, — as nearly all such terms have had, — they maintain that the sensuous meaning must still cling to it. If a figure of speech vividly presenting the vehemence of God's vengeance, and the intensity of its impression, be drawn — as from the nature of the case it must be — from objects and scenes in which intensity of action produces disorganization, the system seizes on that mere material and incidental feature, the disorganization, and refuses to see all the deeper significance of the description. It takes nothing but the husk. No language, much less an oriental tongue, will bear such treatment. It is simply a materializing of human speech; rather it takes away the life, and leaves but the carcass.

A notable, though somewhat extreme illustration of this process appears in the argument of Mr. Blain in regard to the nature of the spirit, or soul. He finds that the Hebrew and Greek words meaning spirit (one of which he invariably misspells) have an original meaning of "breath," that the Greek word "soul," sometimes means life; and on this basis, in defiance of the insuperable evidence to the contrary, and with a heavy rebuke of our "careless translators," and the "folly of our popular expositions," he boldly maintains that the Bible declares the spirit to be but the breath, and the soul but the life, of the body.* The argument, of course, is precisely the same as if one should maintain, that, because the English words "spirit" and "soul" are derived from words signifying to breathe and to blow, therefore the whole body of English theologians believe the soul, or spirit, to be but the breath; and that, when the heart is spoken of as the fountain of sin and the seat of holiness, we mean to refer those qualities to that physical organ in the human body which carries on the circulation of the blood.

It may be well to glance at the process of human speech in all such subjects. The primary reference of all, or nearly all, language seems to have been outward and physical. Outward observation is the earliest and most universal exercise of the human faculties. Material things require first to be named, and material acts to be described. Accordingly, the basis of all

---

* Death, not Life, pp. 27-42.

speech is sensuous, and its primary meaning external and concrete. Intellectual and spiritual existences, facts, and transactions, more slowly attract the attention, and are with more difficulty apprehended and described. In thinking of them, men are accustomed to aid their thoughts by viewing them under the analogies of the material things so much more familiar to them. Under such analogies, they represent them to others. Thus it has come to pass that the terms which now undeniably designate spiritual phenomena, are words originally of physical origin and use, transferred to a secondary and higher meaning. Sometimes they have entirely lost their primary reference; sometimes they retain it in connection with the other and higher meanings. So, also, the longer forms of statement, whereby mental states, emotions, acts, and results are set forth, are almost of necessity analogical. It is peculiarly so in the more concrete and simple languages, and in addresses of a popular cast. Indeed it would puzzle a metaphysician to describe a state of high mental emotion in any other way. His statements, when analyzed, would prove to be a series of physical metaphors, while yet he is speaking of mental phenomena.

Thus, to perceive, was, by origin, to take through; to conceive, to take together; to imagine, to have an image; to apprehend, to lay hold of; to reflect, to turn back; to excite, to summon forth; to provoke, to call forth. So with a multitude of words of Latin origin. In the Saxon usage, a man of hot blood is a passionate man; a man of good blood is of good descent, or ancestry; a man of nerve is a firm man. Heart stands continually for affection or feeling, and brain for intellect. Stiff-necked is obstinate. To be keen, sharp, dull, heavy, to have a long head, a thick skin, a heavy hand, a sharp tongue, a foul mouth, are designations of intellectual and moral traits, though the form of speech has a purely physical aspect. A man is broken down with sorrow, crushed with calamity, lacerated with grief, rent with anguish, melted with emotion, when every faculty of mind and body is sound and whole. He is prostrated with fear, is irretrievably fallen, is ruined, not in body but in soul, when yet the substance and all the powers of his soul remain untouched. He is eaten up by avarice, racked with anxiety, devoured by ambition, consumed with lust, sunk in vice, drowned in sorrow, burned up with fierce and evil passions, — and that, too, when his being and all its essential functions are so far from extinct, that they are in a state of the most intense activity.

These last-mentioned phrases illustrate, to one who has through all his life heard and used such common idioms of speech without ever having carefully examined them, several important principles: First, that the use of strongly sensuous expressions concerning immaterial facts and phenomena is in no danger of misleading the common mind, but is the necessary mode of setting forth those subjects in their intensity. Second, that an assertion couched in figurative language is just as real and substantial as one made in more literal terms, only more significant. Third, that a low and material construction of such phrases gives a result in direct contradiction to their real and well-understood meaning. Fourth, that, from the very nature of material objects, no vivid comparison or illustration can be drawn from them to spiritual things, without involving some incidental element that could be pressed into direct opposition to the true intent of the comparison as a whole. Now, it would be idle to explain to any man, that, in the phrases above cited, the words "crushed," "ruined," "consumed," "devoured," "eaten up," "drowned," do not imply extinction. It would be ridiculous to argue that they do; *and yet this is precisely the kind of reasoning with which annihilationism encounters the Bible.* The words do not even imply suspension of functions, but the greatest activity.

The gross fallacy of dealing thus with the language of the Scriptures becomes still more apparent when we look more closely at their peculiar style of speech. The language of the Old Testament, both in its individual terms and more extended forms of expression, is remarkably concrete and sensuous. Intellectual and moral qualities, acts, and results are constantly represented in physical modes. From a vast multitude of instances consider the following, many of them lost in the translation. The common word for anger primarily means nostrils; fierce anger was a burning; fervent prayer, a heat; pains, writhings; possession (sometimes), a measuring-line; honor, weight; afflictions, straits; prosperity, a large place; a man's conduct, his way or path; his presence, his face; right conduct, straight paths; innocency, clean hands; pride, a high look. The word signifying to transgress means primarily to miss the mark; to bless or pray, to kneel; to worship, to prostrate one's self; to mourn, to smite [the breast]; to exult, to move in a circle or dance;

to swear, to seven one's self, or use the sacred number; to begin, to perforate or open; to favor or delight in, to curve towards; to listen, to make sharp [the ears]; to flatter, to make smooth [the tongue]; to slander (in one instance at least), to walk with or upon the tongue. To spy out a land was to travel over it, or to dig through it. To exact usury was to bite, then to vex. Ardent desire was a thirsting or panting of the soul; vehement affection, a yearning of the bowels. Oppression of the poor (Isa. iii. 15) is literally to grind, or still more literally to beat small, their faces or persons. When David prays (Ps. li. 2), "Wash me thoroughly from mine iniquity," he uses a word which is understood to have originally signified to trample with the feet in washing. A strictly literal translation of the phrase (Dan. vi. 24), "those men which had accused Daniel," would be, "who ate the pieces of Daniel." When men were utterly dismayed and dispirited (Josh. vii. 5; ii. 11), their "hearts melted, and became as water." If the children of Israel are exhorted to be pure and obedient, they are (Deut. x. 16) to "circumcise the foreskin of their heart, and be no more stiff-necked." It was prophesied (Num. xxiv. 8) that Israel should "eat up the nations his enemies, and break [literally, craunch] their bones." David celebrates the completeness of his triumph, when he was delivered "out of the hand of all his enemies, and out of the hand of Saul" (2 Sam. xxii. 1), by the strong figure (ver. 43), "Then did I beat them as small as the dust of the earth; I did stamp them as the mire of the street, and did spread them abroad." When the wicked persecute the righteous (Ps. xiv. 4), they "eat up my people as they eat bread." In Mic. iii. 2, 3, the oppression of evil rulers is described with startling minuteness of imagery: "Who pluck off their skin from off them, and their flesh from off their bones; who also eat the flesh of my people, and flay their skin from off them; and they break their bones, and chop them in pieces as for the pot, and as flesh within the caldron." To be terrified or dismayed is commonly expressed (Job vii. 14; Josh. i. 9, &c.) by a word which literally means and is elsewhere translated (Isa. ix. 4; Jer. li. 56) to be broken, or, more fully, to be broken in pieces.

The dealings of God are described in a similar way. Calamities are his plagues, literally blows; he swallows up the wall of Jerusalem (Lam. ii. 8); he makes his arrows drunk with blood, and his sword devours flesh (Deut. xxxii. 42); and Jeremiah says of him, "He hath broken my bones," "He hath pulled me in pieces," "Thou hast slain, thou hast not pitied" (Lam. iii. 4, 11, 43).

The meaning of these and a great multitude of similar expressions is perfectly clear. To adhere to the primary meaning of the words and phrases is not alone utterly to miss the real meaning of the writer, but, in some instances, to convert the whole into an absurdity. Thus, Daniel was alive and well after his enemies had eaten his pieces. The Israelites certainly were not cannibals. The inhabitants of Canaan had not received the slightest physical hurt, only a terrible alarm, when their hearts melted, and there did not remain any more *spirit* [so the original, Josh. ii. 11] in any man. Jeremiah and his fellows were still alive to make their complaint, though part of their lamentation was, that they were pulled in pieces and slain, and even (Lam. iii. 53) that "they have cut off my life in the dungeon, and cast a stone upon me." God's making his arrows drunk with blood, and devouring flesh with his sword, and his swallowing up the wall of Jerusalem, no man presses further than to express a fearful vengeance *such as those acts vividly set forth.* Nor do such expressions indicate a single and transient action, but often a prolonged course of punishment.

Here comes to view, then, the principle underlying the Scripture representations even of transactions the most spiritual, including alike men's innermost experiences, and God's relations and proceedings towards men. They are all set forth by such material phenomena as are well known and powerfully impressive; but only certain aspects of those phenomena are had in view, to the entire exclusion of certain others which may be, in fact, connected with them. As the most vivid image of firmness, stability, and shelter, God is called "a rock;" although a perverse ingenuity might torture out of the same image the meaning of indifference and insensibility. His vigilance, and power to protect his friends and defeat his foes, are strongly set forth, when it is said, "The Lord is a man of war;" but all other, even the more common qualities of an actual human warrior of those days, are excluded from the thought. He bestows upon his friends a fearless strength when he "exalts their horn like the horn of an unicorn:" with that one trait all resemblance ends. Sometimes God is compared to the "fierce lion" (Job iv. 10; Isa. xxxi. 4), and is described as tearing in pieces (Lam. iii. 10, 11), breaking the bones (Isa. xxxviii. 13), devouring his prey, and rending the caul of their heart (Hos. xiii. 7, 8) ; but here, assuredly, the irresistibleness and terribleness of his punishments are the qualities in view, while, of course, the bloodthirstiness and cruelty of the actual beast of prey, and its bodily laceration of its victim, are wholly out of the question. Sometimes the terror of his anger is denoted by the tempest, the lightning, and the fire (Ps. xviii. 7-17). Its awfully overwhelming power is represented by the wind driving the chaff before it (Ps. i. 4), or the flame sweeping through the stubble (Mal. iv. 1). The completeness of his victory is symbolized in various ways: he is the warrior, setting his foot on the neck of his enemies (Ps. cx. 1), or ruling with a rod of iron (Ps. ii. 9). He is the vintager, treading down the people in the wine-press of wrath, and trampling them in his fury, the blood staining all his raiment (Isa. lxiii.); yea, the " blood came out of the wine-press even unto the horses' bridles, by the space of a thousand and six hundred furlongs " (Rev. xiv. 20). He is the stone grinding them to powder (Matt. xxi. 44). "He shall swallow them up in his wrath, and the fire shall devour them" (Ps. xxi. 9), — two incompatible processes combined in one image of terror. His enemies are brought to naught; they are nothing; they are put away as dross; they consume into smoke; they are trodden down, and are as ashes under his feet; the remembrance of them is cut off from the earth ; their "*place* shall not be."

Now, any one who casts his eye over these collected representations should see, even without any detailed exposition, that the one common element in them all is the simple idea of a terrific overthrow and punishment, overwhelming, resistless. That one fact stands out perfectly distinct through all these varied symbols; and that alone. Press the imagery down to any lower point, and you make the representations *incompatible with each other;* some of them absurd, and some of them intolerable. What shall we say of the stream of blood bridle-deep, and two hundred miles long? Dare we assign it any more definite idea than that of a terrible vengeance? but that one thought it fearfully sets forth. What shall we say of swallowing, pulling in pieces, and rending the caul of the heart? Dare we press it further than to mean an overthrow and punishment as helpless and complete as when a torn victim is undergoing this dismemberment by some resistless beast of prey? Putting them away as dross, treading them down, driving them as chaff, even cutting off the remembrance of them, cutting off their place, are no images of annihilation; but these and all the others are obvious and striking representations of helpless, hopeless overthrow.

The principle thus brought to view is the selection of the most striking facts of the outward world to represent spiritual transactions, and the fixing of the mind upon some one prominent aspect of the material image to the exclusion of all its other bearings; and that, too, while the material image rigidly pressed in all its possible bearings, and especially its lower ones, would contradict the real meaning of the writer. And let it be noted, that, from the nature of the case, it is impossible to select any material symbol in which such intense action as is here represented shall not be incidentally attended with disorganization. No comparison can hold except in certain respects; much less can any perfect analogy be found between things sensual and things spiritual. The sacred writers *could not* select any material symbols of God's anger and its effects, which should be free from the incidental feature of transientness and perishableness.

Now, here the annihilationist steps in, and insists, in every instance, on passing by the clear and striking point of the representation to fix only on this incidental and unavoidable defect growing out of the nature of the case, and cuts down all these varied and impressive representations to a mere dissolution, or rather annihilation. He does it *in defiance of the whole usage of Scripture,* which employs these and kindred terms, as we have seen and shall see further, concerning persons and bodies of men still extant, with every faculty of body and soul in full vigor.

In precisely the same manner in which the annihilation argument is conducted, and with equal strength, an ingenious disputant might show that God is endowed with eyes, ears, arms, hands, feet, a nose, mouth, tongue, heart; is armed with weapons, — sword, bow, spear, shield; rides in a chariot; travels from place to place; possesses all the passions and modes of thinking and acting of an exalted man; has children; lives in a splendid mansion; and the like.

On the same principle, the Pharisees looked for a warrior-Christ, coming with a splendid earthly retinue and pomp to crush out all human oppressors and exalt the Jewish nation to the hight of earthly power. It was the same spirit of gross and sensual interpretation, abandoning the spirit for the letter, the kernel for the husk.

This principle of interpretation is a false one, — specious, perhaps, to those who look only on the surface of speech and only at this one theme in the Scriptures, but refuted by the commonest usage of language, by the entire method of Scripture expression, and by the plain and frequent meaning of these very forms of speech.

Having looked at the fallacy of the fundamental principle, we shall now proceed to consider the details.

CHAPTER III.

THE SCRIPTURE ARGUMENT EXAMINED: DEATH AND LIFE.

IF it can be shown that the doctrine of a future existence was the received doctrine of the Israelitish nation, it would be proper to insist that all the phraseology quoted by annihilationists must be understood as modified or controlled by that supposition. But we are perfectly willing, for the present, to waive that important consideration, and to examine those phrases on the simple ground of Scripture usage.

The chief stronghold of the system under examination is founded upon the use of the words "death" and "life" in the Scriptures. Mr. Hudson correctly remarks, that these are the terms most commonly used to represent the respective destinies of men. And for a good reason: they are brief, striking, and singularly comprehensive. Still they are not, by any means, the only modes of representation: but the destiny of the wicked is frequently described in very varied forms of speech, expressive of the deepest positive suffering; and the future condition of the righteous is represented as one of comfort and joy.

Now, every instance in which death is threatened to the sinner is quoted as proof of his annihilation. It is, says Mr. Blain, "extinction of being, soul, and body." Says Mr. Dobney, death is "a return to that state of blank nothingness from which the Almighty fiat had so recently called" our first parents; while the promised life is "existence only," or, as he waveringly adds in parenthesis, "at all events, chiefly." Mr. Hudson has much to say of the necessity of holding to the literal sense of these terms, although he noticeably refrains from saying, in so many words, that life is mere existence; while yet, as we shall see, the meaning that his argument requires is not the literal sense of the terms. Meanwhile every passage in which death or dying is threatened to the sinner is quoted as proof of annihilation. Mr. Blain accumulates upwards of fifty texts from the Scriptures: Mr. Hudson pushes the matter further still, and adduces all the passages he finds among the early Christian fathers, containing these phrases, to prove that they held the doctrine of annihilation. And yet he is obliged to admit that " these terms are sometimes used in a tropical sense;" * and Mr. Dobney will not "deny that 'life' may sometimes be used in the sense alleged," that is, in a higher or pregnant sense.†

But the attempt to prove the doctrine of annihilation from the threats of death to the sinner, and promises of eternal life to the believer, can not sustain an examination.

1. Death does not *literally* mean, nor does it include, extinction of being, cessation of existence, or even dissolution; nor is life, in its lower sense, simply synonymous with existence. The distinction between the animate and inanimate is not between the existent and

---

* Debt and Grace, p. 172.
† The Scripture Doctrine of Future Punishment, p. 108.

the non-existent. Here are two trees: one is dead, and the other is alive, but they both are in existence, and both are trees. Death does not itself signify even decay or dissolution; for the dead tree is still entire. A dead body is still a body, though dead. It is still in existence: it exists as a body, sometimes for two or three thousand years, — not a living body, still a body.

It is therefore an egregious oversight to say or imply that the common or literal meaning of the word "death" is cessation of being. It does not of itself include, but is distinct from, the dissolution which usually follows physical death: and that dissolution, again, is not extinction, only a change of form; for no matter is annihilated. Accordingly, none of the definitions of the word "death," as found in Webster's Dictionary, include annihilation; while the primary meaning of the word, as there given, turns, not on the extinction of being, but on the *cessation of certain functions*. How thoroughly this harmonizes with and forms the basis of the scriptural use of the word "death," as describing the effect of sin, will presently appear. Meanwhile, let it be settled that "death" does not *literally* and in its lowest use signify extinction of being, nor "life" simply its continuance.

The Scripture itself shall be our witness on this point, even when speaking of subjects not endowed with immortality. "Thou fool! that which thou sowest is not quickened, except *it die*" (1 Cor. xv. 36). "Except a corn of wheat fall into the ground *and die*, it abideth alone; but, *if it die*, it bringeth forth much fruit" (John xii. 24). Is a grain of wheat annihilated in order to germinate? or is there merely a change of condition and mode of action, while its existence and properties remain?

2. But, secondly, there is found, running through all languages, a higher, and what some lexicographers have called a pregnant, sense of these words, "life" and "death," whereby they denote not only the performance or cessation of certain functions, but also the healthful, harmonious, and happy performance of them, or the contrary. They affirm the normal and complete discharge of those functions, especially in the higher faculties of animated beings. Life is then a state of healthful activity, and thus also of prosperity or true welfare.

Indeed, we speak even of the life of something not properly animate to designate its force, spirit, or whatever makes it sound, valuable, or adequate to its proper end. Dead capital is that which lies useless or unproductive. A lifeless poem is simply one which lacks the higher qualities of poetry. A speech falls dead when it fails to make the appropriate impression: or, on the other hand, the speaker's manner is full of animation; and his speech, of life. We speak of a live enterprise, or of lifeless yeast or wine.

Still more common is the use of the words "live" and "life," to express a condition of welfare, prosperity, or enjoyment.

Sometimes in the Old Testament these terms describe simple *bodily* health and activity. Thus in Josh. v. 8: "When they had done circumcising all the people, they abode in their places in the camp till they were whole;" in the Hebrew, "till they lived" or were alive. A vigorous woman was, in the Hebrew, a "living" woman (Exod. i. 19), and a valiant man was one who was "alive" (2 Sam. xxiii. 20). Decay of the generative power in the human system, as one of its most important functions, is described (in Rom. iv. 19) as "the deadness of Sarah's womb," and Abraham's "body now dead." Ahaziah and Hezekiah both inquire, "Shall I recover" — literally, "shall I live" — from this disease? (2 Kings i. 2; viii. 8.)

The Hebrew used the same terms to express a more general welfare, whether of body, mind, or condition. Samson's refreshment after extreme thirst (Judg. xv. 19), and Jacob's rallying from deep grief, are described by the same Hebrew word, as their "living," or coming to life, or, as the translators give it, "reviving;" on the other hand, the extreme terror and mental distress of Nabal (1 Sam. xxv. 37) is described by the words, "His heart died within him, and he became as a stone." The form of shouting wishes of joy and prosperity to the Hebrew monarchs (1 Sam. x. 24; 2 Sam. xvi. 16) was, "Let the king live!" like the modern French cry, "*Vive le roi!*" * When David repaired Jerusalem after its capture from the Jebusites (1 Chron. xi. 8), he "made it alive." When the Psalmist prays that God would restore their former prosperity and happiness to his people, he prays (Ps. lxxxv. 6), "Wilt thou not make us alive again, that thy people may rejoice in thee?" Says Solomon, "Hope deferred maketh the heart sick; but, when desire cometh, it is a tree of life," i.e. clearly, of joy and happiness. Similar is the passage, "A man's life consisteth not in the abundance

---

* We need not continually repeat that we follow the original in these instances from the Old Testament.

of the things which he possesseth" (Luke xii. 15). A very striking instance occurs in 1 Thess. iii. 8 : " For now we *live*, if ye stand fast in the Lord," — we are happy, blessed. The same radical conception of life as denoting, not simple existence, but true functional activity, alone can explain such opposite phrases as "dead faith" (Jas. ii. 17, 20, 26) and "dead works" (Heb. vi. 1; ix. 14). The faith was dead because it put forth none of the true activities of gospel faith ; the works, because they contained within no such vital force. Neither of them had ever been alive : they had not died, though they were "dead." The words here designate condition rather than transaction. The land of Egypt is spoken of as "dying" (Gen. xlvii. 19), when, as explained in the same verse, it was "desolate ;" and Pharaoh names the terrible ruin which the locusts brought upon Egypt, as "this death" (Exod. x. 17).

The Scriptures, especially of the Old Testament, furnish numerous other cases in which "life," clearly, and by the agreement of the best lexicographers and interpreters, signifies true functional action, welfare, prosperity, happiness, and the like ; and "death," its opposite. The above examples are sufficient.

A similar usage occurs in our own habits of speech on serious subjects. We speak of men as being alive to every good enterprise and to every high considera- tion, or as dead to all better feelings and higher pur- poses, to all good, to their friends or family, to society or their country ; of a living death ; of a life worthy of the name ; of the difference being living and exist- ing : —

" That man may last, but never lives,
Who much receives, yet nothing gives."

But, should any one object that this is a theological phraseology, we send him to the Greek and Latin classics to find the same usage there. He may turn to Freund's, Andrews', or Leverett's Lexicon, and find that *vivo*, to live, also means " to live well, live at ease, enjoy life," with references to Cicero, Horace, Lucilius, Catullus, and Sallust. " Since you urge me to labor and ambition," says Cicero, " I will comply ; but when shall we *live ?* " Says Horace, " Master of himself, and joyously does that man pass his time, who can daily say, I have lived." Says the well-known inscription, " *Dum vivimus, vivamus* " — " While we live, let us live." Cicero, in his " Old Age," speaks of a " *vita vitalis*." It were as easy as it is unnecessary to accumulate instances of this kind. It hardly seems a metaphorical meaning of the words : * the lexicons well designate it as a " pregnant " meaning, — one which the words involve whenever they are applied, not to a mere organism, but specifically to an intellectual and sentient being.†

The same usage occurs in the Greek : ζάω, " to live," has also the meaning " to be active, efficient," and the still higher meaning " to live prosperously and truly." ‡

---

* Mr. Hudson in his later work is constrained to make the important admission that words sometimes " break beyond the limits of the letter. But when this lively sense becomes the ordinary sense, that is only a *new literal or proper sense* " (Christ our Life, p. 66). He insists, however, that, in all cases, the primary sense has *primâ facie* evidence in its favor. But even this will depend wholly on the nature of the subject, and the conditions of the speech. Is there are any *primâ facie* evidence that " perceive " designates, in any given case, recognition with the eye ?

† A lower grade of meaning is common enough in the Latin writers in such phrases as " living dew," " living water," " living rock," " dead laws," " dead applause," etc.

‡ See Passow's Lexicon, under the word.

Thus Socrates (Xenophon's Mem., iii. 3, 11) speaks of "whatever noblest things we have learned conventionally, whereby we know how to live," i.e. to live as we ought; and still more distinctly Dio Cassius (69, 19) uses the expression, "having been alive so many years, but having lived (ζήσας) seven years."

In truth, the word "life," instead of denoting simple existence, has for its very point and specialty to express something more,—something superadded. *What that additional idea is, will depend upon the speaker's view, permanent or passing, of the real office, end, and use of life.* According to the elevation of his views, the word becomes more and more "pregnant." Such a process is an absolute necessity of human thought. Its lower planes of meaning are of freshness and preservation, of the power of vegetable development; then of sentient and conscious existence, activity, efficiency, and the like; then of prosperity and enjoyment; and, higher yet, of harmonious moral development, and fulfillment of the great moral aims of human existence. All this will depend on the point of view. It was therefore natural for the Egyptian midwives to describe the vigorous Hebrew women as "alive;" for the populace to say, "Let the king live," when they wished him a prosperous reign; for Cicero, overwhelmed with labor and care, to look forward to a happy leisure as "life;" and for Socrates (Plato's Repub. vi. 495, c.) to describe those who renounced philosophical studies as leading no "true life." In all these instances, the word was used to denote something more than existence; and that something varied with the notion entertained of the proper condition and work of the human being.

Equally natural was it for those taking a still higher view of the functions of a human being to designate the fulfillment of those higher functions as *life*.

3. Here we are brought naturally and directly to the common Scripture use of the terms "life" and "death."

For the word of God contemplates and addresses man chiefly in a far higher light than that of Cicero or Socrates; not simply as a being made to act, think, or receive pleasure, but as a moral, accountable being, made to "fear God and keep his commandments," and thus to live in holy and intimate union with his Maker.

Now, that spiritual state in which man is living in intimate union with God, performing the true work of life, and reaping the blessed fruits, in which all the functions of his being are harmoniously and happily accomplished, the Scriptures abundantly and constantly name LIFE; and its opposite condition they term DEATH. The words describe the *spiritual condition* of the man in this world, and still more emphatically its completed results in another world. Sometimes the present, sometimes the future aspect of the case, is more prominently in view; sometimes the total state is gathered up without special discrimination of its aspects. This use of the terms is a fact which no sophistry can evade.

And let it be observed, also, that no single terms could be found, so appropriate in themselves, or so conformed to the whole scriptural conception of the chief end of man's being. The thought is complex: vital connection with the living God, spontaneous growth and action of an inner principle, harmonious development of the soul after the true law of its being, holiness, and resulting blessedness. All this can be summed up in no one term so fit as "life;" and its opposite, "death." They tell the tale of the highest, truest use, and of the utmost perversion and abuse, — each in one word. Accordingly, it is noticeable that the New Testament never announces the whole condition and destiny of the good by such terms as happiness, blessedness, or felicity. Even Mr. Hudson calls attention to this fact: " It was enough for Christ and the apostles to talk about *life*," — for the obvious reason that no term of less breadth and fullness could adequately set forth the complex good that Christ works in the soul.* The New-Testament view is well exhibited in Rom. ii. 7, where " glory, honor, immortality " [incorruption], are all given as the synonyms

---

* Mr. Hudson does not seem to be aware that this admission is fatal to his theory that eternal life is, in Scripture, eternal *existence*, solely or chiefly. For he holds that, in fact, that future state will be one of holy blessedness. But do the sacred writers, when they speak of that state, constantly ignore its grand characteristic and glory? Or is not the very constancy with which they employ the term "life," conclusive evidence that they comprise therein the whole multiform well-being of the saint?

A constant fallacy runs through Mr. Hudson's representation of the common view. Thus: " He who was the ' Resurrection and the Life ' was dangerously literal in his style of speech, if he simply meant that he came to give happiness to immortal beings." Yet no sound evangelical writer teaches that Christ came simply to give happiness to immortal beings. This constant false assumption is one of the chief points of plausibility in Mr. Hudson's argument. The issue he makes is this, Does "life" eternal mean happiness, or existence? We answer, in the Savior's use, it involves both, and more also. No system but a low style of Universalism lays the chief stress of eternal life on the happiness alone.

of eternal life. Nothing but "life" in its most pregnant meaning can express the divine idea of the work that goes on for ever in the regenerate heart.

"Death," on the other hand, is that state of separation from God, and from the beatific fruition of God, in which all the higher faculties of human nature are working falsely and discordantly; in which the true end of living is discarded, and its true enjoyment lost; and in which there is at last the complete extinction, not of the soul's being, but of its well-being. It sums up the whole penalty of sin; its complex woe, beginning here, matured and perfected hereafter.

Indeed, the very thought and phrase which annihilationists have pronounced absurd *— "a death that never ends"— is found expressed and expanded by a Jewish writer cotemporary with Paul. Says Philo Judæus of the first murderer's punishment, "What was it? That he should *live continually dying*, and that he should in a manner endure undying and never-ending death. . . . Consider how it is that death can be said to be never ending in this man's case. Since there are four different affections to which the soul is liable, two of them being conversant with evil, either present or expected, namely, sorrow and fear, it cuts up by the roots the pair of them which are conversant with good, in order that the man may never receive pleasure from any accident of fortune, nor ever feel a desire for any thing pleasant; and it leaves him only those affections conversant about evil,— sorrow without any mixture of cheerfulness, and unmixed fear; for the Scripture says that God laid a curse upon the fra-

---

* See Storrs' Six Sermons, p. 120, et seq.

tricide, so that he should be continually groaning and trembling. Moreover, he put a mark upon him, that he might never be pitied by any one; so that he might not die at once, but might, as I have said, *pass all his time in dying*, amid griefs and pains and incessant calamities." *

The origin of this mode of speech is not difficult to decide upon. While physical death as the most terrible of natural events would be a ready symbol for the most fearful woes to the spirit,† we believe the actual connection to be historic, originating in the record of the fall and the curse. "In the day that thou eatest thereof, thou shalt surely die." That this included physical death, the Scriptures leave no room to doubt; nor may we reasonably doubt that at once there passed upon the frame the mysterious change which was to bring it surely to the dust. But that this was not all the curse, nor its most immediate and perceptible effect, nor the chief stress of its terror, lies on the face of the record, and is found in God's own unfolding of the sentence.

What was the immediate result of the transgression? The sense of guilt and shame, — "They saw that they were naked;" severance from God, terror, and recoiling from his presence, with total loss of the joys of intercourse with him, — "I heard thy voice in the garden, and I was afraid, because I was naked; and I hid myself." Then comes a further unfolding, in the sentence which announced to the woman pain and sorrow

---

* Philo Judæus, Rewards and Punishments, xii.
† So light and darkness are naturally and almost inseparably associated with the idea of spiritual illumination and its opposite.

and subjection, and to the man sorrow and wearisome discouraging toil, "till thou return unto the ground." The simple returning to dust, then, by the record's own showing, was not the whole penalty involved in the threat "Thou shalt surely die:" it was only an outward token and seal of a comprehensive woe,— the broad and fearful consequences of sin.

Such being the case, it is not essential to inquire whether the first pair understood all that was involved in the penalty, "Ye shall surely die." What further explanation God may or may not have made of a fact that never could be fully comprehended till experienced, we do not know. It will not answer to assert, as some have done, that it would not be just to inflict a penalty of which the full extent was not previously unfolded. In criminal cases, neither the judicial dealings of God nor man sustain the position. The question is never raised. Whatever may be the views of the murderer as to the nature of the penalty, he will, if convicted, suffer that penalty.

The assertion of some that to "die," in the threat involved merely physical decease, is met by the insurmountable fact, that the actual consequences, as set forth in the record, and subsequently announced by God himself, include a great deal more. The simple facts of that momentous transaction at the beginning of human history are these: First the command, with the annexed penalty in one word, "Thou shalt surely die;" next the transgression; then the consequence, not alone an ultimate return to dust, but also an *immediate* severance from God and his fellowship, shame, remorse, dread, and terror before God, sorrow, painful labor, and a curse on the very conditions of toil. Now, what more natural and almost unavoidable than that, thenceforth, the state into which man fell, with all its complex and on-reaching woe, should be described by that one term "death"? Indeed, so thoroughly does this higher and pregnant meaning of the term often predominate, that, in repeated instances, the physical decease is overlooked as not properly deserving the name. Thus the Saviour says (John viii. 51), "If a man keep my saying, he shall never see death."

Men are accordingly represented as being even now in a spiritual condition called "death," to be followed by the full and final consummation which is "the second death," or often simply "death." And as the believer shall never see death, but "hath everlasting life;" even so it is said of the unbeliever, that he "shall not see life, but the wrath of God abideth on him" (John iii. 36). And in the act of believing men have passed in this world "from death unto life" (John iii. 36; 1 John iii. 14). Each term in the Scriptures designates respectively a spiritual state, with all its adjuncts and issues. Each state begins here and is consummated hereafter; the future consummation in the one case being often, though not always, distinguished as *eternal* life; in the other case less frequently as the *second* death.

Let us look at some indisputable instances in which these words designate a moral or spiritual condition of the soul, with certain qualities and issues, and in which the one can not signify either extinction or natural decease, nor the other merely the opposite of this idea.

4

Both terms are applied to the successive states of the repenting prodigal, Luke xv. 24, 32. "This my son was dead, and is alive again; he was lost, and is found." The words clearly describe his state of deep moral degradation and wretchedness, and his recovery from it. They can be tortured into nothing else. It is vain for Mr. Hudson to allege "either supposed death, or relative loss, — 'dead to me.'" There is no hint of any *supposed* decease, while the explanatory phrase, "was lost," refutes the assertion. The servants and the elder brother speak of him simply as "having come;" while the elder brother at once dilates upon the history of the profligate as a known fact, — "hath devoured thy living with harlots." The other alternative — "dead to me" — concedes the whole principle of interpretation which the theory denies. For if a corrupt and profligate man is intelligibly described by the word "dead," dead to his father, the case is perfectly parallel to one's being dead to God and holiness. It designates a moral wreck.

"But she that liveth in pleasure [wantonly] is dead while she liveth" (1 Tim. v. 6). The lewd woman, while outwardly living, is dead, — literally "has died." But she is neither extinct nor deceased: she is in a condition of spiritual death, alienation from God, perversion of being, and rejection of the true end and blessedness of life.

When one of the disciples said, "Lord, suffer me first to go and bury my father," Jesus replied, "Follow thou me, and let *the dead* bury their dead" (Matt. viii. 22). While it is obvious that the second word "dead" refers to the deceased person, it is equally obvious that the first word can not have a similar meaning. The Savior does not utter such unmeaning things as, "Let deceased persons bury deceased persons," much less, "let the non-existent bury the non-existent." The simple apposite meaning recognized by the great mass of skillful interpreters is, "let the spiritually dead, unbelievers, bury the deceased; but do thou, my disciple, come with me to the work that is waiting."* But Mr. Hudson says they are called dead by anticipation, — prolepsis: "Christ regards the lovers of this world as heirs of death." Yet even this shift concedes the point, viz. that the word "dead" describes the *present* state of certain living men, their present character, condition, and prospects, — "lovers of this world or heirs of death." It describes men in a certain moral condition to which certain fearful tendencies and consequences attach.

"I know thy works, that thou hast a name, that thou livest, and art dead" (Rev. iii. 1). The common reader can not miss the meaning. The accompanying explanation renders mistake impossible: "Be watchful, and strengthen the things which remain, that are ready to die; for I have not found thy works perfect before God. Remember therefore how thou hast received and heard, and hold fast and repent. If therefore thou shalt not watch, I will come on thee as a thief,

---

* Mr. Hudson alleges that the Greek word rendered dead (νεκρούς) "always denotes literal death, and commonly signifies corpse." The statement is erroneous. Though the word frequently designates a corpse, it very often designates simply the dead in opposition to the living; and in Homer, when used in the plural, denotes the dwellers of the under-world.— See Passow and Liddell and Scott. Rev. iii. 1 is a *perfectly* clear case, in which it neither designates a corpse nor a deceased person.

and thou shalt not know what hour I will come upon thee. Thou hast a few names even in Sardis, which have not defiled their garments; and they shall walk with me in white; for they are worthy." Here, again, the word "dead" describes the spiritual condition of a church in which the religion was, to a great degree, spurious. As De Wette remarks, it was, on the one hand, destitute of spiritual power and activity, and a fruit-bearing faith ("I have not found thy works perfect," literally *fulfilled*), and, on the other, even fallen into a sinful life (v. 4). But as the Church, being a collective body, contained a few individuals not in this condition, they, "a few names," are specially excepted as the things that remain or are left, not dead, but "are ready to die," endangered by the surrounding spiritual death. Here, again, Mr. Hudson talks faintly of a prolepsis, — "devoted to eternal death," but says he "shall not insist;" although he adds that "the phrase in verse second, 'strengthen the things that are ready to die,' certainly supports the view." But (1) that phrase refutes him; for it discriminates what was left not dead, though endangered, the "few worthy names," from what was dead, "defiled," and needing repentance. (2) The sacred writer clearly distinguishes the two things which Mr. Hudson confounds: the present state of the Church, — "Thou *art* dead," — from its threatened doom, — "I *will* come as a thief," etc. (3) The sacred writer, by the connection, makes it impossible to understand the word "dead" otherwise than as describing the present spiritual condition of that fallen church: "Thou hast a name that thou livest, and art dead." No utterance could be more distinct.

A clear instance is found in Eph. ii. 1–6: "And you hath he quickened who were dead in trespasses and sins; wherein, in time past, ye walked according to the course of this world, according to the prince of the power of the air, the spirit that now worketh in the children of disobedience; among whom, also, we all had our conversation in times past, in the lusts of our flesh, fulfilling the desires of the flesh and of the mind; and were by nature the children of wrath even as others. But God, who is rich in mercy, for his great love wherewith he loved us, even when we were dead in sins, hath quickened us together with Christ (by grace ye are saved), and hath raised us up together, and made us sit together in heavenly places in Christ Jesus." Here are persons described as having been "*dead* in sins," yet all the while in a state of prodigious activity in all manner of lust and service of Satan, but now ' quickened" or made alive with Christ; being "saved by grace." Mr. Hudson regards this as prolepsis; and among several authorities produces one respectable recent name (Meyer) in favor of it.* Against it are such names as Alford, Olshausen, De Wette, Eadie, Ellicott. And the careful reader can judge for himself, by glancing over the passage and the verses following, as far as verse thirteenth, whether the apostle is speaking *merely* of two diverse retributions, one of which would have come, but the other actually will, in

---

* Meyer, however, is not to be understood as siding with Mr. Hudson in viewing this as physical death: in his third edition (1859), he emphatically describes them as sentenced to "eternal death."

the other world; or is speaking of two actual states in this world, in one of which the Ephesians had long lived "in time past," but had now, by the grace of God, been transferred into the other, which is indeed to be made complete hereafter. Look at the tense of the statement, "were dead," "hath quickened" (rather "quickened"); at the specifications of character accompanying, "had our conversation in times past in the lusts of the flesh, fulfilling the desires of the flesh and the mind," but now "his workmanship, created in Christ Jesus unto good works;" at the producing cause of the difference, namely, conversion; and at the description of the two states as coeval with the periods before and after conversion,—"At that time ye were without Christ, being aliens," &c., "but now ye who sometime were far off are made nigh by the blood of Christ." It can not be claimed that the phrase, "hath quickened us together with Christ," looks wholly to the future; for our spiritual quickening here grows out of our union to Christ, while it finds in his resurrection its symbol, its basis, and the pledge of its final completion.

Still more unanswerably clear is the meaning of these terms in Col. ii. 13: "And you, being dead in your sins and the uncircumcision of your flesh, hath he quickened together with him, having forgiven you all trespasses." The preceding verses read thus: "And ye are complete in him which is the head of all principality and power. In whom also ye are [were] circumcised with the circumcision made without hands, in putting off the body of the sins of the flesh by the circumcision of Christ; buried with him in baptism, wherein ye are [were] risen with him through the faith of the operation of God who hath raised him from the dead." Here the circumcision made without hands, and being made alive with Christ and in Christ, are represented as cotemporary past events; and prior to them was the death from which these Christians had been made alive. Accordingly, the statements before and after are of present state and privileges. And, to complete the proof that the quickening and upraising are already experienced, the apostle proceeds in the beginning of the next chapter, "If ye then be risen [raised] with Christ, seek those things which are above." Spiritual affections are enjoined, on the ground of a supposed transition from death to life already wrought. Mr. Hudson, as usual, talks of prolepsis.

In this connection, it may be well to advert to a slightly varied use of the same method of speech. The apostle, in urging the Ephesians to set their affections on things above, and not on things on the earth, adds, "For ye are dead, and your life is hid with Christ in God" (Col. iii. 3). And elsewhere (Rom. vi. 1-11), — he speaks of being "dead to sin," and "alive unto God." What is the propriety or consistency of still applying the term "dead" to those who are no longer dead in sin, but alive unto God? — no longer dead *in*, but dead *to*, sin? How simple the explanation! and how it proceeds from and confirms the fundamental notion of life already exhibited as the possession of certain functional activities! Among other powers of life is *sensibility*, while bodily death is a state of bodily insensibility. This aspect is the one seized upon by the apostle's thought to make a representation paradoxical only in appearance. The higher the Christian's religious life and fulfillment of his true functions, the more completely insensible is he to the work and attractions of sin. His highest life to God, or greatest remove from death in sin, is thus the fullest death *to* sin. This incidental allusion, superficially inconsistent, really in perfect harmony, is thus one of the best proofs of the correctness of this view of life and death.

Another clear text is found John v. 24: "He that heareth my word, and believeth on him that sent me, hath everlasting life, and shall not [doth not] come into condemnation, but is [has] passed from death unto life." The change has taken place, and everlasting life is already commenced as the present portion of the believer. This twofold statement in the past and present tense, mutually explanatory, requires a prodigious hardihood of reckless interpretation to pronounce it a reference wholly to the future. Accordingly, the best modern scholars, Alford, Lücke, Tholuck, Olshausen, De Wette, Meyer, Winer, are perfectly agreed in their concurrence in the received view. "Where the faith is, there the possession of life is. . . . The 'passage over' from death unto life has already taken place," says Alford. Winer remarks, "The perfect is not used for the future (John v. 24): the passage contains no reference to a future event, but to something which has really commenced." * Mr. Hudson, however, talks of prolepsis.

Entirely coincident with this passage, and, if possible,

---

* Winer's New-Testament Grammar, Masson's Translation, p. 289. Mr. Hudson gives a different quotation, which we do not find in Winer's last and matured edition. We have not the older editions at hand.

more explicit, is 1 John iii. 14, 15: " We know that we have passed from death unto life, because we love the brethren. He that loveth not his brother abideth in death. Whosoever hateth his brother is a murderer; and ye know that no murderer hath eternal life abiding in him." In verse 17, the phrase is varied by asking, " How dwelleth the love of God in him?" as an equivalent for the same spiritual state. It requires no comment. One who loves God and his brother is a man who has passed from death unto life; one who does not, now abides in death, and does not have eternal life abiding in him. Mr. Hudson virtually admits here that eternal life denotes a process already commenced in the soul, and continuing for ever. " We think the phrase 'eternal life abiding in him' is best explained of the divine life-giving, working now as a regulative principle, and as a germ of the future life."

The case is very fully stated in John vi. 47, et seq.: " Verily I say unto you, He that believeth on me hath everlasting life." And, after some intervening remarks, " Except ye eat the flesh of the Son of man, and drink his blood, ye have no life in you. Whoso eateth my flesh and drinketh my blood hath eternal life; and I will raise him up at the last day. For my flesh is meat indeed, and my blood is drink indeed. He that eateth my flesh and drinketh my blood dwelleth in me, and I in him," etc. Here is the whole case. They that are not united to Christ " have no life in them;" they that are " have eternal life:" it is produced by, and begins with, their spiritual feeding on Christ, and is consummated at the resurrection. "I will raise him up at the last day."

Perfectly explicit on the point that the life unto God commences in this world is also Gal. ii. 19, 20: "For I through the law am dead to the law, that I might live unto God. I am crucified with Christ, *nevertheless I live;* yet not I, but Christ liveth in me: and *the life which I now live* in the flesh I live by the faith of the Son of God, who loved me, and gave himself for me."

The *immediate* effect wrought by that change as the beginning of an endless life is well set forth in our Lord's conversation with the woman of Samaria (John iv.), where he speaks of the "living water," and adds, "Whosoever drinketh of the water that I shall give him shall never thirst; but the water that I shall give him shall be in him a well of water springing up into everlasting life." And, in his conversation with Martha (John xi.), the Saviour speaks of this life, begun in the believer here, as flowing on uninterrupted for ever; natural decease being disregarded as unworthy to be mentioned. "Jesus said unto her, I am the resurrection and the life; he that believeth on me, though he were dead, yet shall he live. And whosoever liveth and believeth in me *shall never die.*" United to him, the dead lives, and the living never dies. With the same disregard of natural death as unworthy of mention, and as not interrupting the continuity of the true life begun here, Christ says (John viii. 51), "Verily I say unto you, If a man keep my saying, he shall never see death."

In one instance, the life which the Christian gains is

termed the true or "real life" (τῆς ὄντως ζωῆς),— 1 Tim. vi. 19.*

As the believer shall never see that which is truly death, so the unbeliever never experiences true life. "He that believeth on the Son hath everlasting life; and he that believeth not the Son shall not see life, but the wrath of God abideth on him" (John iii. 36). The one has everlasting life now; the other shall not see life at all, being now in a state on which the wrath of God abides.

Regeneration is elsewhere marked as the point of transition, being a resurrection to "newness of life." "Therefore we are buried with him by baptism into death, that like as Christ was raised up from the dead by the glory of the Father, even so we also should walk in newness of life" (Rom. vi. 4). And to leave no doubt that the apostle speaks of a work already commenced, he says in verse 13, "Neither yield ye your members as instruments of unrighteousness unto sin, but yield yourselves unto God as *those that are alive from the dead*, and your members as instruments of righteousness unto God." Holy obedience is proof that they are alive from the dead. Yet Mr. Hudson talks of "prolepsis."

"Awake, thou that sleepest, and arise from the dead, and Christ shall give thee light" (Eph. v. 14). Sinners are summoned to repentance under the form of a call

---

* The received text here reads, "eternal life" (αἰωνίου); against the united voice of the oldest manuscripts, A, א, D, E, F, G, and many other authorities, the decision of critical editions (Lachmann, Tischendorf), and the clear opinion of such commentators as Alford, Ellicott, Olshausen, De Wette, Meyer.

to arise from the dead. In this instance, Mr. Hudson admits that "the metaphor," as he terms it, "is too manifest for doubt."

In addition to all the other forms of statement, we have (John xvii. 3) the assertion that this state called eternal life consists in the true knowledge of God in Christ. "And this is life eternal, that they might know thee the only true God, and Jesus Christ whom thou hast sent." An attempt is made to evade the force of this passage by saying that the expression "will, on the face of it, as easily mean that the knowledge of God, &c., are the way or means of life." But this device is not only a departure from the direct and simple form of the statement; it is in positive contradiction to the usage in connection with this peculiar mode of expression (αὕτη δέ ἐστιν ἡ αἰώνιος ζωή, ἵνα γινώσκωσι, κ. τ. λ. this is eternal life, that they might know, &c.), which elsewhere means that the two things are equivalent; so that the one constitutes the other, or the second consists in the first. Thus John vi. 29: "This is the work of God, that ye [might] believe on him whom he hath sent," i.e. to work the work of God *consists* in believing. "Jesus saith unto them, My meat is to do [literally, that I might do] the will of him that sent me" (John iv. 34); not, "the way or means of procuring my meat;" but "my meat *consists in* doing," &c. "This is the message that ye heard from the beginning, That we should love one another" (1 John iii. 11): the message *consists* in the requirement that we love one another. "And this is his commandment, That we should believe on the name of his Son Jesus Christ" (1 John iii. 23): his commandment *consists in* the requirement that we believe, &c. "And this is love, that we [should] walk after his commandments" (2 John 6),—not, this is the way or means to secure love; but practical love *consists in* so walking. In the same verse, "This is the commandment, That as ye have heard from the beginning ye should walk in it" [i.e. love]; in other words, the commandment consists in this injunction; or, walking in love *constitutes* the commandment, or, according to Lücke, the sum of the commandments. "What is my reward, then? [this] that, when I preach the gospel, I may make the gospel without charge, that I abuse not my power in the gospel;" i.e. my reward consists in this, or this constitutes my reward. "And this is the Father's will which hath sent me, that of all which he hath given me I should lose nothing" (John vi. 39): not, this is the way or means of securing the Father's will (though that is doubtless true); but the Father's will *consists in* this purpose. This thought and form of speech are repeated in the following verse. The above examples include the chief, if not the only cases of this peculiar construction in the New Testament. And we think that the intelligent reader will see that they do not justify the interpretation, "This is the *way* or *means* of life;" but they do most emphatically sustain the meaning: "Eternal life consists in knowing thee the only true God, and Jesus Christ whom thou hast sent." He will also be prepared to learn that the very best modern biblical scholars, with almost one accord, Olshausen, Tholuck, Alford, De Wette, Meyer, Lücke, and others, agree in this interpretation. Says Olshausen, "The idea must not be superficialized by the interpretation that the knowledge of God is one of the *means* to the attainment of eternal life (as if the words ran: ἡ ζωὴ αἰώνιος ἔρχεται διὰ τῆς γνώσεως)." And De Wette admirably says, "This is — therein consists — the eternal life; not, this is the means of the eternal life; for the vital knowledge of God and of Christ is itself the eternal life, which is a life already beginning here, and penetrating the whole life of the human spirit." Olshausen sums up, "In faith and knowledge, consequently, eternal life is embraced." Several of these commentators quote the felicitous statement of the ancient father, Irenæus: "To live without life is impossible; but the existence of life is derived from the participation of God; but the participation of God is to know God, and to enjoy his goodness."

Here, then, is brought distinctly to view an important fact connected with the Scripture use of this mode of expression. Inasmuch as the biblical representation thus clearly presents "eternal life" as a condition or process commencing in this world, and running on in the next world for ever, but receiving in the other world its consummation and glory; so only can we readily and fully explain the fact, that, as the minds of the sacred writers dwell on the one or the other portion of its progress, their speech will apply chiefly now to the present life, now to the world to come: sometimes, too, they view it as a process or activity of the soul; sometimes as a glorious result, and even reward, lying in the future. A similar remark applies to the use of the term "death." For, though both these phrases designate spiritual states, they designate those states always with a direct or implied reference to certain issues or consummations growing out of the present state. Sometimes the glorious blessedness on the one hand, and perhaps still oftener the elaborated and awful woe of a perverted being on the other, in which they issue, are distinctly held forth as the most inviting promise and the most terrific threat, — each under the name of life and of death. And as in Rom. ii. 7, the synonym of eternal life in its culmination is given as glory, honor, incorruption; so on the other hand "death" and "perishing" (i. 32 and ii. 9) find their expansion in "indignation and wrath, tribulation and anguish." In all this we are not prescribing to the word of God, but simply following its guidance.

This particular point now suggested — the variant aspects of life and death, covered at different times by the same terms — and our general position as to their meaning, are both of them illustrated and positively sustained by another common Scripture phrase, "the kingdom of heaven."

"To inherit the kingdom of heaven" is an expression in more than one respect parallel to "having eternal life." In the representation of the final judgment (Matt. xxv. 34, &c.), the righteous are invited to "inherit the kingdom prepared for you from the foundation of the world;" and, in the closing statement, we are told they shall go away "into life eternal." So in the history of the rich young man, the inquiry was for "eternal life;" and the reply, "If thou wilt *enter into life*, keep the commandments." But, when the young man had gone, the Savior's remark was, that "a rich man shall hardly *enter* into the *kingdom of heaven,"*—" enter into the kingdom of God" (Matt. xix. 16-24).

Now, this parallel phrase, "the kingdom of heaven," amply confirms our interpretation of "eternal life," though possessing a still broader diversity of application. Its most distinct prediction appears in Daniel ii. and vii., where four successive human monarchies are to be followed by a kingdom which the God of heaven will set up. Now, without pausing to remark on the folly that should pertinaciously narrow down the "kingdom" to a mere material state like the Babylonish or the Medo-Persian, as equaled by a similar persistency regarding the use of the word "life," let us look at the New Testament idea of the kingdom of God and Christ. It is represented as erected in this world, and flowing on to its completion and glory in the world to come. And, what especially concerns our argument, it is represented, in its relation to the individual believer, as a spiritual state which he actually enters upon in this world: "Who hath delivered us from the power of darkness, and hath translated us into the kingdom of his dear Son" (Col. i. 13). "For the kingdom of God is not meat and drink, but righteousness, and peace, and joy in the Holy Ghost" (Rom. xiv. 17). "Behold, the kingdom of God is within [probably, "among"] you" (Luke xvii. 21). "Thou art not far from the kingdom of God" (Mark xii. 34). This kingdom, as represented in the parables of the mustard-seed and the little leaven, begins with small beginnings, and proceeds with a gradual and steady increase in the believer's heart, as well as abroad in the world, and issues in endless joy, when the Son of man cometh in his kingdom with power and great glory. The representation in this form is precisely kindred with the other, of a state or process commencing here, and continuing till it is consummated in heaven. And, furthermore, the phrase "kingdom of heaven" is used with the same and greater variety of application, according as it is necessary to present one or another aspect of the great idea, the "subjection of all things to God in Christ." Now it is applied to the commencement of the Christian life ("the kingdom of heaven is like unto a merchantman seeking goodly pearls"); now to its progress in the believer; now to the nature of the principle; now chiefly to its consummation, and that, too, considered as a state of *blessedness and reward*, — "inherit the kingdom prepared for you." It has still other applications to the outward aspects and relations of religion, with which we are not now concerned. But, so far as it relates to the individual believer, its applications describe the same process which we have found to be set forth under the term "life," commencing in this world, and continuing uninterrupted for ever. On the other hand, a similar continuous state and process, having its beginning in time and its issue in eternity, is indicated of those who are here under "the power [authority] of darkness," are "full of darkness," "love darkness," "work the works of darkness," are "darkness," and being thus united on earth with the rulers of the darkness of this world, are with them to be cast into outer darkness, yea, "blackness of darkness for ever."

Certain other expressions, closely allied in meaning

to the word "life," point in the same direction. The
Christian is "a new creature," "created in Christ
Jesus unto good works;" he is "born again," "be-
gotten" of God. These terms clearly describe the
Christian's present condition, and they indicate the
bestowment already of a *life* from God.

The same great thought of a life already begun from
God lies everywhere on the face of the New Testament,
under the designation of a present sonship, and often
with a reference forward to its glorious issue. "Beloved, now are we the sons of God, and it doth not yet
appear what we shall be; but we know that when he
shall appear we shall be like him."*

The same view of a present life and death is abundantly set forth under the form of a vital and fruit-
bearing union to Christ, or a withered and sinful separation. "I am the vine, ye are the branches; he that
abideth in me and I in him, the same bringeth forth
much fruit; for without me ye can do nothing. If a
man abide not in me, he is cast forth as a branch, and
is withered; and men gather them, and cast them into
the fire, and they are burned" (John xv. 5, 6). (It is
to be noted that the same essential fact here denoted
by the withered branch is, in Isa. v. 2, somewhat dif-
ferently expressed by the vine bringing forth "wild
grapes.") This vital union to Christ is everywhere
set forth as being "in Christ," or as having Christ "in
us." The time of that union, as well as its present
effect, is defined in 2 Cor. v. 17: "Therefore if any

---

* So in Rom. viii. 23, where our translation misses the real sense, "*waiting out* the adoption" (ἀπεκδεχόμενοι), i.e. looking for its *completion* rather
than simply "waiting for it."

man be in Christ Jesus, he is a new creature: old things are passed away; behold, all things are become new." Its date is conversion; its effect, a new creature. Its nature as a *vital*, a life-producing union, is strongly brought out, where Paul says, " I live, yet not I, but Christ liveth in me; and the life which I now live in the flesh I live by the faith of the Son of God." " Ye are dead, and your life is hid with Christ in God. When Christ who is our life shall appear, then shall ye also appear with him in glory" (Col. iii. 3). It is set forth under the symbol of the union between the members and the head, and of the temple built with living stones upon Christ, the living and the chief corner-stone; and, in various forms of allusion, runs through the New Testament.

But we have not yet seen how deep the view which we maintain lies in the whole Word of God, and how it is re-enforced on every hand, till we have contemplated another Scripture form of statement,— that of health and disease. In this mode, the sinning (and often at the same time suffering) are represented as those in whom the true functions of life are now, in part, impaired or gone, needing and perhaps receiving the healing power of the Great Physician. Sometimes they are spoken of as blind, deaf, lame, insensible; sometimes deeply wounded; sometimes desperately sick; while deliverance is healing mercy. The representation is found alike in the Old Testament and the New. " Is there no balm in Gilead? is there no physician there? Why, then, is not the health of the daughter of my people recovered?" (Jer. viii. 22.) " Lest they see with their eyes, and hear with their ears,

—and convert, and be healed" (Isa. vi. 10). "With his stripes we are healed" (Isa. liii. 5). "Behold, I will bring it [Jerusalem] health and cure, and I will cure them, and will reveal unto them the abundance of peace and truth"(Jer. xxxiii. 6) ; and the cure is explained in the verses following as restoring their captivity, cleansing them from their iniquity, pardoning their iniquities, and procuring them goodness and prosperity. "Return, ye backsliding children, and I will heal your backslidings" (Jer. iii. 22). Among numerous other passages of the same character, in many of which, however, the idea of punishment is entirely predominant, see Isa. i. 5, 6; xxx. 26; Jer. vi. 14; xxx. 12, 13, 14, 17; xl. 11; Hos. v. 13; vi. 1. The Saviour resumes the same thought: "They that be whole need not a physician, but they that are sick" (Matt. ix. 12). "Lest they should be converted, and I should heal them" (Matt. xiii. 15). His miracles of outward healing are confessedly symbolical of the work he came to work on the spirit, which he sometimes wrought, and announced in the very act of outward cure: "Whether is easier to say, Thy sins be forgiven thee; or to say, Take up thy bed, and walk? But that ye may know that the Son of man hath power on earth to forgive sins, then saith he to the sick of the palsy, Arise, take up thy bed and go unto thine house." And so closely are the symbol and its object wrapped together in the sacred word, that the same passage of Isa. liii. 4, "He hath borne our griefs, and carried our sorrows," is quoted by Matt. (viii. 17), and applied to Christ's miracles of bodily healing, and by Peter to his atoning sacrifice for our sins (1 Pet. ii. 24). It was "when we were yet without strength [sick, ἀσθενῶν], Christ died for the ungodly" (Rom. v. 6) ; and the leaves of the tree of life are "for the healing of the nations" (Rev. xxii. 2). Thus, even in that outward healing, the almost constant call for "faith to be healed."

A kindred mode of conception represents the soul as working truly and happily on the one hand, or falsely and disastrously on the other, under the image of the "liberty of the sons of God," and the "slavery" of sin.

Thus it will be seen that the notion of two continuous moral states of the human soul, each commencing in this life with certain tendencies distinctly marked; and reaching across into the other world with developments and issues in kind, only mature and unmingled, is no superficial view, depending on the casual use of a word here and there, but a settled pervading doctrine of the Bible, set forth in a variety of modes, — life, health, the kingdom of God, light, being born again, the new creation, the new man, sonship, liberty, on the one hand ; death, disease, and loss of function, darkness, the old man, continuance in the kingdom of Satan, slavery to sin, on the other. A man may as easily deny the evangelical system, as deny this teaching, which underlies the whole system of the sacred volume. Of these kindred forms of speech, "life" and "death" are the most striking.

We have seen that "life" does not literally signify mere existence, nor death non-existence ; that life designates a certain functional power, attended with certain processes and results,— something superadded to existence; that the usage of common life in various tongues, the language of the Bible included, employs the term in a pregnant sense to comprise true action, welfare, and prosperity; that as the Word of God contemplates man chiefly as a moral being, so it predicates the term of his spiritual condition and activity, with their tendencies and results — and death of the opposite. We have cited instances of this usage in the varied modes of simple statement, antithesis, definition, and clear discrimination, not fairly explicable otherwise; we have seen how it meets the circumstances of its origin; have found certain seeming inconsistencies of usage explained by the fundamental conception; and the whole sustained by similar kindred representations, marked with the same peculiarities, and all, in like manner, derived from outward and physical phenomena.

To complete the showing would carry us over a large number of passages, where, though the proof is not so absolute and unanswerable, the real meaning is so easily recognized that intelligent commentators and lexicographers have recognized it with one accord. They are so understood without force, or continual "prolepsis." They speak in the present tense. They refer to an immediate influence. Thus all those passages concerning Christ: "In him was life, and the life was the light of men." "I am the way, the truth, and the life." "I am the bread of life." "Christ, who is our life." "The life was manifested." "He giveth life unto the world." "For the life was manifested, and we have seen it and bear witness, and show unto you that eternal life which was with the Father, and was manifested unto us." Such allusions as these: "The commandment which was ordained unto life I found to be unto death. Gentiles . . . alienated from the life of God through the ignorance that is in them. As being heirs together of the grace of life. To the one we are a savor of life unto life, to the other of death unto death. His commandment is life everlasting. Among whom ye shine as lights in the world, holding forth the word of life. To be carnally minded is death, but to be spiritually minded is life and peace. The just shall live by faith. And the law is not of faith, but the man that doeth them shall live in them. For we also are weak in him, but we shall live with him by the power of God toward you.* Who died for us that, whether we wake or sleep, we should live with him. Always bearing about in the body the dying of the Lord Jesus, that the life also of Jesus might be made manifest in our body. So, then, death worketh in us, but life in you. As dying, and behold we live. Who his own self bare our sins in his own body on the tree, that we, being dead to sin, should live unto righteousness. A crown of life which the Lord, the righteous judge, shall give me at that day. The words that I speak unto you, they are spirit and they are life. He that hath the Son hath life; and he that hath not the Son of God hath not life. Search the Scriptures; for in them ye think ye have eternal life, and they are they which testify of me. And ye will not come unto me that ye might have life. Now, if the fall of

---

* Mr. Hudson in quoting this verse cuts off the last two words, "toward you," in which, according to Alford, De Wette, and others, lies the emphasis of the verse.

them be the riches of the world, what shall the receiving of them be but life from the dead?"

Now, as these two states are but commenced in this world, and are hastening towards a maturity in the other world, glorious or terrific, in which all that is excellent in the one and loathsome in the other will have brought forth their harvests; so the Scripture designates the totality of well-being in the one harvest, and of woe in the other, by the name of that condition — the seed-grain — of which they are but the luxuriant growth; and calls the one retribution pre-eminently life, eternal life; and the other death, the second death. Naturally;. for all that is inviting in the one and fearful in the other is but the continuation of the process, the eternal fruiting of the tree.

Accordingly, in a large number of cases, these words are used to designate that coming harvest, — the retributions of another world. On this point it is unnecessary to accumulate proof-texts, since there is no controversy about the general fact. We hold, as fully as do the advocates of annihilation, that the future state of the righteous is very commonly called life, eternal life; and the doom of the wicked, though less constantly, death, the second death. But we also hold, that so far from designating, when thus applied, the simple fact of continued existence on the one hand, and final extinction of existence on the other, these terms most clearly set forth the whole complex and thus consummated well-being, and the whole complex and completed ill-being, of God's rational creatures in their state of perpetual retribution. They are comprehensive terms, bearing not merely a physical, but a spiritual import. They designate primarily certain states of the soul, each of which embraces many aspects and consequences: they gather up the totality of those aspects and consequences, and thus often chiefly the weal and woe which stand out so prominent at last.*

The view which we have thus explained has this additional mark of truthfulness, that it is thoroughly consistent with itself. We start with one fundamental conception of the nature of life, which conforms to the truly literal meaning of the word, is supported by the higher uses of human speech, and meets all the shades of application in the Scriptures, even when seemingly exceptional. We have confined ourselves to the usage of the terms themselves, reserving for its proper place the positive proof that the death of the sinner consists in a state of conscious suffering.

We conclude, therefore, that the terms "life" and

---

* In his later book (Christ our Life), Mr. Hudson virtually admits this important point in regard to the word "life." "We disclaim the representation that 'eternal life' in our view signifies *mere* eternal existence. We certainly believe in eternal blessedness, and we think this implied in the phrase 'eternal life.' For all real life, according to its proper laws, is joyous, and can-not be otherwise. Blessedness or well-being is the natural and legitimate *adjective* sense of the phrase in question ; eternal being, its *substantive* import. We insist on this part of its meaning, as implying that they who have not eternal life do not 'live for ever.'" p. 4.

The turn is characteristic and futile. For (1) the statement concerning the substantive and adjective meaning of the *word* is incorrect. Existence is not the thing asserted, though it is involved in "life:" life is always and distinctively more than being. (2) Blessedness or well-being is more than "implied:" it is the thing asserted in the Scripture statements. Is any man bold enough to maintain that these announcements of "eternal life," which form the constant burden of the Scripture promises, mean to include perfection, glory, blessedness, and all manner of well-being, only *by inference?* Is it chiefly and principally *being* that they so enthusiastically set forth? or is it the highest perfection of *well-being?* The answer will decide what is the "substantive" meaning of eternal life in the Scriptures.

"death," on which so largely depends the theory of annihilation, not only give it no countenance whatever, but teach a very different doctrine. The so-called literal meaning is a perversion of language; and the continual resort to assertions of prolepsis, supposed death, and the like, will not relieve the difficulties of the theory, nor satisfy the statements of God's word.

But, as certain objections are or may be made to this view, this important branch of the subject can not properly be dismissed without giving them some attention.

No person who has reflected upon the most familiar use of language will object that we find both a higher and a lower sense in the use of these terms in Scripture. When it is written, " *Look* unto me all ye ends of the earth, and be ye saved ; " " *Hearken*, and your soul shall live ; " " *Come* unto me, all ye that labor and are heavy laden, and I will give you rest," — is it a physical or a spiritual looking, hearkening, coming, that are intended ? and is any difficulty created by the fact, that, in scores and hundreds of other instances in the Bible, these words designate only bodily acts? The *reigning* of Christ over his people is a very different thing from the " reigning " of Ahab; yet the same word, in its lower and its higher senses, describes them both. " Israel," primarily the personal name of Jacob, is also abundantly used as the name of the whole nation, his descendants; sometimes of the ten tribes; and sometimes, in a higher sense, of the true children of God; e.g., " They are not all Israel which are of Israel " (Rom. ix. 6). " Zion " originally designated one of the hills of Jerusalem, and occurs with that simple meaning; but it became a favorite term by which God addressed his people, and especially as the objects of his love. These diverse uses of words, the higher and lower, are freely mingled in the sacred volume. Thus, when the Saviour had just cured a case of both bodily and spiritual blindness, he said (John ix. 39), "For judgment am I come into this world, that they which see not might see."

In a similar way, the lower and the higher meanings of "life" and "death" are freely scattered through the Word of God, often in close proximity, and usually to be discriminated readily by the subject and connection. The higher sense is less strongly marked, in general, in the older Scriptures. This fact, however, only corresponds to the general difference of the two dispensations, in the former of which all that was spiritual was both symbolized and veiled in sensuous forms. But there are many cases in the Old Testament where this usage is so manifest, that not only the mass of common Christians and evangelical expositors, but even rationalist scholars, personally indifferent, have found the pregnant meaning. "Keep thy heart with all diligence; for out of it are the issues of life" (Prov. iv. 23). "In the way of righteousness is life; and in the pathway thereof, there is no death" (Prov. xii. 28). "The law of the wise is a fountain of life, to depart from the snares of death" (Prov. xiii. 14). "As righteousness tendeth to life, so he that pursueth evil pursueth it to his own death" (Prov. xi. 19; so also, iii. 15–18; x. 16, 17; xiv. 27; xix. 23). "See, I have set before thee this day life and good, and death and evil." "I call heaven and earth to record this day against you, that I have set before you life and death, blessing and cursing: therefore choose life, that both thou and thy seed may live" (Deut. xxx. 15, 19). "He that hateth reproof shall die" (Prov. xv. 10). The same phraseology runs through the whole eighteenth chapter of Ezekiel, occurring more than twenty times; also abundantly in the thirty-third chapter, and elsewhere; in Jeremiah, Hosea, Psalms, Nehemiah, and other portions of the Old Testament.

The reader has but to examine these passages — let him read through the eighteenth chapter of Ezekiel, for example — to see in a moment that the words "live" and "die" do not mean simple physical life and death, nor future existence and annihilation. He can not fail to see that they are comprehensive terms, somewhat vague, no doubt, in these passages, but denoting manifold tokens of God's favor and of his displeasure. When standing by themselves, they clearly denote the same thing as when coupled with the explanatory phrases "good and evil," "blessing and cursing" (Deut. xxx. 15, 19). Even Gesenius could not render them less than "welfare, prosperity, happiness," on the one hand, and "ruin, destruction," on the other; and the least that can be understood of "death" in the eighteenth of Ezekiel, and elsewhere, is the meaning which Rosenmüller adopts from Michaelis: "all manner of severer punishment." It is vain to cull out from the neighboring passages (in some of these instances, e.g. Deut. xxx.), and put forward remarks about "prolonging their days in the land," as though this exhausted the idea. This is but one trait in a long catalogue of blessings, with their corresponding curses, running through these whole chapters, and summed up in the exhortation (xxx. 19), "Therefore choose *life.*" And, in this very portion of the blessing, the chief emphasis lies clearly, as the reader may see by examining, on prolonging their days *in the land of Canaan,* the possession of the promised inheritance.

In connection with this last allusion, let us observe more carefully an admirable instance of the Scripture mode of promise, strongly illustrative and confirmatory of the view we are now defending. It is becoming conceded by the best modern interpreters, in accordance with the older English expositors, that nearly all God's outward arrangements with his earlier people were invested with a spiritual significance, at least to the true servant of God. Accordingly, as the promises to Abraham and his seed are by the Apostle Paul applied not merely or chiefly to the lineal offspring, but to the spiritual descendants, of Abraham; so it is also distinctly stated in Heb. xi. 10, 13-16, that under the promise of the earthly Canaan was inwrapped and even apprehended a "heavenly" inheritance: "For he [Abraham] looked for a city which hath foundations, whose builder and maker is God. . . . These all died in faith, not having received the promises, but having seen them afar off, and were persuaded of them, and embraced them, and confessed that they were strangers and pilgrims on the earth. For they that say such things declare plainly that they seek a country. And truly, if they had been mindful of that country whence they came out, they might have had opportunity to have returned; but now they desire a better country, that is a heavenly." A similar statement occurs in verses 39, 40, of the same chapter, while in the fourth chapter, we are informed that the "rest" which God promised his ancient people was not that to which Joshua led them; and the Saviour chose to couch one of the beatitudes in a similar form, "Blessed are the meek, for they shall inherit the earth."

This striking case is sufficient (without adding others that lie at hand) to show how God chose to present spiritual promises of the highest moment under the veil of outer transactions; and also how, under the older dispensation, he chose to leave those topics comparatively dim. It is in perfect conformity therefore with the entire method of that dispensation, that the life and the death of obedience and of sin should have been left somewhat undefined, and should have been enforced largely with material sanctions. Still the higher and comprehensive meaning of the terms is there.* The Scriptures throughout are consistent with themselves in the variant use of this phraseology.

---

* We have not deemed it necessary to reply more at large to the objection of finding two meanings to one word, for the simple reason that not only does every page in the Bible answer it, but a man has only to look under almost any word in the dictionary, with its list of secondary meanings, to see its futility. It will weigh only with the illiterate. Such a writer as Mr. Blain turns it to some popular account, and charges the translators with "error," "corruption," and "perverting God's word" (Death, not Life, p. 30). He and others, the Universalists before him, have made a great outcry against the translation in Matt. xvi. 25, 26, where $\psi v\chi\dot{\eta}v$ is rendered both "life" and "soul." We have a similar and incontrovertible instance in John iii. 8, in which $\pi v\varepsilon\tilde{v}\mu a$ is both "wind" and "spirit." A difference of meaning is demanded by the "so" of the comparison; and, while the meaning "spirit" is unquestioned, the meaning "wind," in the first instance, is proved by the adjunct, — "the wind *bloweth*, . . . and thou hearest *the sound* thereof." With reference to the $\psi v\chi\dot{\eta}v$ of Matt. xvi. 25, 26,

Inasmuch as the Word of God thus uses language both in the higher and the lower signification, all flings at its interpreters for so understanding it fall quite harmless. Thus says Mr. Blain, " It is a notorious fact, that, in our theological works, a nondescript dictionary is formed with definitions as follows : To be dead

and the fuller passage in Mark viii. 35–38, it may be remarked (1) A difference of significations is indispensable to escape a flat contradiction in the statement, " Whosoever shall lose his life shall save it." The annihilationist does not escape this necessity, for he makes one life the life here, the other " the *resurrected* life " — two distinct things, though couched under one word, and even spoken of as though identical, — " it." (2) The word ψυχή, designating primarily the interior invisible principle, sometimes signifies specially the life which was connected with it, and sometimes views it as the seat of thought, affection, will, i.e. as a soul. Instances where it means life need not be given. Instances in which it designates the soul or its affections are the following: Matt. xi. 29; xxii. 37; John x. 24; Acts xiv. 2, 22, and many others. (In one instance in the New Testament (Rev. vi. 9), it means even a departed spirit, as often in classic Greek.) (3) In the passage before us, the preceding verse shows that one of its references is to the natural life here; the passage following, especially in Mark, proves the other reference to be to the future or higher welfare, " When the Son of man cometh in his glory." (4) Still more particularly, the connection of the two things, not alone by the use of the same word, but the blending of them in one common pronoun, " Whosoever will save his life shall lose *it*," renders it proper to carry the same word and thought, "life," through both clauses of the antithesis, while we are forced to understand the *lower* and the *higher* life. And this view is sustained by John xii. 25. (5) The best mode of translating in the two closing questions, " What shall it profit a man if he shall gain the whole world and lose his own soul? or, What shall a man give in exchange for his soul?" may admit of a question. In favor of the view of Alford, who would translate " *life* in the higher sense," is the one consideration of carrying through the same meaning of the word and the same shade of thought. In support of the view of De Wette, Alexander, and others who understand the soul itself, the seat of that life, is the more common meaning of ψυχή in this application, the similar expression in Luke ix. 25, " lose himself," and the very fact that it is another shade of meaning, and that a climax. The plain meaning of the passage is, that he who will lose his life in a lower sense for Christ, shall save it in the highest sense conceivable.

means to be more conscious; to die is to live on in woe; to lose life is to preserve a miserable existence; life means happiness; to burn up, to make a living salamander; to destroy is to preserve whole; to devour, perish, consume, etc., means to make indestructible and immortal." And Mr. Hudson writes in the same strain: "We find that the wicked will die, and yet not die," etc. Deferring a portion of these terms to their proper place, and waiving some inaccuracies, we accept the statement on the whole. The wicked will die, and yet in another sense not die; for " to die is to live on in woe," as Adam began to do on that day when he ate the forbidden fruit. "To be dead," if not " to be more conscious," is, at least, to be in a state of intense action, as the Ephesians, while dead in sins, were " walking according to the course of this world," and "fulfilling the desires of the flesh and of the mind." To lose life in one sense may be compatible with preserving a miserable existence; just as to lose life in another sense is compatible with preserving a blessed existence, or simply preserving life (John xii. 25). To those who are disposed to make such flings as these, it might be not altogether unsuitable to commend the study of verses 4 and 5 of Prov. xxvi., in one of which we are told, "Answer not a fool according to his folly;" and in the other, "Answer a fool according to his folly."

One evasion of a different kind is brought to view in the above quotations. "Life means happiness," says Mr. Blain, concerning our interpretation. And Mr. Hudson implies, that, according to the opponents of annihilation, life means " endless felicity." Mr. Dobney also assumes that we understand it as meaning "an eternity of bliss." Much of the speciousness of their arguments turns on confining the higher meaning of life, which we claim, to this signification. It is needless to say that this is a great misconception. Endless felicity, as we understand the Bible, is but one aspect of that true life, — an important aspect, but not the most important, nor by any means the radical idea of that complex term. And the conclusiveness of our view is seen in the fact that the one fundamental conception of the phrase easily and naturally meets all the various modes of its usage.

It is also attempted to evade the view now presented, especially in connection with the threat of death as the penalty of sin, by averring that we make the death itself to consist in sin or sinning. Thus Mr. Hudson in both his books, substantially: Adam did not, "*in the day*" when he ate the forbidden fruit, receive temporal or physical death, nor certainly eternal death, i.e. future misery; and "theologians are more and more conceding that 'spiritual death' as consisting in a sinful state should not be called penalty, lest God should seem to punish sin with sin." * And again: "His continuing to sin can not be called his punishment." No doubt this is adroitly put, but is very easily answered.

---

* Christ our Life, p. 41; see also Debt and Grace, p. 167. Mr. Hudson is replying to an argument which some bring against his theory of death by laying emphasis on the phrase, " *In the day* thou eatest thereof, thou shalt surely die;" whereas Adam did not become extinct on that day: therefore the "death" was something different from extinction, and the soul, though dead, is yet immortal. We have not cared to press that view. Death might that very day have begun its work by the implantation of its seed in his system; the mortal change tending steadily to the end. This would meet the demands of the statement.

In the act of sinning, the man inflicted a permanent injury on his whole moral nature; an incurable wound, or rather *disorder*, which brought with it false working, further sinning and suffering, internal and external, ripening for ever. If this be not punishment, thorough-going and terrible, what is punishment? One disconnected act of sin may not be the penalty of another, or of itself; but when the first involves the sinner in such entanglements and necessities, or begets in him such uncontrollable passion or folly, as to lead into the second and all its disastrous consequences, is not that a true and awful punishment? Is it not one of the daily and most fearful *penalties* of crime that it leaves no way of retreat, but both induces and often drives the criminal to plunge even deeper? Does habitual intoxication carry any form of punishment so dreadful as the insane passion which urges the victim again and again hopelessly to the cup, and thereby to all its bitter dregs? "Spiritual death," then, if that be the mode by which it shall be designated, does not consist in isolated acts of sinning, but in a permanent disease or distortion of the moral nature, a proneness to sin, a hopeless entanglement with it and all its woes.

Nor does it avail to refer to passages from the Bible, in which death (as well as its opposite,—life) has the lower meaning. The lower does not preclude other instances of the higher.

To set aside the force of the Scriptures, which affirm a death already commenced, and therefore not a cessation of existence, various methods are adopted. But the chief resort is to the figure *prolepsis*, anticipation: men are called dead because soon to die. Mr. Hudson naïvely remarks of this word *prolepsis,* " We shall find it a convenient name." He certainly does so.

That there is such a figure as prolepsis, and that there are instances of it in the Bible, there is no occasion to deny. The failure of this appeal, however, as an attempt to cut down the meaning of the word "death," appears in several ways. 1. The very few cases cited as proleptical assertions of death are, in several instances, more than doubtful. They are as follows, in Mr. Hudson's words (when speaking of the threat " Thou shalt surely die ") : " Just so said the affrighted Egyptians when God had smitten their first-born, ' We be all dead men ; ' and the trembling Israelites, when the troop of Korah was destroyed, ' Behold, we die ; we perish, we perish.' And God himself employs similar language in addressing the presumptuous Abimelech, ' Behold, thou art but a dead man for the woman which thou hast taken.' A phrase similar to that in our text occurs (Exod. x. 28) : ' Get thee from me ; take heed to thyself; see my face no more : for, in that day thou seest my face, thou shalt die.' Yet Pharaoh would not have falsified his words if Moses, incurring his wrath, had lived many days under sentence of death. Still more in point is the passage in 1 Kings ii. 36, 37, where Solomon gives charge to Shimei respecting the tenure of his once forfeited life : ' It shall be, that on the day thou goest out and passest over the brook Kidron, thou shalt know for certain that thou shalt surely die.' The last phrase is the same as in Gen. ii. 17, ' Dying thou shalt die ; ' and the expression, 'Thou shalt know for certain,' makes no difference, since Shimei knew his danger on the fatal day no more certainly than before: the circumlocution is simply emphatic." Add to these Matt. ix. 24, "The maid is not dead, but sleepeth," which he interprets " is called *not dead,* because she will soon be alive;" and Rom. viii. 10: "And, if Christ be in you, the body indeed is dead because of sin; but the spirit is life because of righteousness."

But in the last passage, the real meaning of which has been much controverted, a sound interpretation is that of Alford: " The body still remains dead, under the power of death physical," in which he substantially agrees with De Wette. Death is going on in the body, doing its work.

A more legitimate exposition of Matt. ix. 24 is that of Alexander: "She really was dead, but only for a time, and therefore *not dead* in the ordinary acceptation of the term." Physical death includes not only the departure, but the *returnless* departure, of the spirit: in this sense she was not dead. Not only does this exposition retain strictly the ordinary lower meaning of the word; it is confirmed by the additional words "*but sleepeth,*" showing the point of the remark to lie in the return of the spirit; and still further sustained by Christ's words in reference to Lazarus, where he begins by saying, "Our friend Lazarus *sleepeth,* but I go that *I may* awake him out of sleep;" and, when the disciples failed to comprehend, he plainly tells them " Lazarus is dead," though immediately hinting at the miracle which made his departure a sleep rather than a common death. The threat of

Pharaoh affords no ground for asserting a prolepsis: he threatens, in a certain contingency, immediate death, — death in that very day. There is no cause for saying he meant any thing else. The threat of Solomon to Shimei was also doubtless intended to intimate the most summary vengeance. And we find, that, to all appearance, the execution was as speedy as the possibility of the case admitted.

The exclamation "We die, we perish," meant, in the mouths of Israelites and Egyptians, death is close upon us, just before us, stares us in the face. This *may* be called a prolepsis; but it is cutting very close to do so. Just so, when Jacob and Joseph respectively were about to die, they began by saying, "I die" (Gen. xlviii. 21; l. 24); though Jacob certainly lived long enough to utter a whole chapter of predictions afterwards. If any one chooses to call this a prolepsis, it certainly shows how small a matter a prolepsis may be, and how close an argument may come to a quibble. In the two remaining passages, "We be all dead men," "Thou art but a dead man," the appearance of prolepsis is more distinct from the use of the word "dead" in the translation; whereas the expression in the original is precisely the same as that of Joseph and Jacob, translated "I die," and is so translated in these passages in the Septuagint, — "Behold thou diest," "We all die." * But if we waive this point, and admit, according to the English version, a prolepsis, that pro-

---

* The Hebrew מֵת may be either a participle used for the finite verb, or an adjective used as a substantive. Fürst gives it either way in these passages. Perhaps the latter usage is the more common.

lepsis is not only obvious, it does not admit the possibility of misapprehension.

2. So far as any of these can be considered cases of anticipation, it is of a death immediately at hand. "We die," "We be all dead men," "Thou art a dead man," indicate that the parties are at death's door.

3. The exclamation of "trembling Israelites" and "frightened Egyptians," as Mr. Hudson calls them, and the threats of Pharaoh or even of Solomon, if the latter bore upon the case, are but a slender basis on which to modify the solemn legislation of God, the calm words of Christ, or the doctrinal utterances of Paul and John.

4. It is vain to cite even clear cases of prolepsis against certain other passages which are just as clearly not proleptical. We have adduced many passages that can not be so understood without violence both to text and context, but which yield perfectly easy meanings, consistent with each other and with the radical idea of death, and with scores of other passages in which the same thought occurs.

5. The attempt, in this mode, to evade the Scripture teaching concerning a continuity of condition from this world to the next, called death, is also frustrated by equally numerous representations concerning the continuance of one and the same life, extending unbroken from this world into the next.

6. The resort to prolepsis is still further frustrated by the fact, that the same view of continuous conditions, life and death, is also presented under entirely different forms of speech.

7. The assertion of an habitual prolepsis (for habitual it is made) on the subject of the sinner's death, is itself the assertion of an habitual use of the term "death" concerning the sinner's condition, with an application quite different from the literal or lower use of the word. In the incautious language of Mr. Hudson (Christ our Life, p. 54), those numerous passages "seem to describe a coming death as *if its proper work were already done.*" Precisely so.

If any thing were wanting to show the entire futility of the attempt to force "death" into meaning "extinction" throughout the Bible, it is found in the complete breaking-down of that attempt, even in the collateral uses of the word. There are numerous instances in which the word "dead" does not describe bodily decease, nor the moral disease or future doom of the soul. In these cases, the meaning will be found a legitimate outgrowth of the radical signification which we advocate, and entirely incompatible with the fundamental meaning insisted on by the annihilationists. Of this class are such expressions as these: "Likewise reckon ye also yourselves to be dead indeed unto sin, but alive unto God" (Rom. vi. 11). "For I, through the law, am dead to the law" (Gal. ii. 19; Rom. vii. 4). "Faith without works is dead" (Jas. ii. 20). "Dead works" (Heb. vi. 1; ix. 14). "The law being dead" (Rom. vii. 6). "Sin was dead" (Rom. vii. 8).

Now, let us look at Mr. Hudson's exposition of the phrase "dead to sin," to which we invite the reader's careful attention. After a faint suggestion (which he does not venture to maintain) to translate "dead *by* or *in* sin," he proceeds thus: * "But if we translate the phrase νεκρούς τῇ ἁμαρτίᾳ, 'dead *to* sin,' the sense of the term 'dead' will not be figurative, but quite literal. Christians have no life in the direction of sin. *Their love for it has died out* [the Italics are ours], and their capacity for it is dying out. They have too much of the life that quickens to retain much of the life that kills." Now, let the reader look at this poor juggle. What is "literal" death? It is extinction, says Mr. Hudson, — extinction of the *man* himself; first the body, then the soul: and here is quite "literal" death, — "Reckon YOURSELVES to be dead." What is it? extinction of the *man?* No: the *man* still lives, and is to live on for ever: only his "love for sin" has died out. But even this, if you look closely, is but a figure; for not a faculty has perished, — only he has learned to turn his faculties in a different "direction." He who loved sin loves God. And so this "*literal*" death, this annihilation of a *man*, turns out to be a transfer of his affections from one object to another! Can it be that a man should not see that he has surrendered his whole argument, and admitted that death sometimes denotes a spiritual state? Still, he could not well do better. It is true that the term is applied in a different moral relation from the customary one, — sufficiently explained by its adjuncts; yet it exemplifies the same fundamental meaning for which we contend.

Equally ineffectual is his method of dealing with those other phrases, "dead faith," "dead works," "the law being dead," "sin was dead." "Here, however,"

---

* Christ our Life, p. 49.

he says, "death is predicated, not of *persons*, but of *things*; which certainly can not be spiritually dead, or 'dead in trespasses,' as that phrase is commonly understood." Well, and who ever supposed that they could? But they can be dead in a sense fully kindred to that meaning, — they can have ceased or failed to perform their proper function, can be destitute of all true efficacy, power. And this is precisely what is meant. Accordingly, in the next sentence, the author admits it against himself. "And the metaphor, if it be such [he seems to agree with us now, that it is hardly a metaphor], grows out of the conception of things that have force and power, as 'vital,' 'living,' and, again, as 'dead,' when they have lost their power." This is very well said, but not strengthening to his own cause. And now he proceeds, endeavoring to give the matter a different direction: "A law that is invalid is a 'dead letter;' and the parchment that contains it is waste paper [quite figuratively; for the parchment is still carefully preserved]. All things that grow out of date, or obsolete, may be very properly said to lose all the life they ever had; [how much is that in the case of 'dead works,' for example?] and the forms in which they were embodied in due time crumble away and vanish, or remain only as monuments [some diversity in the two suppositions] or ruins of that which is no more. Nothing could be more like literal death." But the reader will be pleased to observe through all this haze of statement that the "law" itself has not ceased to exist, nor perhaps been repealed, only lost its proper *functions;* that sin has not ceased to exist or even to act mightily, but simply to do its peculiar work on this individual; that the works were dead, not because non-existent, nor because they had lost any thing whatsoever, but because they never had any vitalizing, functional energy or true significance in them; the faith was dead, not as having perished, but because it failed to exhibit those activities which are the marks and issues of a living power performing its true work. Thus on each and all these collateral uses of the phraseology, as well as on the chief instances, the narrow sensual interpretation breaks down, and is inconsistent with itself; while the plain fundamental meaning which we have found not only fits the main drift of the Bible and its particular assertions, but adapts itself to all the incidental uses of the word, even the opposites of a dead faith and dead works, — of the law being dead, and of being dead to the law; of being dead in sin, and being dead unto sin.

We have, then, on the one hand, the legitimate and ordinary meaning of the words " life," " death," as denoting the presence or the absence of certain functions and activities tending to certain results in existent beings, traced in their higher and pregnant application from a material to an intellectual and spiritual use even in common life, and especially through the Word of God; we find that fundamental conception consistently applying in cases outwardly diverse; and especially we find that conception to be the one which will meet, and which *alone* will fully and easily meet, all the exigencies of that phraseology in its comprehensive power as applied to the state and prospects of the human soul, — a meaning too, not dependent on a word, but impregnably sustained by various other representations running through the warp and woof of Scripture, and read there unmistakably by the great mass of Christian men.

We have, on the other hand, a meaning assigned to the words "life" and "death" as the *literal* meaning (a meaning ascribed as unwarrantably as it is ostentatiously and pertinaciously); then we follow the writers who set out with this *literal* meaning of "death" as "extinction," not only to find the meaning breaking down in a large number of passages, and unsuitable in a great number more; not only refuted by other modes of representation, and, as we are presently to see, contradicted by positive statements to the contrary, but we track them in their devious paths casting away this "literal" meaning piecemeal; making it now a cause of death, now a "supposed death" (when there was no such supposition); now a "relative loss," now a "loss of force and power;" now the state of "the lovers of pleasure regarded as heirs of death," now a doomed condition, or a certainty of death — and that certainty spoken of as already existing in the past — while yet some of the very parties have now the certainty of not dying (Eph. ii.); and finally this "literal" death or extinction completely vanishing into a transfer of a living man's affections.

The truth is, that no man, however ingenious, can carry consistently through the Bible an endeavor to palm off this spurious meaning of "extinction" upon the word "death." The main argument is a total failure.*

---

* See Appendix, note A.

CHAPTER IV.

THE SCRIPTURE ARGUMENT EXAMINED: "DESTRUCTION," AND OTHER TERMS.

HAVING examined the terms "death" and "life," which constitute the most plausible portion of the argument for annihilation, the other phraseology, which is treated in the same arbitrary and material mode, may be more briefly dispatched. The same persevering attempt is made to ingraft the meaning of annihilation upon various other terms. But the refutation is easy.

1. *Destroy, Destruction.* "The Lord preserveth all them that love him; but all the wicked will he destroy" (Ps. cxlv. 20). "Fear him which is able to destroy both soul and body in hell" (Matt. x. 28). "Art thou come to destroy us" before our time? (Mark i. 24.) "The wicked is reserved to the day of destruction" (Job xxi. 30). "Broad is the way that leadeth to destruction" (Matt. vii. 13). "Vessels of wrath fitted to destruction" (Rom. ix. 22).

Mr. Blain quotes and refers to some forty-two such texts, and informs us that such terms are used five hundred times in the Bible. But as the same Greek word ($\mathit{\dot{α}πόλλυμι}$ and $\mathit{\dot{α}πώλεια}$) is also translated by the words "perish," "perdition," "lose," and "lost," it will be convenient to add those words also before replying.

2. *To perish, perdition.* "Kiss the Son, lest he be angry, and ye perish from the way, when his anger is kindled but a little" (Ps. ii. 12). "As many as have sinned without law shall also perish without law" (Rom. ii. 12). "None of them is lost but the son of perdition" (John xvii. 12). "We are not of them who draw back unto perdition" (Heb. x. 39). Some thirty-five other passages containing these terms are cited by Mr. Blain.

3. *Lose, lost.* "He that findeth his life shall lose it" (Matt. x. 39). "But if our gospel be hid, it is hid to them that are lost" (2 Cor. iv. 3). Some six other texts more or less resemble these.

The words here quoted, in a very large number of passages of the Bible, refer simply to physical ruin or death; as where Joshua "destroyed" the cities of Canaan and their inhabitants, and Rahab "perished not."

But there is another use, perfectly clear and undeniable, in which these terms do not refer even to the loss of physical life, much less of existence, but correspond almost precisely to our comprehensive phrase *ruin,* and *being ruined or undone.* The ruin may be of the most various description, — a destruction of the well-being in whatsoever form, but, when applied to the prospects of the sinner, of his whole highest welfare here and hereafter. The Greek word translated lost, perished, destroyed, has this for one of its most familiar meanings. Ἀπόλωλα — I am lost, destroyed, or perished — was a common Attic phrase, meaning, according to Passow, "I am in the last degree miserable or unfortunate." So in the Scriptures.

The prodigal son was "lost," though neither dead nor annihilated, but in a most forlorn and wretched state. Christ was sent unto the "lost" sheep of the house of "Israel," to "seek and to save that which was lost," —ruined, though still existing and bitterly active. And if we wish for Christ's own exposition of what the "lost" sheep of the house of Israel were, read in Luke xv. 4–7: "What man of you having an hundred sheep, if he *lose* one of them, doth not leave the ninety and nine in the wilderness, and go after that which is *lost*, until he find it? . . . I say unto you, that likewise joy shall be in heaven over one sinner that repenteth, more than over ninety and nine just persons which need no repentance." A sinner alienated from God is already lost, in a state of ruin begun: his repentance is the recovery. Precisely so said God to Israel, "O Israel, thou hast destroyed thyself; but in me is thy help" (Hos. xiii. 9). Yet Israel was not extinct either nationally or individually, but reduced to a most calamitous and desperate condition. "My people are destroyed [cut off] for lack of knowledge" (Hos. iv. 6). But the people were existing still. Indeed, the "destroying" ranges through almost every form of calamity that can befall a nation or individual, up to the eternal penalty of sin. "Egypt was corrupted [*destroyed*, margin] by reason of the swarms of flies" (Exod. viii. 24). Said Pharaoh's servants, "Knowest thou not yet that Egypt is destroyed?" (Exod. x. 7.) Said Job of his great afflictions, "He hath destroyed me on every side" (Job xix. 10). And God says concerning him to Satan, "Thou movedst me to destroy him [swallow him up] without cause" (Job ii. 3).

The king of Babylon, who by his wars had exhausted the resources of his kingdom, is told, "Thou hast destroyed thy land, and slain thy people" (Isa. xiv. 20). We are told of Uzziah (2 Chron. xxvi. 16), "When he was strong, his heart was lifted up to his destruction;" upon his profane attempt to burn incense, he was smitten with leprosy, and obliged to abandon his palace and his government, dwelling by himself to the day of his death. "The rich man's wealth is his strong city; the destruction of the poor is their poverty" (Prov. x. 15). Clearly the meaning is, not the annihilation of the poor, or even the cause of their death, but the source of exposure to many forms of grievous suffering, trial, and danger. "In the multitude of people is the king's honor; but in the want of people is the destruction of the prince" (Prov. xiv. 28), — a cause of his weak and inglorious condition, liable to defeat and overthrow. "Pride goeth before destruction, and a haughty spirit before a fall" (Prov. xvi. 18). "But when his disciples saw it, they said, To what purpose is this waste?" — ἀπώλεια, destruction, i.e. simply misapplication or perversion (Matt. xxvi. 8). The ravaging of plain and valley is thus predicted (Jer. xlviii. 8): "The valley shall perish and the plain shall be destroyed." The utter overthrow of hope and courage is described as a perishing of heart (Jer. iv. 9): "And it shall come to pass at that day, saith the Lord, that the heart of the king shall perish, and the heart of the princes; and the priests shall wonder."

Without citing numerous other similar instances which abound, especially in the Old Testament, we remark in brief, that any reader of ordinary intelligence who shall run over, with a concordance, the passages of the Bible containing these words, will see that the attempt to force these passages to the aid of annihilation is destitute of all true foundation. He will see that the simple and generic idea of the words is not extinction, but *ruin*, — ruin of very various kinds, — very often indeed designating the demolition of a city with its buildings, and the taking of physical life; but also applied, with equal freedom, to the impoverishment, exhaustion, or devastation of a land, the miserable condition and dispersion of its inhabitants, the humiliation of a living monarch, the calamitous state of a surviving man, the downfall of a haughty sinner, the entire misapplication of a precious ointment. He will thus see that the word does not carry with it, by its proper force, the idea of extinction; and therefore, though applied to designate the awful ruin which shall overtake the sinner in another world, the attempt to sustain by its use the doctrine of annihilation, however vaunting and persevering, is simply preposterous.

4. *Consume, devour.* Some six or eight passages in which these words occur are materialized into extinction: "They that forsake the Lord shall be consumed" (Isa. ii. 28). "They shall consume; into smoke shall they consume away" (Ps. xxxvii. 20). "A fearful looking-for of judgment and fiery indignation, which shall devour the adversaries" (Heb. x. 27).

Can not a living man be, in Scripture imagery, devoured or consumed, without the destruction or impairment of his conscious being? Read a few passages and see. Says Jacob, in describing his physical endurances, "In the day, the drought consumed me; and the frost by night" (Gen. xxxi. 40). The Psalmist describes the deep grief which roused his faculties to a constant wakefulness: "Mine eye is consumed because of grief" (Ps. vi. 7). "Mine eye is consumed with grief, . . . my bones are consumed" (Ps. xxxi. 9, 10). Of the effect of God's heavy chastisements, he says, "I am consumed by the blow of thine hand" (Ps. xxxix. 10). He says of the wicked, "They are utterly consumed with terrors" (Ps. lxxiii. 19). Of the active zeal that filled all his being with life, he says, "The zeal of thy house hath eaten me up" [consumed me] (Ps. lxix. 9). In like manner the word "devour," though very often including the taking of human life, has a wide range of special meaning under the general idea of inflicting grievous evils. We read of strangers "devouring the land" (Isa. i. 7); of "shame devouring the labor of our fathers from our youth, their flocks and their herds, their sons and their daughters" (Jer. iii. 24); of "secretly devouring the poor" (Hab. iii. 14); of Christians warned not "to bite and devour one another" (Gal. v. 15); of men who "devour widows' houses" (Mark xii. 40); of a "deceitful tongue" that "loveth all devouring words" (Ps. lii. 4); and other similar utterances, which clearly show the futility of the endeavor to materialize these words into meaning annihilation.

5. *Tear in pieces, break in pieces, grind to powder.* "On whomsoever it shall fall, it will grind him to powder" (Matt. xxi. 44). "Now, consider this, ye that forget God, lest I tear you in pieces, and there be none to deliver" (Ps. l. 22). "The adversaries of the Lord shall be broken to pieces" (1 Sam. ii. 10).

One would suppose that such texts as these were sufficient to open the eyes of any one to the absurdity of the kind of interpretation with which we are contending. As though the Almighty would, like some hungry beast of prey, literally "tear in pieces," or, like a falling stone, crush into a shapeless mass! One is almost ashamed to refute such a gross conception by citing the numerous passages which show it to be only a vivid representation of deep contrition, oftener of heavy affliction, and especially of an irresistible and crushing overthrow and vengeance. "A broken and contrite heart" (Ps. li. 17) is literally a heart "broken in pieces and shivered." Job asks his friends (chap. xix. 2), "How long will ye vex my soul, and break me in pieces with words?" "They [the wicked] break in pieces thy people, O Lord, and afflict thine heritage" (Ps. xciv. 5). "The fourth beast" (Dan. vii. 23) was to "devour the whole earth, and tread it down, and break it in pieces;" yet the fifth kingdom (Dan. ii. 44) was to "break in pieces and consume all these [previous] kingdoms." Said the Lord to Jeremiah, "Arise, and speak unto them all that I command thee: be not dismayed at their faces, lest I confound [*break to pieces*, margin] thee before them." He addresses the enemies of Judah (Isa. viii. 9), "Associate yourselves, O ye people, and ye shall be broken in pieces; and give ear all ye of far countries: gird yourselves, and ye shall be broken in pieces; gird yourselves, and ye shall be broken in pieces. Take counsel together, and it shall come to naught." In David's song commemorative of his deliverance "out of the hand of all his enemies, and out of the hand of Saul," he says,

"Then did I beat them as small as the dust of the earth, I did stamp them as the mire of the street, and did spread them abroad" (2 Sam. xxii. 43): in other words, they were completely routed and overthrown by him. "To break all one's bones" is a frequent expression for heavy affliction. Job speaks thus of his grievous sufferings coupled with the triumph of others over him: "He teareth me in his wrath who hateth me; he gnasheth upon me with his teeth; mine enemy sharpeneth his eyes upon me. . . . God hath delivered me to the ungodly, and turned me over into the hands of the wicked. I was at ease, but he hath broken me asunder: he hath also taken me by the neck, and shaken me to pieces, and set me up for his mark;" and more in the same strain (Job xvi. 9–14). Yet all this time Job was in a state of the highest mental activity. It is also true that these terms are often applied to defeats and overthrows in which life is taken; but, even then, how completely the meaning rises above the mere form of the imagery is well illustrated in the song of Moses, where, after distinctly stating in repeated forms that the enemy were "drowned in the Red Sea," he continues, "Thy right hand, O Lord, hath *dashed in pieces* the enemy" (Exod. xv. 6). A man is crushed and prostrated, not annihilated, whether by deep contrition, severe affliction, or entire defeat.

6. *Cut off.* Some five texts containing this phrase are cited in proof of annihilation. "For evil-doers shall be cut off; but those that wait upon the Lord shall inherit the earth" (Ps. xxxvii. 9). "The face of the Lord is against them that do evil, to cut off the re-

membrance of them from the earth" (Ps. xxxiv. 16). "For such as be blessed of him shall inherit the earth; and they that be cursed of him shall be cut off" (Ps. xxxvii. 22). See also verse 28.

The very form of the above expressions shows the primary reference to *temporal* blessings and calamities, — "inherit the earth;" "cut off from the earth." They would leave the question of future existence out of sight. It is therefore hardly needful to show that they do not and can not signify annihilation by quoting such passages as these concerning the Messiah: "He was *cut off* out of the land of the living" (Isa. liii. 8). "And after threescore and two weeks shall Messiah be cut off" (Dan. ix. 26); and other passages almost equally decisive. But if it should be said that these passages, first cited under the form of temporal good and evil, involve also future retributions, we reply, If so, they affirm that the one class shall possess, and the other shall be cast out from, all the promised blessings of the heavenly land. In Matthew, we read a much stronger expression than simply to be cut off from a land; the Lord of the evil servant will "cut him asunder," i.e. cut him in two. If applied to physical life, the expression, literally taken, would assert its extinction, of course; but how different a meaning is here conveyed is made evident at once by the next words, "and shall *appoint him his portion with the hypocrites: there shall be weeping and gnashing of teeth*" (Matt. xxiv. 51). The phrase "cut off" commonly refers simply to physical death, but sometimes involves the additional idea of a threatened removal from the blessings of God's people in this life; while, in some instances, it even expresses a release from life's afflictions: "That he would let loose his hand, and cut me off; then should I yet have comfort" (Job vi. 9). The Psalmist, however (Ps. lxxxviii. 16), exclaims concerning his pitiable deprivation of earthly joys, "Thy terrors have cut me off."

7. *Blot out.* Two texts containing these words are adduced to prove annihilation: "Let them be blotted out of the book of the living, and not be written with the righteous" (Ps. lxix. 28). "I will not blot out his name out of the book of life" (Rev. iii. 5). In the first of these passages, the last precisely explains the first part. Let them "*not be written with the righteous,*" as sharers of their blessings, — perhaps here in the land of the living. "To blot out our transgressions," an often-recurring phrase, does not mean to annihilate them, but to pardon them, i.e. overlook their claims to punishment. To "blot out the handwriting of the ordinances which was against us" (Col. ii. 14) is not to annihilate those ordinances, but to set aside their demands and punitive consequences.

The fundamental image is that of record-books, some containing certain records of sins as though debts to God, others containing the registry of ancient Israel as heirs of the promised land, and one (in the New Testament) containing the names of the heirs of the kingdom of heaven. To blot out the transgressions or the handwriting of the ordinances was figuratively to erase that record; that is, to release the claim. To blot out the name from God's book (Exod. xxxii. 32 and Ps. lxix. 28) was to take away all title to the promises, and perhaps to send to a premature death; not to blot out a name from the Lamb's book of life is to leave the man a recognized, recorded heir of all Christ's promised love, entitled to the privileges of enrolled citizens of his kingdom. He, therefore, whose name is blotted out from that book of life, is for ever banished from the kingdom of heaven.

8. *Not be, naught, as nothing.* A few texts containing these words are also forced into the service of the system; with what success, the reader shall see. Ps. xxxvii. 10, "For yet a little while, and the wicked shall not be: yea, thou shalt diligently consider his place, and it shall not be." Mr. Blain triumphantly asks, "Where is hell, then?" We answer, In the other world; for this passage speaks clearly of the overthrow and disappearance of the wicked in this world. So the phraseology, "Thou shalt consider his place;" so the next words, "But the meek shall inherit the earth;" so similar statements in the same psalm, "I have seen the wicked in great power. . . . Yet he passed away, and lo, he *was not:* yea, I sought him, but he could not be found;" that is, on earth. Even Job describes his own desired disappearance in similar terms (Job vii. 21): "For now shall I sleep in the dust; and thou shalt seek me in the morning, but I shall not be:" see also Job xx. 8, and other places. The same remark applies to another quoted passage (Job viii. 22), "The dwelling-place of the wicked shall come to naught," or not be; where the whole argument respects God's dealings with men in this world. Another passage: "They shall be as though they had not been" (Obad. 16). But here the prophet is speaking of the entire *temporal* overthrow and extermination of the

Edomites: the land shall be as clear of them as though they had never been. The same thought is expressed two verses later: "There shall not be any remaining of the house of Esau." Job can hardly be accused of expressing the hope of annihilation, when, having uttered the wish that he had "given up the ghost at birth," he adds, "I should have been as though I had not been; I should have been carried from the womb to the grave." He clearly means that so transient an appearance, followed by an immediate and final disappearance from this life, would have been almost the same as not having lived here at all: he would have escaped the flood of earthly afflictions that came upon him.

And let it be observed, in passing, that it is vain to appeal to those passages which speak of death as the land of silence and darkness; for *these passages are quite as often employed in case of the righteous* as of the wicked, and they manifestly describe the case merely according to the *appearance* of things. It is the view from this side, the land of the living. To us it is darkness and silence, where "there is no work nor device."

But there are one or two passages like these: "They that war against thee shall be as nothing, and as a thing of naught; and they that strive with thee shall perish" (Isa. xli. 11, 12). "Correct me; but . . . not in thine anger, lest thou bring me to nothing" (Jer. x. 24). But how perfectly manifest the meaning, even to the commonest reader. To be *as* nothing and *as* a thing of naught, in warring against God, is but the popular expression for utter insignificance, e.g., "All nations before him are as nothing; and they are counted to him less than nothing, and vanity" (Isa. xl. 17). Is that annihilation? Just so a multitude of phrases which it is superfluous to quote, all having the same general meaning of insignificance (or sometimes discomfiture): "Mine age is as nothing before thee" (Ps. xxxix. 5). "Circumcision is nothing, and uncircumcision is nothing, but the keeping of the commandments of God" (1 Cor. vii. 19). "An idol is nothing in the world" (viii. 4). "Though I be nothing" (2 Cor. xii. 11). "If a man thinketh he is something, when he is nothing" (Gal. vi. 3). So the phrases, "Brought their counsel to naught," "Bring to naught" (Neh. iv. 15; Ps. xxxiii. 10; Acts v. 36; 1 Cor. i. 28), mean to show the insignificance of a thing in its complete overthrow. To "set at naught" (Prov. i. 25; Mark ix. 12; Rom. xiv. 10) is to treat as insignificant and with contempt.

With this plain idiom thus running through the Bible, it is astonishing that any man can even impose upon himself so as to find annihilation in it. Still more astonishing in reference to the other passage, "Lest thou bring me to nothing" (which is cited by Mr. Blain); for a man who could not read in his Hebrew Lexicon that the word means simply and strictly "to make little or few," might at least read in the margin the translation "diminish" (Jer. x. 24).

9. Some prominence is given to four texts, containing the word "end": "Whose end is destruction" (Phil. iii. 19). "Whose end is to be burned" (Heb. vi. 8) (where the wicked are spoken of under the image of thorns and briers). "Oh! let the wickedness of

the wicked come to an end" (Ps. vii. 9). "The end of the wicked shall be cut off" (Ps. xxxvii. 38). The texts are somewhat oddly brought together. But look at the first two: the argument is, that "end" here means final cessation of existence. What, then, shall we say of these texts? — "Let me die the death of the righteous, and let my last end be like his" (Num. xxiii. 10). "Mark the perfect man, and behold the upright; for the end of that man is peace" (Ps. xxxvii. 37). Do these passages declare the annihilation of the righteous at death? No. The word "end," which has a variety of meanings in Scripture, when used in such texts as this, simply denotes in a general way the close of the earthly career or probationary state: "Make me to know mine end, and the measure of my days, what it is" (Ps. xxxix. 4); or perhaps, more exactly, sometimes the close of this state as the beginning of the final condition. Indeed, that it sometimes denotes a final condition, even in this world, is undeniable: "Though thy beginning was small, yet thy latter end should greatly increase" (Job viii. 7). "So the Lord blessed the latter end of Job more than the beginning" (Job xlii. 12). "And the end everlasting life" (Rom. vi. 22). All reliance upon this phraseology is suicidal.

The two remaining passages are somewhat different: "Let the wickedness of the wicked come to an end." Waiving all other remarks, the reader who shall peruse the whole psalm will see that the one subject in view is the wickedness and its ebullitions in this world, from which the Psalmist prays for deliverance. The other passage is translated by Rosenmüller, De Wette,

Maurer, and apparently by Olshausen, "The posterity of the wicked shall be cut off."*

10. *Burn, and burn up.* The materialist interpretation lays considerable stress on nine or ten texts in which these terms are used concerning the enemies of God, and argues as though the vengeance of God were strictly similar to a wood fire, and the human soul to a combustible material, and the operation of the one upon the other was in either case much the same. Mr. Blain actually italicizes the word "ashes" in quoting Mal. iv. 3: The wicked " shall be ashes under the soles of your feet in the day that I shall do this." The passages cited (in addition to this) are the following: "A fire goeth before him, and burneth up his enemies round about " (Ps. xcvii. 3.) "And the fire shall devour them" (Ps. xxi. 9). "Whose end is to be burned" (Heb. vi. 8). "Cast them into the fire, and they are burned" (John xv. 6). "He will burn up the chaff with unquenchable fire" (Matt. iii. 12). "As therefore the tares are gathered and burned in the fire, so shall it be in the end of this world" (Matt. xiii. 40). "For behold the day cometh that shall burn as an oven; and all the proud, yea, and all that do wickedly, shall be stubble: and the day that cometh shall burn them up, saith the Lord of hosts, that it shall leave them neither root nor branch" (Mal. iv. 1). "Our God is a consuming fire" (Heb. xii. 29). "Fire came down out of heaven, and devoured them" (Rev. xx. 9). "A fearful looking-for of judgment and fiery in-

---

* Gesenius translates the word "end" here [אַחֲרִית] *eventus felix*, "happy close;" and Delitzsch, "the future (i.e., the earthly future) which he had imagined." The word itself admits either meaning.

dignation, which shall devour the adversaries" (Heb. x. 27).

It requires but a moderate familiarity with this kind of imagery in the Bible, to see the entire fallaciousness of the interpretation. This particular mode of expression runs through the Bible, and especially the Old Testament, so abundantly, as to render the meaning unmistakable. God's anger is a fire or a flame; afflictions and sufferings are its heat and burning effect, sometimes a burning in general; and when that vengeance is perfectly irresistible, appalling, and overwhelming, it is represented, as could be done in no other way so graphically and so consistently, as a devouring and consuming fire, driving over the helpless stubble, or sweeping through the dry thorns and briers, or reducing the tares and chaff to ashes. This is the simple fact of the case, capable of easy proof.

Not alone God's anger, but anger generally, is described as heat. The phrase, "he was angry," is, in Hebrew, "it was hot to him;" and the primary allusion probably to the flush upon the cheek. Heat and anger, associated in all languages, are still more closely interwoven in the Hebrew. Severe anger is חָרוֹן, burning. Ahasuerus "was very wroth, and his anger burned within him" (Est. i. 12).

The expression of that anger is a sending forth of flames or of coals, especially when infliction of suffering is implied. Even Leviathan is thus described (Job xli. 19-22): "Out of his mouth go burning lamps, and sparks of fire leap out. Out of his nostrils goeth smoke, as out of a seething pot or caldron. His breath kindleth coals, and a flame goeth out of his mouth."

Judah said to Joseph, "Let not thine anger burn against thy servant" (Gen. xliv. 18). Of God it is said (Jer. vii. 20), "Behold mine anger and my fury . . . shall burn, and shall not be quenched." "Shall thy jealousy burn like fire?" (Ps. lxxix. 5; lxxxix. 46.) "So a fire was kindled against Jacob, and anger also came up against Israel" (Ps. lxxviii. 21). Numerous other passages use these phrases and the like to describe in general the exhibition of anger, in whatever mode, but so as to involve the infliction of suffering.

In other cases, the suffering inflicted is clearly the prominent thought represented, as the effect of the fire. The calumniator is one in whose lips "there is as a burning fire" (Prov. xvi. 27). See also Ps. cxx. 4, Prov. vi. 27, for similar expressions with similar meaning. Jeremiah describes his deep sorrow "with which the Lord hath afflicted me in the day of his fierce anger," by adding in the next words, "From above hath he sent fire into my bones, and it prevaileth against them" (Lam. i. 13). The Psalmist, in his "prayer of the afflicted" (Ps. cii. 3), complains that his "bones are burned as a hearth." And Job, in his deep troubles, utters the same cry: "My skin is black upon me, and my bones are burned with heat" (Job xxx. 30). The deliverance of the Israelites from the terrible oppressions of Egypt was God's bringing them "forth out of Egypt, from the midst of the furnace of iron" (1 Kings viii. 51; Deut. iv. 20; Jer. xi. 4). God's threats of the terrible evils he would bring upon the house of Israel for its sins, describe him as about to gather them in Jerusalem like "silver and brass and iron and lead and tin into the midst of the furnace, to blow the fire upon it, to melt it; so will I gather you in mine anger and in my fury, and I will leave you there and melt you; yea, I will gather you, and blow upon you in the fire of my wrath, and ye shall be melted in the midst thereof. As silver is melted in the midst of the furnace, so shall ye be melted in the midst thereof; and ye shall know that I the Lord have poured out my fury upon you" (Ezek. xxii. 19-22). Here is terrific trial, but of course no annihilation: and the silver is melted as well as the tin; the fire only separates the two. So we read of a "fiery trial" (1 Pet. iv. 12), of being "tried with fire" (1 Pet. i. 7), and of being "saved so as by fire" (1 Cor. iii. 15). David describes his afflictions by saying, "We went through fire and through water" (Ps. lxvi. 12). "The rust of them [of your gold and silver] shall eat your flesh as it were fire" (Jas. v. 3). The Saviour describes the bitter troubles and persecutions which were to rage around the track of the gospel, "I am come to send fire on the earth; and what will I, if it be already kindled?" (Luke xii. 49.)

But oftener yet the thought conveyed, while still involving the notion of suffering, at the same time sets forth prominently the resistless, overwhelming discomfiture which God's anger will inflict upon the wicked. Nothing can so well describe the appalling power of that punitive anger, and the utterly helpless condition of its objects (together with the keenness of their tortures), as the surging, devouring conflagration. It is sometimes used even of severe human vengeance; thus (Judg. ix. 20): "Let fire come out from Abimelech, and devour the men of Shechem, and the house of

Millo." Num. xxi. 28 : "For there is a fire gone out of Heshbon, a flame from the city of Sihon : it hath consumed Ar of Moab, and the lords of the high places of Arnon." Here is only a threat of thorough overthrow. But more particularly God's irresistible vengeance, in whatever form, is represented under this figure. Thus (Nah. i. 6) : "His fury is poured out like fire, and the rocks are thrown down by him;" which is sufficiently explained by the preliminary questions of the same verse: "Who can stand before his indignation, and abide in the fierceness of his anger?" Jeremiah (in Lam. iv. 11) describes in general the overthrow of the land : "The Lord hath accomplished his fury; he hath poured out his fierce anger, and hath kindled a fire in Zion, and it hath devoured the foundations thereof." The vengeance which God will execute by the Assyrian is spoken of (Isa. xxxi. 9) as the work of " the Lord, whose fire is in Zion, and his furnace in Jerusalem." Of the devastation already inflicted by God upon his people, it is said that the vineyard " is burnt with fire ; it is cut down " (Ps. lxxx. 16). And the whole comprehensive and appalling chastisement in store for the sinning house of Israel, though often drawn out in detail, is constantly summed up in the sweeping threat of a fire that shall come upon it; sometimes a fire that can not be quenched: " O house of David, thus saith the Lord: Execute judgment in the morning, and deliver him that is spoiled out of the hand of the oppressor, lest my fury go out like fire, and burn that none can quench it, because of the evil of your doings" (Jer. xxi. 12; see also iv. 4; xvii. 27 ; Isa. xxx. 27 ; Ezek. xxi. 32; xxxix. 6, etc.). If any additional proof were needed that this phraseology simply describes any kind of overwhelming and irresistible vengeance, it is found in the reiteration contained in the first and second chapters of Amos, where, in the same words, with only a change of names, the punishments of Damascus, Gaza, Tyre, Edom, Ammon, Moab, and Judah, are all alike described as "sending a fire upon" those cities and nations, which shall "devour the palaces thereof" (Amos i.).

The same methods of speech — probably from the necessity of the case, and certainly in conformity with the usage which represents the joys of heaven under the forms of this world — are employed to describe the punishments of the wicked hereafter. Indeed, that flame is sometimes apparently represented as a continuous fire following them into the other world : " For a fire is kindled in mine anger, and shall burn unto the lowest hell" (Deut. xxxii. 22). Sodom and Gomorrha "are set forth for an example, suffering the vengeance of eternal fire," — the temporal overthrow passing into an endless woe of which it was the fearful symbol. In the New Testament it is the everlasting fire, the unquenchable fire, the fire that never shall be quenched, the lake which burneth with fire and brimstone. In the last of these phrases, the additional features would seem to have been drawn from some such scene as that of Sodom, where the lurid light, the suffocating smoke, and the torturing heat, all combine in one image of horror.

To the assertion that such phraseology as "burn" and "burn up," together with the other references to that punishment as a fire, denotes annihilation, we offer, then, the following decisive replies (waiving the fact, that, even in earthly fire, the elements remain undiminished, though changed in form): 1. The strange inconclusiveness of thus arguing from a figure, that because heat decomposes fuel, therefore God's anger must decompose a spirit. 2. The positive fact that this figure itself is abundantly used to denote extreme suffering and resistless vengeance, when the *subject continues to exist*, and even to describe himself as burnt and consumed. 3. The epithets often accompanying, which describe, not an extinction, but a long-continued infliction. It is " eternal," " unquenchable," " that never shall be quenched." To evade this consideration requires the double artifice of maintaining that " eternal," not once, but in all cases where it applies to the punishment of the wicked, shall not only be shorn of the meaning of *endless* duration, but of *all* duration whatever, and signify only " final " or " irreversible ; " and that the incessant continuance of the flame, which in one solemn passage (Mark ix. 43–48) is twice repeated, should be a superfluous circumstance.* Yet the Old Testament passages from which this latter representation is drawn most clearly denote protracted suffering.— See Jer. xvii. 4 ; xxi. 12 ; xvii. 27 ; iv. 4, and the contexts. 4. The additional decisive fact, that the fire of punishment is definitely described in the New Testament as the agent of conscious, continued

---

* The meaning of these phrases will be more fully considered hereafter. We say, *twice* repeated, but, if we follow the received text, it is *five* times. Tischendorf omits three of them, in verses 44, 45, 46. He is supported by manuscripts B, C, L, Δ, ℵ, together with the Coptic and Armenian versions; opposed by manuscripts A, D, E, F, G, H, K, M, S, U, V, X, Γ, and the Latin versions, Vulgate, Gothic, Ethiopic, and both Syriac. The case is doubtful.

anguish, and not of extinction. The rich man, who "in hell lifted up his eyes, being in torments," said, " I am *tormented* in this flame." "The devil that deceived them was cast into the lake of fire and brimstone, where the beast and the false prophet are; and shall be *tormented* day and night for ever" (Rev. xx. 10). The worshiper of the beast and his image "shall be *tormented with fire and brimstone* in the presence of the holy angels and in the presence of the Lamb; and the *smoke of their torment* ascendeth *up for ever and ever;* and they have *no rest, day nor night*" (Rev. xiv. 10, 11). "The furnace of fire" into which the wicked shall be cast at the end of the world is described as a place where "there shall be wailing, and gnashing of teeth" (Matt. xiii. 42, 50). These passages, so full and explicit, are conclusive that fire symbolizes an irresistible overthrow of perpetual suffering, and not of extinction.

11. "*Put under his feet.*" With the same eagerness, even this phrase is claimed as teaching annihilation. Mr. Blain quotes 1 Cor. xv. 25, 26: "For he must reign till he hath put all enemies under his feet. The last enemy that shall be destroyed is death." With characteristic sensuousness of interpretation, he adds, "To have eternal groaning and cursing in a 'footstool' would not seem to be pleasant. This is a Bible expression for utter destruction of enemies: see Mal. iv. 3, and Rom. xvi. 20." Archbishop Whately seems to admit this position.* On this we need only remark, that the Apostle Paul elsewhere uses this very expression to describe the complete subjection of

---

* Blain's Death, not Life, p. 21; Whately's Future State, p. 177.

the whole universe to Christ, — of all created things, rational and irrational; of all intelligences, rebellious or obedient: see Heb. ii. 7, 8; Eph. i. 20–23; with which compare Phil. ii. 9–11. According to this mode of dealing with Scripture, therefore, the subjection of Christ's empire to his authority would consist in its annihilation!

We have examined the chief passages and phrases on which the advocates of annihilation rest their position. In every one of them, the attempt utterly fails. Its only speciousness consists in viewing the imagery detached and materialized. To the common reader, the Scripture explains itself as he reads these phrases in their place. The whole tenor of the Bible, transfused as it is with such vivid metaphors, guides him aright; indeed, the case is so clear, that he raises no question: but when a few of the most intense expressions are *isolated from their surroundings* and ingeniously combined, and the glowing metaphors converted into literal propositions, he is surprised, perhaps, at the form and strength of the language. It becomes necessary to clear up the matter by showing him the same expression in unmistakable connections: therefore the almost superfluous extent at which we have examined these phrases.

Perhaps, in concluding this portion of the subject, no more satisfactory exhibition can be made than the forms under which a single living speaker in the Bible describes his own present deep sufferings. The reader will observe that a large portion of all the phrases on which annihilationists rely, and others besides, are found in Job's description of his state. Let him weigh these several modes of expression: "The arrows of the Almighty are within me, the poison whereof *drinketh up my spirit;* the terrors of God do set themselves in array against me" (vi. 4). "Thine eyes are upon me, *and I am not*" (vii. 8). "For he *breaketh me with a tempest,* and multiplieth my wounds without cause. He will not *suffer* me to *take my breath,* but filleth me with bitterness" (ix. 17, 18). "Wherefore hidest thou thy face, and holdest me for thine enemy? Wilt thou break a leaf driven to and fro? and wilt thou *pursue the dry stubble?*" "And [I am] he [that] as a *rotten thing consumeth,* as a garment that is motheaten" (xiii. 24, 25, 28). "He *teareth me* in his wrath who hateth me; he gnasheth upon me with his teeth: mine enemy sharpeneth his eyes upon me. They have gaped upon me with their mouth; they have smitten me upon the cheek reproachfully; they have gathered themselves together against me." "I was at ease, but he hath *broken me asunder:* he hath also taken me by my neck, and *shaken me to pieces,* and set me up for his mark. His archers compass me round about; he *cleaveth* my reins asunder, and doth not spare; he *poureth out my gall* upon the ground. He *breaketh me with breach upon breach;* he runneth upon me like a giant. I have sewed sackcloth upon my skin, and defiled my horn in the dust. My face is foul with weeping, and on my eyelids is *the shadow of death*" (xvi. 9, 10, 12–16). "My breath is corrupt; *my days are extinct;* the graves are ready for me" (xvii. 1). "He hath fenced up my way that I can not pass, and he hath set *darkness* in my paths. He hath *destroyed me* on every side, and *I am gone;* and mine hope hath he removed like a tree. He hath also *kindled* his wrath against me" (xix. 8, 10, 11). "They came upon me as a wide breaking-in of waters: in the desolation, they rolled themselves upon me. Terrors are turned upon me: they pursue my soul as the wind." "He hath cast me into the mire, and I am become like *dust and ashes.* Thou liftest me up to the wind; thou causest me to ride upon it, and *dissolvest my substance.*" "I went mourning without the sun; I stood up, and I cried in the congregation. I am a brother to dragons, and a companion to owls. My skin is black upon me, and my bones *are burned with* heat" (xxx. 14, 15, 19, 22, 28–30).

A glance at the various modes of expressing the overpowering afflictions of a living being is sufficient to show the futility of using them, or the like of them, as arguments for annihilation. By the whole showing of Storrs, Blain, Hudson, and their coadjutors, Job was an annihilated man while uttering these words. The language describes indeed a reality, a terrible reality; but that reality *is not annihilation.* It is the overwhelming anguish of a living, conscious being. Let the man who rests his hopes of annihilation on such phraseology pause, and ponder well its meaning in the Word of God.

CHAPTER V.

THE SCRIPTURE ARGUMENT EXAMINED: THE RESURRECTION AND THE SECOND DEATH.

SOME of these writers attempt to lay stress upon certain passages which speak of the resurrection as an object of promise and desire to the believer. Mr. Dobney quotes specially three passages,—John vi. 39, 40, in which the Saviour says of the believer, that he shall "have everlasting life, and I will raise him up at the last day;" Luke xx. 35, "But they which shall be accounted worthy to obtain that world, and the resurrection from the dead," etc.; Phil. iii. 11, "If by any means I might attain unto the resurrection of the dead." With these he combines 1 Cor. xv. 12–32, and, after some twenty pages of discussion, sums up as follows : —

1. "There is a resurrection of the dead, generally. 2. The final judgment of each individual, with its award to heaven or hell, is consequent upon the resurrection. 3. The resurrection state was that which the apostles longed for, earnestly desiring to find themselves in their house from heaven, or heavenly house; that is, their second or spirit body. 4. Future conscious existence is connected with, and dependent upon, or identical with, resurrection; so that, no resurrection, no future life. 5. The resurrection grows out of the

mediatorship of Christ; so that, no Mediator, no resurrection, and therefore no future state." *

Some of these points we do not care to discuss now, though we dissent from them. We would remark, in passing, that the denial of consciousness immediately after death can not by any fair means be reconciled with Luke xxiii. 43, 2 Cor. v. 6–8, Phil. i. 21–24, the appearance of Moses and Elijah, and Christ's argument in Matt. xxii. 31, 32. And how far the fifth proposition is consistent with the writer's own theory will incidentally soon appear.

The main point of the writer appears in his third proposition, — that " the resurrection state was that which the apostles longed for ;" from which he would argue that none but the righteous attain the " resurrection state," or, as he would interpret his own meaning, continue in existence after the resurrection.

The fallacy is here covered over in the phrase " resurrection *state*," a phrase of the writer's own coining. If this phrase means the state of having been raised from the dead, the Bible is perfectly explicit that all men will share that state. " There shall be a resurrection of the dead, both of the just and unjust " (Acts xxiv. 15). " The hour is coming, in the which all that are in the graves shall hear his voice, and shall come forth: they that have done good, unto the resurrection of life; and they that have done evil, unto the resurrection of damnation " (John v. 28, 29). Nor does this writer venture to deny it. It is, then, not simply a living again from the dead which the apostle desired and Christ promised his disciples ; that *must* come. What

---

* Future Punishment, p. 164.

was it? Clearly, as the context in Philippians shows, the *blessed* resurrection, the resurrection *in Christ* to those joys and glories which he elsewhere describes as " the crown of glory," " the prize of his high calling," and which Peter calls the " incorruptible inheritance," the resurrection to " eternal life." Here is nothing about the resurrection *state*. It is " the resurrection " *par eminence*, no doubt; being " the only resurrection which is the completion of the man in his glorified state." The apostle speaks, therefore, not of the fact of a resurrection, but the mode and circumstances of the blessed resurrection; just as " life " means true life, — life worthy of the name. Eadie well remarks on Paul's expression, " The reference is to the resurrection of the just — Luke xx. 35 ; that resurrection described also in 1 Thess. iv. 16, etc. The resurrection of the dead was an article of his former creed, which the apostle did not need to change in his conversion ; but it was the resurrection to eternal life secured by Christ that the apostle aspired to reach." This is the simple explanation necessitated by the Scriptures ; for it is a clear scriptural doctrine, that the wicked shall be raised. These passages have no bearing on the question of their continued existence afterward.

But the fact of their resurrection at all is a fact of ominous significance, and of the gravest difficulty to the advocates of annihilation. They feel it. Says Mr. Hudson, " It is hard that they are raised up by a miracle that ends in their destruction, or that accomplishes nothing but a judgment, which in this view must appear simply vindictive. If they have no immortality, why are their slumbers disturbed ? " Surely, why? The Scripture gives clear information why the wicked are raised; it is to "the resurrection of condemnation;" "that every one may receive the things done in his body according to that he hath done, whether it be good or bad;" that God may render to them that obey not the truth "indignation and wrath, tribulation and anguish, upon every soul of man that doeth evil;" that they may "go away into everlasting punishment." This is simple and consistent. But the deniers of immortality must find here an abortive and meaningless miracle. And here they scatter in various confusion. Some of them, accordingly, by Mr. Hudson's own admission,* openly deny that "the resurrection of the unjust signifies their being made alive." This brings them in direct collision with the Word of God. Others hold, with Mr. Blain, that the man already once destroyed is brought into existence again to be destroyed with a second and final destruction. This, waiving all difficulties on the score of identity, makes the man suffer the penalty of the law twice over, and still leaves the futility of the second process unsolved. Mr. Hudson endeavors to escape the ominous fact by reducing the resurrection itself to a *minimum*; making it, indeed, no proper resurrection at all. Hear him: "Damaged seeds that are sown often exhaust their vitality, and perish in the germination; and we have noted the fact, that of insects which pass through the chrysalis state to that of the psyche, or butterfly, many, from injuries suffered in their original form, utterly perish in the transition." Then, after suggesting

---

* Debt and Grace, p. 247; Christ our Life, p. 4.

that the effect of the gospel, even upon the wicked, may be somehow to prolong a dim though unconscious existence after the bodily decease, dividing " death itself" into two installments, he concludes his explanation thus : " And for judgment, it is as if the unjust, hearing the voice of God in the last call to life, *should be putting on a glorious incorruption, and should perish in the act.*" *

We will not pause to inquire too curiously into the precise correctness of these matters of natural history, nor into the closeness of the parallel attempted. We will ask two questions : 1. What shadow of resemblance is there between this representation of an ineffectual struggle to come to life and " perishing *in the act,*" on the one hand, and, on the other, the Scripture doctrine that all the dead shall alike " hear the voice of the Son of God, and come forth ; " that they shall all appear before the judgment-seat, give account of the deeds done in the body, receive sentence from the Judge, and the wicked shall go away into everlasting punishment ? The Word of God teaches a resurrection as truly of the unjust as of the just, followed by the most solemn transactions. Mr. Hudson teaches an abortive attempt at a resurrection, or rather an abortive effort of the wicked to put on incorruption, — a process which seems itself to require a further elucidation. 2. What solution does this scheme offer to his own question, " Why disturb their slumbers at all ? " For let it be remembered the Scriptures represent this resurrection, not as a natural process, but as a grand

---

* Debt and Grace, pp. 264, 265.

miracle of the Son of God. To what end this transcendent miracle, this vast and inconceivably wonderful and solemn preparation? The Scriptures answer, that it is the fitting introduction to a still more solemn series of transactions, and a destiny commensurate. Mr. Hudson can not answer his own question; he simply evades it by depreciating and substantially denying the fact.

The whole Scripture doctrine of the resurrection, therefore, instead of lending any support, furnishes a most momentous objection, to the scheme of annihilation.

Equally ineffectual is the appeal to the phrase, "the second death." The term might have been considered in connection with other phrases denoting the destiny of the wicked. "The second death is to be taken," says Mr. Hudson, "in the literal sense." By the "literal" sense, he chooses to mean extinction. And it deserves special attention, that, in his quotations on this subject here and throughout his volume, wherever the words "death," "destruction," "exclusion from life," and kindred terms occur, we have this perpetual juggle on the "literal" sense of terms, which are often quoted from other writers as though denoting in those writers nonexistence, but without foundation. A great mass of quotation throughout these books is irrelevant and worthless, by reason of this pertinacious persuasion. Thus we are told, for example, that the Jews understood the phrase "second death" to mean "exclusion from life."* But did they mean by "life" bare

---

* Debt and Grace, p. 178.

existence? No. In the same way, the commentator Hammond is quoted in the use of the term "destruction," as though he thereby advocated the doctrine of annihilation. The persistency of this mode of reasoning strikes us as one of the most thoroughly sophistical procedures in the two volumes of Mr. Hudson; and it extends through them.

The phrase "second death" occurs but four times in the Bible; all these instances being in the Apocalypse, in one of which its meaning is explained. The course of Mr. Hudson on this subject is quite peculiar. 1. He resorts to Jewish Rabbins to explain a New-Testament phrase. 2. Of these twelve or thirteen quotations from "*early* Jewish books," five, being from the Jerusalem Targum, date as low as the seventh century; and others, at somewhat uncertain periods. 3. The quotations show no settled usage among the Rabbins; in one instance, the phrase being applied to the despair of Rachel at being childless (Gen. xxx. 1), in another, to the punishment threatened in Exod. xix. 12: "Whosoever toucheth the mountain shall surely be put to death." 4. Not one of the quotations seems clearly to sustain the meaning of annihilation, even in the Rabbins. Some of them are blind, others turn simply on the meaning of these very terms "life" and "death;" which terms, for aught that appears, are used in the biblical sense.*

---

* The quotations are as follows: "Let Reuben live in eternal life, and not die the second death." "This hath been decreed by the Lord: That this sin shall not be forgiven them until they die the second death." "Every idolater who says that there is another God besides me I will slay with the second death, from which no man can come to life again." "Behold, this is written before me: I will not give them long life, until I have taken

The appeal to the Rabbins to determine the meaning of a New-Testament term, which is explained in the same book in which it occurs, is as unjustifiable as it is ineffectual. The four instances in which the phrase occurs are Rev. ii. 11; xx. 6, 14; xxi. 8. In the last-mentioned passage, it is explained. After declaring that "he that overcometh shall inherit all things; and I will be his God, and he shall be my son," the sacred writer proceeds: "But the fearful and unbelieving, and the abominable and murderers and whoremongers and sorcerers, and idolaters, and all liars, shall have their part in the lake which burneth with fire and brimstone: which is the second death."

The second death, then, consists in *having their portion* in the lake which burneth with fire and brimstone. But this is not a process of extinction, but of continuous and endless suffering; for this lake of fire and brimstone is the same into which, according to the previous chapter, the Devil shall be cast, and " shall be *tormented day and night for ever.*" So, also, in the chapter following, this same class of persons are spoken of as being in existence, but excluded from the joys of the New Jerusalem: " Blessed are they that do his com-

---

vengeance for their sins; and I will give their glory to the second death." " Every thief, or robber of his neighbor's goods, shall fall by his iniquities, that he may die the second death."• " We learn from this place (Num. xiv. 37) that they died the second death." " Because he [Cain] was doubly guilty, he was slain with a twofold death, — the latter far more severe than the former." " They shall die the second death, and shall not live in the world to come, saith the Lord." " They shall die the second death, so as not to enter into the world to come."

Some of these passages seem very clearly not to signify annihilation. Two or three of them may, or they may not. It is as difficult as it is unimportant to determine what they do signify.

mandments, that they may have right to the tree of life, and may enter in through the gates into the city; *for without are* dogs and sorcerers and whoremongers and murderers and idolaters, and whosoever loveth and maketh a lie" (Rev. xxii. 14).

The foregoing passage designates most distinctly the nature of the "second death," as no extinction, but endless suffering, being "tormented day and night for ever." One other passage only seems to describe its nature, viz. Rev. xx. 14, 15. No doubt the whole passage in which it occurs is attended with some difficulties of interpretation, and is still the subject of controversy. On this account, it is less suitable for ascertaining the meaning of the phrase than the clear passage already cited. Still, as it has been made the ground of objection to the view now taken, it deserves a brief examination. In this chapter and the preceding is set forth the victorious progress of him who is called the Word of God, and the overthrow of his enemies. First, the beast and the false prophet are overthrown, and cast into the "lake of fire burning with brimstone." Afterwards, Satan, having been suffered at large for a time, is "cast into the lake of fire and brimstone where the beast and the false prophet are, and shall be tormented day and night for ever and ever." Then follows the judgment-scene, the white throne, the books opened, all the dead summoned before God, "death and hell [*hades*] delivering up the dead which were in them; and they were judged, every man according to their works. And death and hell [*hades*] were cast into the lake of fire. This is the second death, the lake of fire.* And whosoever was not found written in the book of life was cast into the lake of fire." Here it is objected that the casting of death and *hades* into the lake of fire must be, so it is affirmed, their annihilation; and consequently the casting of the wicked into the lake must be the annihilation of the wicked. To this we reply, 1. Satan (verse 10) is cast into the lake, not to be annihilated, but forever tormented,—a satisfactory refutation. The same thing is indicated in regard to the beast and the false prophet, when it said they were "cast *alive* into the lake." With this, also, is connected the statement in chap. xiv. 10, 11, that the worshipers of the beast "shall drink of the wine of the wrath of God, which is poured out without mixture into the cup of his indignation; shall be tormented with fire and brimstone in the presence of the holy angels, and in the presence of the Lamb: the smoke of their torment ascendeth up for ever and ever, and they have no rest day nor night." 2. The one point of the representation throughout is the *victory* of Christ over all his foes, and the *overthrow of their power*. The beast and false prophet — representatives of living beings — are overcome and punished, and their ascendency overthrown. Satan, a personality, is overcome and punished, and his power broken. All human foes are overcome, and cast into the same place of *punishment* with Satan. And, to set forth the absolute completeness of the victory, death and *hades*, which, in the New Testament, are represented as foes of the redeemed and of the Redeemer's

---

* This last clause, omitted in the received text, is found in the three oldest manuscripts, and admitted by the latest scholars and editors.

kingdom, are here personified; and they too are *pun-ished* like the rest, and their power overthrown. For this representation of hostility see 1 Cor. xv. 26: "The last enemy that shall be destroyed is death." Verse 55: "O death, where is thy sting? O grave [*hades*] where is thy victory?" Matt. xvi. 18: "Thou art Peter, and upon this rock I will build my church; and the gates of hell [*hades*] shall not prevail against it." * The representation is not of extinction, but of overthrow and punishment. If it be said that the overthrow of death and *hades* is their extinction, that is an incidental fact, if fact it be, and grows out of the circumstance that they are both personified abstractions, and not living beings. The living beings, or representatives of living beings, as appears from the passage under discussion, continue in existence and in suffering. Mr. Hudson, however, remarks of the phrase, "shall be tormented day and night for ever," "We think the language describes their utter and irrevocable destruction [annihilation] in a dramatic form." † On which all that need be said is, that a more utter perversion of language, perhaps, can not be found, unless it be in the advocates of this system and of universal salvation. 3. The extinction of death and *hades*, if we should grant that consequence, has no bearing upon the question of endless punishment. The "second death" remains, from which no deliverance comes. The "death and *hades*" here spoken of are simply the personifica-

---

* Even in Matt xi. 23, Luke xvi. 23, Rev. i. 18, xx. 13, if the idea of a direct hostility is not implied, that of opposition or antithesis to heaven and the kingdom of Christ always remain.

† Debt and Grace, p. 215.

tion of *physical death*. This is overcome, being reckoned as one of the enemies of Christ's redeemed; just as, in 1 Cor. xv. 26, we are told, " The last enemy that shall be destroyed is death " (compare verses 54–57).* This is the whole aim of the present passage, to set forth the overthrow of *thanatos* and *hades* — physical death — as hostile to Christ and his subjects. *All death is not abolished*, when the first death and the grave are overthrown, and cast into the lake of fire. There is another death remaining, which consists in being " tormented day and night for ever and ever." " This is the second death, the lake of fire." Into that are cast all the foes of Christ and his subjects, — the beast, the false prophet, the devil, all the wicked, and death itself, the attendant of sin and long the terror of the righteous. Accordingly, in the next chapter (xxi. 4) we read, " There shall be no more death" to the people of God, while (verse 8) the unbelieving shall reap " the second death," having their portion in the lake that burneth with fire and brimstone.

---

* So Alford, Düsterdieck, Brückner.

CHAPTER VI.

THE RATIONAL ARGUMENT EXAMINED.

A CHIEF reliance of the advocates of annihilation is on the rational argument. By Mr. Hudson and Mr. Hastings, this reliance is made quite prominent. The latter writer declares that " the doctrine of eternal anguish and torture of the lost is in itself so utterly opposed to our natural conceptions of God as revealed in the Bible, that it staggers the faith of the *most devout;* how then can it be received by the unbelieving ? In the language of Bishop Newton, ' Imagine it you may, but you can never seriously believe it.' Hence many minds *reject revelation entirely,* because it teaches, as they suppose, a doctrine so utterly repugnant to common sense and divine goodness." In the midst of other remarks to the same purport, namely, the entire incredibleness of the doctrine, he proceeds: " We say, first decide from the Bible whether the doctrine of eternal torment be true, and then, if we find no such thing is there taught, reject and oppose it as the most *terrific blasphemy,* the most audacious and unmitigated libel ever uttered against a God of love." *
The reader can judge how much meaning there is in

---

* Pauline Theology, pp. 76, 78. Except in the last sentence, the Italics are his.

the faint exhortation to examine the Scriptures, coming from one who so peremptorily declares the impossibility of believing the doctrine. With smoother and more temperate phrase indeed, but with a distinctness which the reader is requested to ponder, Mr. Hudson, after a metaphysical discussion of the whole subject, extending through a hundred and fifty-seven pages, advances to the Scripture testimony with the remark, "If our doctrine of evil be true, *it gives us a valid theism.*" *

As we are not discussing this subject to convince rejecters of the Bible, but for the satisfaction of those who receive it as the Word of God and as the ultimate authority, it is unnecessary to follow out this subject in its full extent. The question is with us, at present, simply a question of testimony to a matter of fact. If the testimony is distinct and valid, metaphysical or other objections must, as in all other questions of fact, go for nothing. Still, as some of these arguments are quite common, and admit of a very ready answer, we will give them a passing notice.

They are drawn from the nature of evil, and the nature of God.

Evil, it is affirmed, must be temporary, because (1) it is not needful to God's universe in any mode, and (2) because it is in its own nature frail.

As to the first point, sin is not indeed necessary, nor is it the necessary means of the greatest good. But no man who believes that God has made the best system can deny that the power freely to commit sin was

---

* Debt and Grace, p. 158.

indispensable to the best system of moral agency. And, though not necessary in itself, sin is a fact; and having become a fact, and a universal one, some better reason than this must be given to show why, *having once entered the system*, it may not continue for ever. Though not necessary, it came; much more, it may remain.

As to the frailty of evil, Mr. Hudson has devoted to this point some pages, of which the chief allegations are, that sin is a derangement and disease of man's faculties; that its pains are marks of decay and heralds of death; and finally, that sin " has no substance, is not an entity, is the antithesis of being." The first two of these statements are much the same with certain teachings of the Bible, which, however, the writer does not choose to find there. But when it is affirmed that its pains are signs of decay and " heralds of death," in the sense of coming non-existence, the statement has no foundation. All high emotions exhaust the bodily powers; but the pains of sin no more reduce the existence of the soul than do the joys of holiness. Indeed, the vast depths of its being and inextinguishable vitality are oftenest exhibited in the anguish of its sins. And for the " nothingness " of evil, its being " no substance," and the like, men may amuse themselves with such phraseology as long as they please. It is nothing at last but word-play. Whether sin be " an entity " or not, it is one of the most universal, ineradicable, and appalling *facts* in the history of the human race. For six thousand years it has been exhibiting a terrific power. Its " frailty " of nature remains to be proved.

But what is there in the nature of God to indicate

that all evil shall be banished from his universe? It may be alleged that his power, benevolence, and wisdom are guaranties of such a result.

But the first two considerations are of themselves entirely inadequate. We will grant that he has the perfect power to expel all evil by the extinction either of its perpetrators or of their evil propensities. But the use that he will make of that power depends entirely on other attributes.

We will concede that his benevolence will seek and secure the highest good of his universe. But *how* is that end to be accomplished? The whole question hinges at last on this other: Is the wisdom of God a perfect guaranty to us that he will secure the highest good of his universe by bringing all sin to an end? And this, again, is but the same as asking, Do *we ourselves* so certainly know the whole method in which Infinite Wisdom would govern a universe, that we can pronounce with confidence on the mode in which it will deal with sin? in other words (for it comes to that), Are we ourselves possessed of infinite wisdom,— the wisdom of God? If not, then we can not affirm that Infinite Wisdom requires the banishment of sin and sinners from his universe.

But we are not left to a negative result, though that alone annihilates the objection with which we are dealing. We have positive and unmistakable evidence on the question, whether the wisdom or any other of the perfections of God necessarily, or even certainly, excludes sin from this universe of which he is sovereign. It is the evidence of fact. The perfections of God did not prevent sin from entering the world, nor have they prevented its remaining age after age during the whole history of the human race thus far, for at least six thousand years. Now, whatever force there might seem to be in the argument that the wisdom of God requires him finally to drive out sin from his universe, it might be urged with tenfold force that he never would suffer it to enter a universe where all was holiness and harmony, and that he never would suffer it to remain in that universe for an hour. Facts show, then, that the argument is absolutely worthless. And it is not easy suitably to characterize the hardihood of an argument which boldly affirms God's perfections to be incompatible with the existence of that which he has permitted to continue from the beginning of the world until now.

But perhaps it is said, the *eternal* continuance of evil is a very different thing from its tolerance in this world. How different? Not in principle, certainly, but only in degree. It is only more of the very same thing. If there is nothing incompatible with God's perfections in its existence to-day and the past six thousand years, how is there to-morrow, or any other day, or six thousand years, or through all eternity? It is only repeating precisely the same process one day at a time; and the process goes on for ever.

The statement of Archbishop Whately on this point is clear and unanswerable: "The existence of any evil at all in the creation is a mystery we can not explain. It is a difficulty which may perhaps be cleared up to us in a future state; but the Scriptures give us no revelation concerning it. And those who set at defiance the plain and obvious sense of Scripture, by contending (as some do) for the final admission to eternal happiness of all men, in order (as they themselves profess) to get over the difficulty by this means, and to reconcile the existence of evil with the benevolence of God, do not, in fact, after all, when they have put the most forced interpretation on the words of the sacred writers, advance one single step towards their point. For the main difficulty is not the *amount* of the evil that exists, but the existence of *any at all*. Any, even the smallest, portion of evil is quite unaccountable, supposing that the same amount of good could be attained *without* that evil; and why it is not so attainable is more than we are able to explain. And if there be some reason we can not understand why a small amount of evil is unavoidable, there may be, for aught we know, the same reason for a greater amount. I will undertake to explain to any one the final condemnation of the wicked, if he will explain to me the *existence* of the wicked; if he will explain why God does not cause all those to die in the cradle, of whom he foresees, that, when they grow up, they will lead a sinful life. The thing *can not* be explained. . . . All we can say is, that, for some *unknown* cause, evil is unavoidable. Now, it is a manifest absurdity to attempt to explain and limit the operations of an unknown cause.

"It would indeed be very consolatory to be able to make out, *on sufficient grounds*, that the total amount of suffering, past, present, and future, in the universe is far less than we had imagined. But even if we could satisfy ourselves of this, — if we could discover that not a hundredth part of the evil that we believe to exist really does exist, still, as I have said, the diminution of the *evil* itself would not at all diminish the *difficulty*, I may say the impossibility, of explaining how it comes to pass, that, in the work of a benevolent Creator, there should be any evil at all.

"Unthinking people, however, are apt to fancy that a difficulty is itself diminished if the *thing* is diminished *about which* the difficulty arises. For instance, it is admitted, as is well known, to be impossible for man to annihilate any portion of material substance. We can destroy its form, as by tearing this book into shreds; or we can divide it into particles invisible to our eyes, as by burning it, so as to disperse part of it into vapor and smoke, and scatter away the ashes that remain: but we can not annihilate, that is, cause to exist no longer, the material substance. And, as impossibility does not admit of different degrees, it is equally impossible to annihilate the smallest as the largest quantity of matter. And yet, perhaps, some people, if they were told that some chemist had succeeded in annihilating a few grains of sand, though they might not absolutely believe the report, yet would not be so much startled at the extravagance of it, as if it had been said that he had annihilated some huge mountain. Again: it is thought by most to be impossible (at least, they would have great difficulty in admitting it) to convert, as some ancient chemists attempted to do, the baser metals into gold; and I suppose most persons, if they were told of some one having changed several tons of lead into gold, would at once reject the account as an idle tale; but if they were told that it was *only a few grains*, some, I imagine, would feel less confidence in the falsity of the report. And yet, if the difficulty is to conceive how lead can become gold, that difficulty is not at all lessened by lessening the quantity of the metal.

"And so it is with some unthinking persons in respect of the present subject. If they can devise some theory which will explain away great part of the supposed amount of evil in the universe, they hastily conclude that they have explained away some part, at least, of the difficulty presented by the existence of evil. Our distress and alarm, indeed, would be diminished by a diminution of the evil that exists; but the *difficulty* would remain precisely the same. And of this, as I have said, no explanation can be framed by human reason, or is to be found in Scripture." *

And so there is no difficulty encountered in the doctrine of the *continuance* of sin and suffering in eternity, which is not already encountered in the *fact* of its existence in and through all time. And the argument which breaks down before these present facts is good for nothing as a basis of future predictions.

But perhaps it may still be argued, there are special reasons why evil is admitted and tolerated in this present world, — disciplinary uses to the sinner himself, salutary impressions and influences on the universe, or exhibitions of the character of God, or grounds unknown to us; but these reasons will cease with the present life. We answer, that, in the first place, this reply concedes the main point, and admits that the permission of sin and misery *for sufficient reasons* is

---

* Whately's Future State, p. 175.

perfectly compatible with God's perfections, and therefore just, so long as valid reasons exist. If those good reasons always exist, then evil may be permitted for ever. The question then changes to this: Can any man prove that God, who has seen good reasons for suffering the introduction of sin, and its existence for many thousand years already, with every prospect of its continuance for a still longer period, can have no good reason whatever for suffering its continuance in the world to come? And this question involves two inquiries: First, Does any man *know* the reasons, all the reasons, why God permitted sin to enter and occupy this universe at all? Second, Does he know that those reasons will all cease hereafter? He is a bold man who ventures to answer the first of these questions in the affirmative; for he claims to have fathomed the whole mind of God. And bolder yet, if possible, is the man who ventures to affirm the second, while he can not affirm the first; who dares to assert that the methods of God must certainly change, while yet he does not know on what they are founded.

It is therefore entirely unnecessary to follow out in detail the argument, in whatsoever form presented, which endeavors, by its theory of God, or its "theodicy," as the phrase is, to prove that sin must come to an end. It has a fatal lack of fact for its basis.

And not only so, it is sadly *in conflict* with all the facts which seem related to the case. The history of the human race, and of the angelic race thus far, has a very unfortunate bearing on it. Had God never suffered moral evil to break in on his universe, very likely we should have thought that his perfections constituted an incontrovertible argument that he never would suffer it. Had he even on the first irruption of sin instantly hurled it out, by whatsoever method, annihilation or restoration, we might still have had some confidence in this argument against its permanence. Had he blotted out the sinning race, and started another, pure and spotless; had he manifested some special haste to bring the sinful race to an end; did he continue in existence only those fallen beings who were on probation, or those only whose probation would surely bring them to repentance, and cut off at once all those who, he knew, would never repent,— we might still allow some weight to the argument. Or could some man show very clearly and certainly some great end to be accomplished by permitting sin for many thousand years, which must wholly cease at some particular time; or some valid reason for continuing one finally impenitent sinner for a long term of years, and for repeating the process millions on millions of times, which reason *can not* possibly exist except in their particular circumstances,— the reasoning would have some force. But, unfortunately, every one of these particulars is against the argument. God did not exclude nor banish sin. He did not narrow it down to the least possible time, nor the fewest possible individuals. He has not exterminated the sinning race, but has suffered it to drag on its protracted and sinful career. He has continued in existence for an unknown length of time a race of sinful beings to whom we have no knowledge that any offer of recovery was ever made. He prolongs on earth the lives of multitudes of sinners who do not repent, and who, he knew beforehand, would not repent. Thousands and millions of these sinners he suffers thus to prolong their lives on earth, not only to no purpose so far as their own final welfare is concerned, but, *as far as we can see*, to no purpose as a warning to other sinners; yea, rather to introduce other sinners into the world, and to be the means of keeping countless thousands away from God. Such are the facts. They *prove* that the permission of sin and suffering is perfectly consistent with the perfections of God; that the reasons for their continuance do not necessarily contemplate the recovery, or even the probation, of the sinner; and that those reasons are wholly beyond our complete apprehension. The aspect of the case, from the facts which lie before us, affords no objection whatever to the eternal continuance of evil. On the other hand, it shows that if God see adequate reasons, he may properly continue this state of things for ever; and, in our entire inability to fathom the reasons for its present and past existence, holds out, of itself, a very strong presumption that he may deem it wise to suffer the continuance of evil in the future world. No man can allege a ground for the final extinction of all sin, that did not exist still more strongly for its original exclusion. No man can give a reason for the annihilation of the sinner at the end of fourscore years, which did not exist *a fortiori* for his non-creation, or for his extinction at the first transgression. No reason can be given why evil should be exterminated when probation has ceased, which would not bar its permission where no probation was offered, or where probation was known to be fruitless.

There is still one other shape in which the opposing

argument may be advanced. Thus: The protracted existence of sin and suffering is compatible with God's perfections, only because of his coming final and perfect triumph over it. We answer, First, This fully concedes the main principle at issue, namely, that the permission of sin for a good reason is perfectly defensible, while somewhat presumptuously asserting that there can be but one good reason. Secondly, The reason assigned overthrows the position which it endeavors to sustain; for if it be, as the argument admits and assumes, more honorable to God, and more truly *a triumph*, to show his mighty ascendency in the universe, after the protracted admission of sin and suffering, than by its utter exclusion, then, on the same principle, *a fortiori*, it is a still grander triumph in him to show that ascendency and glory over the *eternal* opposition of sin.

Considered thus in whatsoever light, the argument drawn from the perfections of God against the future existence of evil, is, in view of the plain facts of this universe, entirely fallacious, and hardly even specious.

It is quite customary with the advocates of annihilation (as well as the teachers of universal salvation) to garnish their argument with extracts from a letter of Rev. John Foster, in which, while admitting that "the language of Scripture is formidably strong" in support of the doctrine of eternal punishment, he descants dismally but powerfully upon the terrible aspect of the case. The point of the whole is contained in the following paragraph: "Under the light (or the darkness) of this doctrine, how inconceivably mysterious and awful is the whole economy of this human world! The immensely greater number of the race hitherto, through all ages and regions, passing a short life, under no illuminating, transforming influence of their Creator (ninety-nine in a hundred of them, perhaps, having never even received any authenticated message from Heaven), passing off the world in a state unfit for a spiritual, happy, and heavenly kingdom elsewhere,— and all destined to everlasting misery. The thoughtful spirit has a question silently suggested to it of a far more emphatic import than that of him who exclaimed, ' Hast thou made all men in vain ? ' "

But Mr. Foster best answers himself by another picture, equally lugubrious and direful, which he has drawn of the aspect of things in this world hitherto, and irrespective of any future state. He writes to Mr. Harris in the following strain : "I hope, indeed may assume, that you are a man of cheerful temperament; but are you not sometimes invaded by the darkest visions and reflections, while casting your view over the scene of human existence *from the beginning* to this hour? To me it appears a most mysterious and awful economy, overspread by a dreadful and lurid shade. I pray for piety to maintain a humble submission of thought and feeling to the wise and righteous Disposer of all existence. But to see a nature, created in purity, ruined at the very origin, etc., the grand remedial visitation, Christianity, laboring in a difficult progress; soon perverted; at the present hour known and even nominally acknowledged by very greatly the minority of the race; its progress distanced by the increase of the population; thousands every day passing out of the world in no state of fitness for a pure and happy state elsewhere, — oh, it is a most confounding and appalling contemplation!"

Thus the condition and history of things in the present world are described by Mr. Foster in the same mode in which he paints the retributions of the future world; and, by his own showing, it appears that the same kind of impeachment against God's character may be drawn from the one as from the other. The objection is therefore null.

PART II.

POSITIVE DISPROOF OF THE DOCTRINE OF ANNIHILATION.

CHAPTER I.

BELIEF OF A FUTURE EXISTENCE AMONG THE EARLIER JEWS.

WHEN we would weigh the teachings of Christ and his apostles on the subject of punishment, it is important to know what views prevailed among their immediate hearers. Those inspired teachers knew how their words could not fail to be understood, and spoke accordingly. And it may be well to consider, not only what was the then existing view, but what had been the early education, of that people.

Now it can be conclusively shown that the belief of another state of existence was familiar to that people from ancient times.

1. It is incredible, not to say impossible, that the Israelites should have lived in Egypt for many generations, without being thoroughly conversant with the belief of a future state. The doctrine of the continued existence of the soul after death, and in a state of re-

ward or of suffering, was one of the most prominent religious beliefs of the Egyptians. All attempts to cast doubt or confusion on this prime fact of the Egyptian religion is idle, if not dishonest.*

Herodotus, the oldest Greek historian, indicates the remote antiquity, as well as the prominence, of this doctrine among the Egyptians, when he says that "they were the first to broach the opinion that the soul of man is immortal." † But we do not depend upon the testimony of foreigners. The Egyptians themselves have made their own clear record. Delineations of judgment-scenes in the other world are among the most abundant of the old Egyptian records. They are found on the papyri, in the temples, and especially in the tombs. Here, with some variety of detail, abundantly recurs the same fundamental representation. The deceased person, in charge of the god Horus, is brought toward Osiris, the judge of the dead. Near the gates of Amenti, the region of the blessed, stand the scales of Justice; and the god Anubis, placing in the one scale a vase representing the good actions of the deceased, and in the other the emblem of Truth, ascertains the result. If found wanting, Osiris inclines his scepter in token of condemnation, and remands the soul, in the form of an unclean animal, back to earth; and all communication with Amenti is hewn away behind him. But, if his virtues predominate, Horus, tablet in hand, leads him forward to dwell in the presence of Osiris and the mansions of the blessed. A full account of these paintings may be found in Wilkinson's

---

* See Hudson's unworthy attempt: Future Life, p. 268.
† Herodotus, Book ii. sect. 123.

Popular Account of the Egyptians.* The same writer, in the notes of Rawlinson's Herodotus, makes the following declaration,—the declaration of an eye-witness: "This [doctrine of immortality] was the great doctrine of the Egyptians, and their belief in it is everywhere proclaimed in the paintings of the tombs. But the souls of wicked men alone appear to have suffered the disgrace of entering the body of an animal, when, weighed in the balance before the tribunal of Osiris, they were pronounced unworthy to enter the abode of the blessed. . . . There is every indication in the Egyptian sculptures, of the souls of good men being admitted at once, after a favorable judgment had been passed on them, into the presence of Osiris, whose mysterious name they were permitted to assume. Men and women were then called Osiris, who was the abstract idea of 'goodness;' and there was no distinction of sex or rank when a soul had attained that privilege." †

Proofs on this subject are abundant and incontrovertible. The question is set at rest. Bunsen, in his great work on Egypt, speaks thus: "The Egyptians were the first who taught the doctrine of the immortality of the soul,—a fact mentioned by all Greek writers from Herodotus to Aristotle, and one brilliantly confirmed by the monuments." ‡ In addition to the delineations of the monuments, a papyrus has been discovered in the Tombs of the Kings at Thebes, and recently translated by Mr. Birch, of the British Museum,

---

* Vol. ii., pp. 375-383.
† Rawlinson's Herodotus, vol. ii. pp. 168,169.
‡ Egypt's Place in Universal History, vol. iv. pp. 639 et seq.

entitled the Book of the Dead. It describes the acts or adventures of the soul of the deceased, and contains his prayers, invocations, and confessions on his long journey through the celestial gates. Bunsen gives an analysis of the work, with extracts, and proceeds to say, " The main points in the formulas of the Book of the Dead may be summed up as follows: According to the creed of the Egyptians, the soul of man was divine, and therefore immortal. It is subject to personal moral responsibility. The consequence of evil actions is banishment from God [in migration through animal bodies]. Faith transfers venial sins to the account of the body, which is, in consequence, doomed to annihilation. Man, when justified, becomes conscious that he is a son of God, and destined to behold God at the termination of his wanderings." *

The celebrated Egyptian scholar, Lepsius, adds his testimony. He describes the Book of the Dead as " essentially a history of the soul after death;" confirms the reference of the doctrine of immortality by Herodotus to the Egyptians; adding, " It is now sufficiently known from the monuments, that the Egyptians pos-

---

* Id. vol. iv. p. 648. Bunsen also remarks, " It is only by considering how very deeply this sense of immortality was ingrafted on the Egyptian mind, that we can comprehend the passion for the monstrous and colossal proportions of the Pyramids, and, at the same time, the glorious emblematical and artistic character of those works of the Old Empire. As animal worship is merely the Egyptianized African form of an early Asiatic conception, so is also the combination of the care for the preservation of the body, and, if possible, its protection from destruction, connected with the doctrine of immortality. The soul was immortal; but its happiness, if not the possibility of its continuing to live, depended on the preservation of the body. The destruction of the body consequently involved the destruction of the soul." — Vol. iv. p. 657. The closing remark seems to be offered as conjectural. No proof is cited.

sessed, from the earliest times, very distinct ideas about the transmigration of souls and of judgment after death." *

The records on these monuments date back to a period earlier than the residence of the Israelites in Egypt. Certain side-questions about the exact nature and history of the doctrine of transmigration have been raised; but the fundamental fact of a belief in immortality is indisputable. "No one," says a learned writer, "has ever disputed the fact that the ancient Egyptians believed in a future state ; and, as appears from the work of Röth (Die Egypt), they had this belief even before Jacob and his sons took up their residence in Egypt." †

---

* Lepsius' Introduction to Egyptian Chronology (Bohn's Antiq. Library), pp. 392, 365.

† Rev. S. Tuska in the Bibliotheca Sacra for October, 1860.

Prior to the modern discoveries, much confusion hung over this subject; and differences of opinion still exist as to some of the details. But the fundamental fact is no longer an open question. Mr. Hudson, however, by referring to these differences of detail, apparently endeavors to leave the impression that there is a doubt whether the Egyptians believed in the soul's existence after death. — Future Life, p. 268.

Mr. Alger, in his History of the Doctrine of a Future Life (A.D. 1864), very properly treats this as a question most perfectly settled by the three sources of knowledge now accessible; viz., the papyrus-rolls, the ornamental cases of the mummies, and the paintings in the tombs. He cites eminent modern authorities for the following results: " Souls at death pass down into Amenti, and are tried. If condemned, they are either sent back to the earth, or confined in the nether space for punishment. If justified, they join the blissful company of the Sun-god, and rise with him through the east to journey along his celestial course. . . . The condemned soul is either scourged back to the earth straightway, to live again in the form of a vile animal, as some of the emblems appear to denote; or plunged into the tortures of a horrid hell of fire and devils below, as numerous engravings set forth; or driven into the atmosphere, to be vexed and tossed by tempests, violently whirled in blasts and clouds, till its sins are expiated, and another probation granted through a renewed existence in human form " (p. 103).

Now, the Israelitish people resided in Egypt many generations in the midst of such views publicly held and conspicuously promulgated. To suppose them ignorant of a future state at the exodus is preposterous. The unquestionable records of the Egyptian monuments now for ever refute the alleged incredibility of finding the knowledge of a future state in the Hebrew documents. They make it incredible that it should not be there, — incredible that the long series of inspired men, from Moses to Malachi, should have been so far below Egyptian priests and kings as never to have alluded to a great truth which had been published to the empire long before the days of Moses.

2. The Hebrew view of the nature of the soul was such as to lay a natural foundation for a belief in its continued existence after death. The human being is specially distinguished from the animal world in his creation; and the soul is specially distinguished from the body, and allied to God, its creator.

This view of the human soul, though not drawn out in metaphysical statements and definitions, lies upon the face of the sacred volume from the beginning. The first chapter of Genesis sets forth the distinction between man and the animals, and his special alliance to God. The Creator proposes to "make man in our image, after our likeness;" and it is solemnly recorded, "So God created man in his own image." The Hebrew reader could not understand this as referring to any thing connected with the body; for he was taught (Exod. xx. 4) that God could not be imaged forth in

---

Mr. Alger, it should be remarked, does not find the doctrine of eternal punishment taught in the New Testament.

a body. The spirit alone could be made after the likeness of the spirit God. The thought is confirmed in the following chapter, where man's special relation to God in his nature is indicated in the fuller narrative of his creation. God "formed man of the dust of the ground;" and as a distinct and distinguishing act, we are told, he "breathed into his nostrils the breath of life, and man became a living soul." Thus the tenant of the human body was from the special inbreathing of God. "Two elements are united in man, — an earthly and a divine; which latter no other creature shares with him." *

The same high view of human nature is assumed throughout the older Scriptures, sometimes with apparent allusion to this account of man's nature and origin. Man walked and talked with God (Gen. ii. iii.). He was to be inviolate; " for in the image of God made he man " (Gen. ix. 6). " Thou hast made him a little lower than the angels," or rather (in the original), " Thou hast made him lack little of God " (Ps. viii. 5). Elihu exclaims, " There is a spirit in man: and the inspiration of the Almighty giveth them understanding " (Job xxxii. 8). " The Lord, which . . . formeth the spirit of man within him " (Zech. xii. 1). " Who knoweth the spirit of man that goeth upward, and the spirit of the beast that goeth downward to the earth ? " (Eccles. iii. 21.)

In this high doctrine of man's nature, and especially of the peculiar origin and alliance of his soul as the very inbreathing of the eternal God, was laid the firm basis of the almost inevitable conclusion — the immor-

---

* Hengstenberg on Ecclesiastes, p. 121.

tality of the soul, and its survival of the body's dissolution. In one striking passage, the conclusion is stated with the clearest reference to its foundation. The best comment on Gen. ii. 7 is found in Eccles. xii. 7, where the diverse destination of body and soul at death is distinctly stated, and with an allusion to their different origin and alliance : "Then shall the dust return to the earth as it was ; and the spirit shall return unto God who gave it."

Thus Elijah prayed : "O Lord my God, let this child's soul come into him [within, or into the midst of him] again. And the Lord heard the voice of Elijah ; and the soul of the child came into [the midst of] him again, and he revived " (1 Kings xvii. 21, 22).

It is not pretended that the Hebrews had nice metaphysical notions, or used precise phraseology to define this nobler part of human nature. It is never so in common life. But it is a fact beyond the reach of cavil, that throughout the Old Testament there runs the underlying and outcropping distinction between the earthly, perishable frame of man, and that higher portion of his being, variously termed his heart, soul, or spirit, which brought him into alliance and communion with God. "Bless the Lord, O my soul; and all that is within me, bless his holy name " (Ps. ciii. 1). "With my spirit within me will I seek thee early " (Isa. xxvi. 9). Sometimes it is even termed the "glory" of his being, and is distinguished from the body, which is joined with it to make the whole man : " Therefore my heart is glad, and my glory rejoiceth ; my flesh also shall rest in hope " (Ps. xvi. 9). Sometimes the soul and body are together put for the whole being of the man: "My soul thirsteth for thee, my flesh longeth for thee;" "My soul shall be satisfied as with marrow and fatness, and my mouth shall praise thee" (Ps. lxiii. 1, 5). "But his flesh upon him shall have pain, and his soul within him shall mourn" (Job xiv. 22). Sometimes over against the frailty of the one portion of his being is set the eternal joy of the other in its union with God: "My flesh and my heart faileth; but God is the strength of my heart, and my portion for ever" (Ps. lxxiii. 26). Quite often the soul, as the nobler part, is put summarily to designate the man himself: "Many there be which say of my soul [myself], There is no help for him in God" (Ps. iii. 2). "How say ye to my soul [to me], Flee as a bird to your mountain" (Ps. xi. 1). "Say unto my soul, I am thy salvation" (Ps. xxxv. 3).*

Through the entire Old Testament runs this distinc-

---

* From this designation of the man by the animating and interior portion of his nature arose a still further extension of the term to designate a human being in the most general terms: "Seventy souls," persons, irrespective of age or sex (Exod. i. 5; xvi. 16; Gen. xlvi. 18, 27, etc.). It is used of servants: "The souls they had gotten in Haran" (Gen. xii. 5); "If a man be found stealing any of his brethren" [a *soul* of his brethren] (Deut. xxiv. 7). Of captives: "Give the persons," literally *souls* (Gen. xiv. 21). With the proper adjective, it even designates a dead man, but never a dead animal: "Shall come at no dead body," literally dead *soul*, i.e. person (Num. vi. 6). The universal application of a law is indicated by the use of the word "soul" for "person:" "If a soul touch any unclean thing" (Lev. v. 2). In view of this last fact, so manifest, one can appreciate the force of the following passage from a tract by Thomas B. Newman, with his own capitals: "What dies? The SOUL that sinneth, it shall die." The Scripture, of course, means simply that the individual, whoever he may be, shall die.

It is not denied that the particular Hebrew word "soul" [נֶפֶשׁ] which primarily denotes the vitalizing principle, and thence an animate being, is frequently applied to all living creatures; e.g., Gen. i. 24; ii. 7, 19, etc. — See the next note.

tion between the earthly body and the higher principle, the animating spirit which brings the man into communion and union with the ever-living God, from whom it came; and which clings to him in unshaken hope and deathless love. It forms the natural basis for the almost inevitable doctrine of the continued existence of that exalted portion of our being.*

3. Accordingly, an existence beyond this life is recognized on the very threshold of the Bible, in the translation of Enoch; and, in the same palpable form, is reiterated in the translation of Elijah.

It is recorded that "Enoch walked with God; and he was not, for God took him" (Gen. v. 24). Now, it did not require the explanation of the writer to the Hebrews (Heb. xi. 5.) to unfold the meaning of this statement. A good man who walked with God while on earth,—and the fact is twice affirmed,—God *therefore* takes. Whither? To annihilation? To extinction of all conscious joy? Is that the mode in which

---

* This position, it will be perceived, does not rest on the nice or unvaried usage of a particular term or terms, but upon the accompanying utterances, the explanatory phrases, and unmistakable drift of whole passages; not upon a few such utterances, but upon a multitude of them, constituting the entire strain of such outpourings as the Psalms. Meanwhile many specific passages like those we have quoted definitely refer this alliance and communion with God to the inner portion of our being, in distinction from the perishable body.

It is therefore idle to tell us of certain diverse uses of the words "soul," "spirit," "heart" (נֶפֶשׁ, רוּחַ, לֵב), to disprove the Hebrew belief; as idle as to attempt a disproof of the modern belief in a soul or spirit, because *we* use these words so variously at times: e.g., the heart of the subject, the heart of the Andes, heartless; the spirit of a poem or a discussion, the high spirit of a horse, proof-spirit, etc.; every soul on board perished, a soulless wretch.

God shows his love for a good man? The thought is ridiculous. He took him to himself, to heaven; to be with him on high with whom he walked below. No man could miss the meaning.* And the sacred writer explains (Heb. xi. 5): "He was translated, that he should not see death." This narrative, occurring almost at the beginning of the sacred history, is very striking and weighty. It gives a key-note to the whole strain of the Scriptures.

Once again, long afterwards, the eyes of the whole nation were directed to that home of the holy by the ascension of the grandest of the Israelitish prophets to the presence of God. Elijah, in the repeated phrase of Scripture, "was taken up by a whirlwind into heaven," in a chariot of fire (2 Kings ii. 1, 11). It needed not his re-appearance on the Mount of Transfiguration to intimate, that, though absent from earth, he was present with God. Malachi foretold his return (iv. 5); and there is the most ample evidence, both in the Gospels and the Talmud, that the whole nation looked for his coming.

4. The patriarchs, who died by natural deaths, are described as having gone to join the company of their ancestors beyond this life.

It will not be forgotten how Christ silenced the Sadducees, in their denial of immortality, by that phrase from the Old Testament, "I am the God of Abraham, of Isaac, and of Jacob;" adding, that "God is not a God of the dead, but of the living" (Luke xx. 38).

---

* Such was the interpretation, for example, of Ecclesiasticus. xliv. 14; xlix. 14; and of Josephus, Antiq. 1, 3, 4.

The statement, he would say, made by God long after the death of the patriarchs, proved that they were not extinct; for God does not stand in such relations to extinct beings. Though dead, they live.

Other passages very distinctly intimate the continued existence of these patriarchs. We refer to those passages where each of them is said to be "gathered to his people," or "gathered to his fathers." This is the phrase employed concerning Abraham, Isaac, Jacob, Moses, and Aaron (Gen. xxv. 8; xxxv. 29; xlix. 29; Deut. xxxii. 50). To Abraham also there was given the previous assurance, "Thou shalt go to thy fathers in peace" (Gen. xv. 15).

Now, this phrase does not mean simply to die, or to be buried, or to be buried in a family tomb; for three reasons, the third of which is absolutely decisive. (1) Death and burial are both mentioned in the same connections, as facts distinct from this: "Thus Abraham gave up the ghost and died, an old man and full of years, and was gathered to his people; and his sons Isaac and Ishmael buried him" (Gen. xxv. 8, 9). Here the joining his people is mentioned as though the sequel of death, and as entirely distinct from his burial. Sarah, indeed, was the only occupant of the tomb in which he was buried. Precisely the same statement is made of Isaac (Gen. xxxv. 29). So Jacob "charged them, and said unto them, I am to be gathered unto my people: bury me with my fathers in the cave that is in the field of Ephron the Hittite" (Gen. xlix. 29). Here the being gathered to his people is the event over which he had no control; but the burial is the subject of direction. Moses was commanded

(Deut. xxxii. 50) to "die in the mount whither thou goest up, and be gathered unto thy people; as Aaron thy brother died in Mount Hor, and was gathered unto his people." Here, again, death and the being gathered to his people are distinguished; while burial in a family tomb is out of the question, since neither Moses nor Aaron was buried with their ancestors. The phrase in question is almost invariably preceded by the additional statement, "died." (2) The distinction between burial in one common tomb, and "being gathered to one's people," is also made prominent by the separation of the two events by a considerable interval of time. Jacob "yielded up the ghost, and was gathered unto his people" (Gen. xlix. 33); but it was only after embalming and seventy days of mourning, and a journey to Canaan, that we are told his sons "buried him in the cave of the field of Machpelah" (Gen. l. 13). (3) It is a decisive fact, that the phrase is employed concerning those who were not deposited in the tombs of their ancestors. Abraham was buried beside his wife only. Moses (and apparently Aaron) was buried in an unknown and solitary place. So also David, Omri, and Manasseh, each "slept with his fathers;" although David was buried in the city of David, Omri in Samaria, and Manasseh "in the garden of his own house, in the garden of Uzza" (1 Kings ii. 10; xvi. 28; 2 Kings xxi. 18).

There is, therefore, conclusive reason for understanding the phrase "gathered to his fathers" in its unperverted meaning of joining them in the other world. Such is the clear decision of the best modern commentators of various schools, — Baumgarten, Gerlach, Knobel, Delitzsch.*

It is with this thought that David comforts himself concerning his dead child (2 Sam. xii. 23): "I shall go to him; but he shall not return to me." The patriarch Jacob apparently expressed the expectation of joining his lost son Joseph, at the time when he supposed *his body* to have been irrecoverably devoured by wild beasts: "For I will go down into the grave (*sheol*) unto my son, mourning" (Gen. xxxvii. 35).

To the same purport the record of Elijah's miracle. The prophet prayed, "O Lord, my God, I pray thee let this child's soul come into him again; . . . and the soul of the child came into him again, and he revived" (1 Kings, xvii. 21, 22): an apparent recognition of the separate existence of the departed soul.

5. We may not properly omit to mention that this view is strongly re-enforced by the repeated designation

---

* Says Gerlach, on Gen. xv. 15, "Thou shalt go to thy fathers, or thy people, in peace, is the gracious expression for a life after death." Says Baumgarten, "A continuance after death is assuredly expressed therein." Knobel remarks more at length, on Gen. xxv. 8, "Abraham was gathered to his fathers, i.e. was associated with his ancestors in *sheol* [the underworld]. The phrases 'to go to his fathers,' 'to be gathered to his fathers,' and the very common one 'to sleep with his fathers,' all have the same meaning. They signify neither to die merely, since בָּרַע and מִיתָה are commonly connected with them; nor to be buried in a family tomb with one's ancestors, since the interment often is also expressed at the same time by קָבַר, and since the terms are applied also to those who were not buried with their fathers, but elsewhere, like Moses, David, Omri, Manasseh, as well as of those in whose place of burial not more than one of their fathers lay, e.g. Solomon, Ahab." Delitzsch takes the same ground on Gen. xxv. 8: "That Abraham was buried is first stated further on; the union with his relatives who had gone before thus takes place first, not at his interment, but already in the moment of death. . . . The union with the fathers is not a mere union of corpses, but of persons."

of the whole present life, however protracted, as a pilgrimage. "The days of the years of my pilgrimage are a hundred and thirty years, few and evil have the days of the years of my life been, and have not attained unto the days of the years of the life of my fathers in the days of their pilgrimage" (Gen. xlvii. 9); "I am a stranger with thee, and a sojourner, as all my fathers were" (Ps. xxxix. 12). The writer of the Epistle to the Hebrews certainly puts this construction on these utterances; for he says that the patriarchs "confessed that they were strangers and pilgrims on the earth; for they that say such things declare plainly that they seek a country, — a better country; that is, an heavenly" (Heb. xi. 13, 14, 16).

6. Another, and a decisive indication, amounting to a positive proof of a belief in the continued existence of the departed, is found in the practice of magical invocations of the dead, — a practice which, among other species of witchcraft, Moses was obliged to prohibit by law. In Deut. xviii. 10, 11, he commands, "There shall not be found among you any one that maketh his son or daughter to pass through the fire, or that useth divination, or an observer of times, or an enchanter, or a witch, or a charmer, or a consulter with familiar spirits, or a wizard, or a *necromancer*," literally a consulter of the dead.

The clear comment on this law, and conclusive proof of the strong hold of the belief and practice upon the nation, is found in the interview of Saul with the Witch of Endor (1 Sam. xxviii. 7-20). Saul went with the demand, "Bring me him up whom I shall name unto thee." The woman's reply shows that this was a common pretension of the whole class of wizards: "Behold, thou knowest what Saul hath done, how he hath cut off those that have familiar spirits, and the wizards, out of the land; wherefore then layest thou a snare for my life to cause me to die?" When Saul had re-assured her, she inquires in the most sweeping way, "Whom shall I bring up unto thee?" He calls for Samuel. The sequel need not be related.

Now, no difference of opinion as to the actual nature of the subsequent transactions can disguise that there was a class of persons in Israel who pretended to summon the dead into communication with the living, and that, while the belief in their power to do it was so extended as to require a special exertion of the monarch's authority to banish them from the kingdom, it was also so deep-seated, that even that monarch himself was the victim of the delusion. And, furthermore, this prevalent belief in the ability to bring up the dead must have rested on an equally prevalent belief that the dead were still in being.

7. But there are found also in the earlier times clear indications of the nature of that future; allusions to it as a state of retribution. It is the scene of joy and recompense to the righteous, and of vengeance to the wicked. Sometimes these respective future prospects are contrasted with each other, sometimes they are indicated separately.

How plainly does the writer of the sixteenth Psalm declare his confidence that God, who is his trust, will rescue him from the grave, and receive him to eternal joy in his presence! The first part of the Psalm (ver. 1–7) expresses his confidence and his delight in God, and the intimacy and firmness of his adhesion to him. With God at his right hand (ver. 8), nothing shall disturb his tranquillity. Not only shall his spirit be glad (ver. 9), but his " flesh also " — his body or person — "shall rest in hope" of future deliverance. "For thou will not leave my soul in hell [*hades, sheol*]; neither wilt thou suffer thine Holy One to see corruption. Thou wilt show me the path of life [the way to life, to God's presence]. In thy presence is fullness of joy; *at thy right hand, there are pleasures for evermore*" (ver. 10, 11). Here is the plainest hope of a life of pleasure for evermore at the right hand of God, after deliverance from the grave. The Messianic bearing of the Psalm makes no difference in regard to the doctrine of a future life, uttered primarily in the person of David.

The seventeenth Psalm contrasts the bright future hopes of the Psalmist with the earthly transient enjoyments of the men of this world. The Psalmist, with strong confidence in his integrity of purpose (ver. 1-4), appeals to God for defense from his deadly foes (ver. 5-9). He describes their pride and ferocity (ver. 10-12), and, in connection with a fresh petition for deliverance (ver. 13), he reminds himself of the evanescence of their many sensual joys (ver. 14): "Men of the world, which have their portion in this life, and whose belly thou fillest with thy hid treasure: they are full of children, and leave the rest of their substance to their babes." Immediately (ver. 15) he breaks out exulting: "As for me, I will behold thy face in righteousness; I shall be satisfied, when I awake, with thy likeness." Now, when we consider that to which this hope stands contrasted, — the portion of the men of the world in this life, as well as the Psalmist's own sufferings, inflicted by them in their hostility; and when we look at the phraseology of his hope, — the beholding of God's face in righteousness, the awaking, the satisfaction with God's likeness, — it is not easy to dissent from the statement of Rosenmüller, that "these things can hardly be understood otherwise than concerning the hope which the prophet entertained of a blessed vision of God in the future life, when he should have awaked from the sleep of death." Indeed the brilliant but skeptical scholar, De Wette, even maintained that David could not be the author of the Psalm, because it clearly expresses the hope of immortality. Tholuck says well: "Wondrously enlightened by the Holy Ghost, he [David] speaks with a clearness which seems possible to Christian minds only, of the glories of heaven, where the struggle with sin shall be changed into perfect *righteousness*, faith into face-to-face vision, satiation with the divided goods of this life into satiation with the one perfect good, which renders every thing besides unnecessary." *

Psalm seventy-third describes in full the writer's perplexity, distress, and danger, as he viewed the grand enigma of Providence in the sufferings of the godly, and

---

* Hengstenberg does not receive this exposition; but his objections are singular enough. They are solely that, "according to it, not merely would there be expressed here a knowledge of eternal life, more clear and confident than we could almost expect to find in a psalm of David, but specially that the Psalmist would declare his entire resignation in regard to earthly things, which, in that case, he wholly abandons to the wicked, and directs all his hope to the heavenly." Therefore he can not suffer him to express so clear a knowledge or so entire a resignation.

the undisturbed prosperity of the heaven-defying wicked, and the solution of that enigma in which his soul found peace in the assurance that the relative position of the parties shall be speedily reversed at death by the mighty and righteous Governor of the world. In the earlier part of the Psalm, he describes the occasion of his repining: "The prosperity of the wicked," often up to the very hour of their death (ver. 4.), their exemption from suffering, and their accumulation of riches and pleasures in the fullest degree through their whole life, while they defy both God and man (ver. 6–12). The contrasted sight of his own suffering lot had bred in him deep gloom (ver. 13–16), till he went to the sanctuary, and understood their end (ver. 17), which will be an instantaneous waking from an empty dream to a fearful reality of "destruction," "desolation," and "terrors" (ver. 18–20). After an expression of amazement at his own former stupidity, the writer exults in the consciousness of God's continual support; breaks out in the joyful assurance, "Thou shalt guide me with thy counsel, and afterward receive me to glory;" declares God to be his supreme portion in heaven and earth (ver. 25); and asserts that, even though or when "flesh and heart faileth, God is the strength of my heart, and my portion for ever." In this passage, the obvious meaning of the language is sustained by the whole scope of the Psalm. The source of the writer's distress was the unbroken prosperity of the impious wicked *up to the very hour of death* (ver. 4–17), as compared with the daily

---

* To avoid this, Ewald and J. Olshausen find it necessary to change the Hebrew text of verse 4, — conjecturally.

chastisements of the righteous. At the "end" only does the difference appear. The destruction, desolation, and terror of the wicked must be even subsequent to their dissolution; for there are "no bands in their death: but their strength is firm." The "dream" is dispelled "in a moment." On the other hand, the Psalmist is consoled under his daily chastisements with the assurance that the God who has hitherto held him by the hand will guide him by his counsel here, and "afterward receive him to glory;"* and that He who, of all objects in heaven and earth, is his chief good, will be his strength and portion when heart and flesh fail; yea, "to eternity." The judicious Alexander well remarks, that the reference to a future state in verses 16-19, 24, is "evident, if interpreted in any natural and reasonable manner."

The forty-ninth Psalm, though more obscure in method and expression, is a development of the same fundamental theme. It is intended to vindicate the government of God, and, in the words of Alexander, "to console the righteous under the trials arising from the prosperity and enmity of wicked men by showing these to be but temporary, and by the prospect of a speedy change in the relative position of the parties." In like manner, Tholuck describes it as "a didactic psalm concerning the uncertain prosperity of the proud and rich, their certain death, the victory of the godly, and their final reception with God." The writer solemnly calls the attention of the whole world to his solution of the great problem (verses 1-5). He points to the

---

* It makes no material difference if we adopt De Wette's translation, — and "afterward with honor receive me."

iniquity of his pursuers (not "heels") as they compass him about, boasting in their riches, and while powerless to redeem themselves from death with all their wealth (verses 7–9), yet regardless of the common lot that awaits alike the wise man and the fool (verse 11), and dreaming of perpetual prosperity (verse 12). But there comes an hour when "the righteous shall have dominion [shall triumph] over them," and that time is the hour of death. How so? for the Psalmist had already admitted (verse 10) the transparent fact, that the righteous, too, must die. Wherein, then, is the triumph? It is that "God will redeem my soul from the power of the grave; for he will receive me" (verse 15); while all the good things of the wicked pass away at death: "When he dieth he shall carry nothing away; his glory shall not descend after him, though while he lived he blessed his soul" (verses 16, 17). It is precisely the case of the rich fool of the New Testament, not so fully carried out. And so manifestly is this obvious interpretation of the language indispensable to even a tolerable fulfillment of the opening promise of the psalm, that a late German (rationalist) commentator (J. Olshausen), who denies the reference to the future, makes this fatal admission: "Though the poet in the introduction proceeds with no little self-confidence, yet does his solution of the problem which he treats turn out to be very unsatisfactory. Surrounded by the baseness of enemies, insidious and wholly reliant upon their worldly resources, he looks around for consolation, and without difficulty finds it, — sorry enough, however, — chiefly in the thought, that even his luxury can not rescue the rich man from death, and he must leave it all behind; while altogether short-lived and even trivial (*beiläufig*) is the defense and deliverance from death which in his conception the righteous may hope from God."

Sorry indeed, if that were all! The naked statement of such an exposition is a sufficient refutation. Strange that men should deem it needful to put a restraint on the obvious meaning of language in order to educe such inanity; and passing strange that the sweet singer of Israel can not be suffered to make the least allusion to a future world, when even the cat-worshiping Egyptian had recorded his convictions of a judgment to come, a thousand years before!

A very distinct assertion of the future retribution is found in Eccles. xii. 13, 14: "Let us hear the conclusion of the whole matter: Fear God, and keep his commandments; for this is the whole duty of man. For God shall bring every work into judgment, with every secret thing, whether it be good, or whether it be evil." That the judgment here spoken of is a future one, as Hengstenberg well remarks, is clear from verse 7 of the same chapter, where the writer speaks of the appearance of the spirit, separated from the body, before God, to receive the recompense for its works.

Still more distinct, if possible, is the utterance of Dan. xii. 2, 3: "And many of them [i.e., the many, the multitude; see Rom. v. 15, 19] that sleep in the dust of the earth shall awake, some to everlasting life, and some to shame and everlasting contempt. And they that be wise shall shine as the brightness of the firmament; and they that turn many to righteousness, as the stars for ever and ever."

This passage is from the closing declarations of Daniel's prophecy. He who had depicted so fully and repeatedly the rise and fall of the great earthly monarchies, and the triumph of the kingdom which the God of heaven should set up, and who just before the present passage minutely specifies the conflicts that should rage around the seat of that kingdom, now, in accordance with prophetic custom, flashes one clear glance down to the end and issue of the whole struggle on earth. Then the message is to be sealed up (verse 4) "to the time of the end;" and the prophet himself is directed (verse 13), "Go thy way till the end be; for thou shalt rest, and shalt stand in thy lot at the end of the days." The collocation of the passage thus strongly justifies the obvious interpretation; while the language itself, in its details, will hardly admit any other. It has indeed been questioned whether the verse next preceding refers to the ultimate "time of trouble" at Christ's coming, or to a nearer series of terrific trials in the time of Antiochus Epiphanes. But Professor Stuart, who takes the latter view, is perfectly decided that the passage in question "opens the prospect of the future and final destiny of men, the righteous and the wicked, and shows us the final result of the Messianic period." *

These are some of the passages in the Old Testament which more specifically refer to the future state of rewards and punishments.† But it would be doing great

---

* For a fuller vindication of this view, see Stuart's Commentary on Daniel on this passage.

† Such passages have been selected as were easily apprehensible by ordinary readers. Passages like Job xix. 25-27 have been intentionally omitted, because less available in a popular discussion.

injustice to the older portion of the sacred volume were we to intimate that these comprise the main portion of such allusions. The doctrine here distinctly stated seems to underlie a multitude of promises and threats, as an implication without which they are empty. Such passages as the whole thirty-seventh Psalm; Ps. i. 3–6; Prov. x. 28, 30; xi. 7, 19, 21, 23; xii. 3, 21, 28; xiv. 32; xv. 24; and the like,— consider what they amount to, except as they involve such a reference. Without it, what does it mean to say. "As righteousness tendeth to life, so he that pursueth evil pursueth it to his own death;" "In the way of righteousness is life, and in the pathway thereof is no death?" Unless these threats and promises reach forth into another world, all these high-sounding words, and others like them, mean only this,— that a wicked man shall have a little earlier decease than a good man; a threat not always fulfilled.

The case seems to us one of remarkable strength. We start with the now settled fact, in itself of great weight, that the nation among whom the Israelites resided four hundred years had for many hundred years previous held and publicly recorded the doctrine of an existence and retribution after death. We find the Hebrew doctrine concerning the origin and character of the soul laying the proper basis for a belief in its continued existence when the body dies. We find the record, in both the antediluvian and the Mosaic ages, of good men, by reason of that goodness, taken directly from this world to dwell with God. We find this whole present life designated as a pilgrimage. We find the successive deaths of patriarchs, prophets, priests, and kings, even when they were laid in unknown or solitary graves, described as being gathered to their fathers. We find the practice of conjuring by pretended communication with dead persons, familiar spirits, to have gained such a hold on the general belief, that the law of Moses specially prohibited the offense; and even the first monarch of the nation, in his time of exigency, resorted to the practice. And, finally, we meet with not a few passages which of set purpose present the doctrine of a judgment and twofold retribution after death, so distinctly, that they can be set aside only by a denial both of the obvious meaning of the language, and the obvious scope of the argument.

CHAPTER II.

BELIEF OF A FUTURE EXISTENCE AMONG THE JEWS IN THE TIME OF CHRIST.

WHEN our Saviour and his apostles began their mission, they addressed themselves first to the Jewish nation. Their teachings were professedly but the fuller development of " the law and the prophets." Moreover, their utterances on the subject of a future destiny, unless specially guarded by them to the contrary, must, of course, be understood in the light of the known and acknowledged views of the nation.

Now, even if there were any reasonable doubt what were the notions of the earlier Jews upon this subject, no such doubt hangs over the views that prevailed in the time of Christ. It is susceptible of decisive proof that the prevalent belief of the people at that time recognized a future state of rewards and punishments. This proof is found more full and minute in profane writers, as they are called, but briefly and conclusively confirmed in the New Testament.

The fullest and most competent secular witness is the celebrated historian Josephus. He was a native Jew, belonged to the order of the priesthood, and not only was a man of learning, but had been specially initiated into the ways of each of the three sects into which the Jewish nation was divided. For a long time he governed Galilee, afterwards commanded the Jewish army, and, upon the conquest and destruction of Jerusalem, went with Titus to Rome, where he wrote the History and Antiquities of his nation. No man could be more competent as a witness.

Now, Josephus informs us in many passages that the Jewish people were divided into three sects, the Pharisees, the Sadducees, and the Essenes. Of the Pharisees he informs us (Antiq. book xviii. chap. i. sect. 3), "They also believed that souls have an immortal vigor in them, and *that under the earth there will be rewards or punishments according* as they have lived virtuously or viciously in this life ; and the latter are to be detained in an everlasting prison, but the former shall have power to revive and live again : on account of which doctrines, *they are able to persuade the great body* of the people." Again (Wars of the Jews, ii. § 14) : "They [the Pharisees] say that all souls are indestructible ; that the souls of good men alone are removed into other bodies ; but that the souls of bad men are subject to eternal punishment." *

Concerning a second of these Jewish sects, the Essenes, we are told by Josephus (Antiq., xviii. 5), "They teach the immortality of souls, and esteem that the rewards of righteousness are to be earnestly striven for." Again (Wars, ii. 8, 11) : "For their doctrine is

---

* It is commonly understood that the removal " into other bodies " (strictly *another body*), here ascribed to the souls of the righteous, simply designates the new or spiritual body. Any question which may be raised on this point does not in the slightest degree affect the positiveness of Josephus's testimony to the doctrine of immortality and future eternal rewards and punishments.

this: That bodies are corruptible, and that the matter they are made of is not permanent, but *that the souls are immortal, and continue for ever;* and that they come out of the most subtile air, and are united to their bodies as in prisons, into which they are drawn by a certain natural enticement; but that, when set free from the bonds of the flesh, they then, as released from a long bondage, rejoice and mount upward. And this is like the opinion of the Greeks, that good souls have their habitation beyond the ocean in a region that is neither oppressed with storms of rain or snow, nor with intense heat; but that this place is such as is refreshed by the gentle breathing of a west wind that is perpetually blowing from the ocean: while they allot to bad souls a dark and tempestuous den, full of never-ceasing punishments. And, indeed, the Greeks seem to me to have followed the same notion when they allot the islands of the blessed to their brave men, whom they call heroes and demi-gods; and to the souls of the wicked the region of the ungodly in *hades,* where their fables relate that certain persons, such as Sisyphus and Tantalus and Ixion and Tityus, are punished; which is built on this first supposition, — that souls are immortal. And thence are those exhortations to virtue and dissuasions from wickedness collected, whereby good men are made better in the conduct of their life by the hope they have of reward after their death, and whereby the vehement inclinations of bad men to vice are restrained by the fear and expectation they are in, that, although they should lie concealed in this life, they should suffer deathless punishment (ἀθάνατον τιμωρίαν) after their dissolution. These are the divine doctrines of the Essenes about the soul, which offer an irresistible attraction to those who have once had a taste of their philosophy." The reader will observe in this passage how distinctly the writer represents the future punishment to consist in continual suffering.

His statements are made still more distinctly significant by the account which he gives of the remaining sect, the Sadducees: "The doctrine of the Sadducees is this: That souls die with the bodies" (Antiq., xviii. 1, 4). Again (War, ii. 8, 14): "They take away the belief of immortality, and the *punishments and rewards in hades.*"

This testimony is explicit. The Pharisees and Essenes believe in a state of endless rewards and suffering after death. The Sadducees discard that doctrine. It only remains to ask which of these sects represents the prevailing and received belief. Josephus himself informs us that " the Sadducees are able to persuade none but the rich, and have not the populace obsequious to them, but the Pharisees have the multitude on their side" (Antiq., xiii. 10, 6); that the Pharisees " are able greatly to persuade the body of the people" (xviii. 1, 3); that the doctrine of the Sadducees " is received but by a few," who, when they become magistrates, " addict themselves to the notions of the Pharisees, because the multitudes would not otherwise hear them" (xviii. 1, 4).

Fully coincident with this is Josephus's remonstrance with his comrades against suicide (War, iii. 8, 5), in which he urges, that " the soul is ever immortal, and is a portion of the divinity that inhabits our bodies;" that " those who depart out of this life, according to the law of nature, and pay that debt which was received from God, when he that lent it is pleased to require it back, enjoy eternal fame. Their houses and their posterity are sure; their souls remain pure and propitious to prayer, and obtain a most holy place in heaven, from whence, in the revolution of ages, they are again sent into pure bodies; while the souls of those who have acted madly against themselves are received by the darkest place in *hades*." Again (War, i. 33, 2): the learned Jews Matthias and Judas are represented as rousing a sedition against Herod by the consideration that, " it was a glorious thing to die for the laws of their country; that for those thus perishing remained an immortality of soul, and an endless fruition of happiness." And when forty of the rebels were brought before Herod, and interrogated " how they could be so joyful when they were to be put to death," they replied, " because they should enjoy greater happiness after they were dead." And once more, at the siege of Masada (War, vii. 8, 7), Eleazer the leader of the Sicarii urges his men to dispatch one another rather than fall into the enemy's hands, by a burning appeal to the doctrine of immortality: " The laws of our country and God himself, have, from ancient times, and as soon as we could use our reason, continually taught us, and our forefathers have corroborated the same doctrine by their actions and by their bravery of mind, that it is life which is a calamity to men, and not death; for this last affords our souls their liberty, and sends them by a removal into their own place of purity, where they are to be insensible to all sorts of misery. For, while souls are tied down to a mortal body, they are partakers of its miseries: and really, to speak the truth, they are themselves dead [observe his use of the word "dead"]; for association with what is mortal befits not that which is divine." And he goes on to a considerable extent, pressing on them the hope of a blessed immortality, presenting even the example of the Indians "who have such a desire for immortality that they cheerfully hasten to their death," and asking, "Are we not therefore ashamed to have lower notions than the Indians?" Such appeals even to the populace on the ground of reward and punishment hereafter, however perverted may have been the application, are the best possible proof of the universal hold of that doctrine on the popular belief.*

These reiterated testimonies, uttered by a learned Jew whose life was cotemporary with the epistles of Christ's apostles, present an insurmountable difficulty to those who incline to deny the prevalence of the doctrine among the Jews of Christ's day; for, unfortunately for them, the statements can not be rejected as spurious, or of questionable genuineness. Their total meaning can not possibly be mistaken, nor can the perfect competency of the witness be called in question. In all these respects, the testimony is impregnable.

The only possible resort remaining is to impeach the veracity of Josephus. This, accordingly, is attempted by one leading advocate of annihilation. But how? By bringing any counter testimony to refute these assertions? By showing any inconsistency in his several

---

* We have chosen for the most part to follow the common, awkward translation of Josephus. In some instances, we have substituted Traill's version as more accurate.

statements on this subject? By proving that he is not, in the main, a veracious narrator? By showing that, in this particular subject, he had some special temptation to fabricate a deliberate falsehood,— total, circumstantial, reiterated, and easy of refutation? None of these things.

Mr. Hudson endeavors to dispatch this troublesome witness by accumulating from various writers a few general criticisms upon him,— some of them wholly irrelevant, some of them unfounded, and all of them falling short of an impeachment of his testimony on this point,— and then summarily "dismissing Josephus as an unreliable witness" (Debt and Grace, p. 336).

Mr. Hudson is not ashamed to quote in his argument certain epithets applied by a late female writer (Charlotte Elizabeth) to Josephus's personal history, such as "traitor," "apostate," "groveling sycophant," "fulsome flatterer," "sordid, craven tool of the pagan foe," although he admits that the language "is perhaps too expressive of indignant feeling," and fails to inform us what it has to do with the matter in hand, supposing it to be true.

Among the cited criticisms upon Josephus, there are, however, two classes of remarks which might seem to have force.

First, it is alleged that he is not always trustworthy. "Another writer observes, It must be owned, that, in his account of the Scripture times, he has taken a bold liberty to add, alter, retrench, and even sometimes contradict it; which is a fault for which no other apology can be made than that he was of the sect of the Pharisees, and gave too much credit to their trifling traditions." The same writer shows that the whole account given by Josephus of the visit of Alexander to Jerusalem (Antiq., xi. 8, 5) is unquestionably fabulous, and is "at a loss to determine whether he was himself the author of the story, or was imposed upon in taking it as a narrative or tradition of some other Jewish writer" (Debt and Grace, p. 335). A note on the same page mentions another account of Josephus (War, vi. 9), which "is shown to involve insuperable difficulties."

Now, the reader will observe that even this critic does not charge Josephus with proved intentional falsehood, but admits that his deviations from Scripture history were because "he gave too much credit to" Pharisaic "traditions," and that, in his account of Alexander, he may have been "imposed upon." It should be added that his adhesion to the Scripture narrative in his Antiquities, though the book was written for heathen readers, is, for the most part, singularly close; most of the deviations being by way of expansion, while others show inadvertence, and others indicate that he probably had before him a different reading, as is sometimes the case in matters of number.* But no inadvertence, no difference of text, no imposition, no credulity, could mislead him in the doctrines of his cotemporary sects.

We may go further than does his critic, and admit that, in his topography, he is sometimes inaccurate, as in the dimensions of the temple, which he perhaps embellished, — writing, as he did, far from the place, without exact data, and prone from national vanity to

---

* In some instances, the suggestion of Josephus actually relieves a difficulty.

magnify its glory.* Still, no such motive can be found in the present instance; and if there could, it would hardly cover the case of a deliberate and circumstantial invention of alleged facts concerning his own belief and that of the whole nation.

Secondly, it is alleged that "his doctrine" is, so to speak, "un-Jewish" and "the account given by Josephus is in a nomenclature to which the Jews had been strangers, which is unknown to the Talmud, but with which the Greeks and Orientals were quite familiar." † This view is backed by several quotations, ‡ — one from Pococke, that, "in giving the views of the sects he names, respecting the other world, he [Josephus] seems to have used words better suited to the fashions and the ears of the Greeks and Romans than such as a scholar of the Jewish law would understand or deem expressive of his meaning;" one from Matthaei, that "Josephus was pre-eminently inclined to accommodate his accounts to the understanding of the Gentiles;" one from Bretschneider, that "his extant writings would be more valuable if he had separated their views from the modifications which he has seen fit to give them, out of respect to the Grecian readers for whom he wrote." Harmer is quoted, who speaks of his "solicitude to make his representation of the opinions and practices of that nation, in those writings that were designed for the perusal of the unbelieving Gentiles, as little exceptionable to them as possible;" and who also says that "some of the learned have remarked that

---

* Robinson's Researches, i. 415.
† Debt and Grace, p. 224.   ‡ Ib. p. 335.

he has even expressed himself in such a manner as might lead his readers to imagine that the Pharisees believed rather a transmigration than a proper resurrection."

These are the statements. On which it may be observed, 1. That no one of the writers quoted questions the fundamental veracity of Josephus's statements. They simply aver that, in stating his views, he has "*used words*" suited to the fashions of the Greeks and Romans," and that " he was pre-eminently inclined to *accommodate his accounts to the understanding* of the Gentiles :" at most, that he has given " modifications " to his statements out of respect to the Gentiles, has made them " as little exceptionable to them as possible," or has in one case used a perhaps intentional ambiguity.

2. Inasmuch as both the treatises from which we have quoted were, in the form in which we have them, expressly written for and to be understood by Gentile readers, it was the most obvious dictate of common sense to adapt his phraseology to their "fashions" and "understandings;" and, in alluding directly to any supposed resemblance to Gentile views, Josephus was doing only what is common enough even in Christian writers, and, in the very act of making the comparison, he asserts the difference. If in any respect he may be thought to have modified the Jewish notions, that softening-down is a very different thing from an out-and-out fabrication. Even the alleged ambiguity concerning the resurrection (if designed) was, at most, a shrinking from an outspoken statement of belief. If his words could be interpreted by some of his readers in harmony with the doctrine of transmigration, it is still true that

they can be understood strictly of a proper resurrection, and that, in *any case, they positively assert a future retribution;* and it is true that his reiterated doctrine is of a twofold retribution, — eternal happiness and endless suffering.

3. The difficulty of invalidating the testimony of Josephus is well illustrated by the two remaining specifications. "His dissuasion from suicide is quite Platonic: 'The bodies of all men are corruptible, and are created out of corruptible matter; but the soul is ever immortal, and is a portion of the divinity that inhabits our bodies.'" The last clause contains the alleged Platonic phrase. But if that one mode of statement indicates connivance with Platonism, then on equally valid grounds does the Apostle Peter's expression (2 Pet. i. 4), "That by these ye might be partakers of the divine nature," indicate a collusion with Brahminism. Such expressions, when occurring singly, are too common, and too readily suggested to any mind, to attract attention. But Mr. Hudson endeavors to settle the case by one other quotation from Josephus: "To the passage already cited, in which he speaks of the soul as a 'portion of the divinity that inhabits our bodies,' we may here add the following: 'Those souls,' he says, 'which are severed from their fleshy bodies in battles by the sword, are received by the ether, that purest of elements, and joined to that company which are placed among the stars: they become good demons and propitious heroes, and show themselves as such to their posterity afterward.'" The reader will appreciate the force of this argument, when he learns that the sentiment ascribed by Mr. Hudson to Josephus is *part of a*

speech which Josephus ascribes to the heathen emperor Titus.*

4. The declarations of Josephus, as the reader will observe, are not found alone in his formal statement of doctrine, but they stand also naturally interwoven in the details of his narrative, as comprising the motives addressed to his countrymen by himself and other Jews to nerve them up to courage and to fortitude. The terrors of hell were urged by himself to dissuade his countrymen from suicide. The joys of heaven were presented by Eleazer and Matthias and Judas, to persuade their followers to brave deeds; and the followers of the two last mentioned sustain themselves in the hour of condemnation with the hopes of blessedness after death. These accounts are not only intrinsically natural and probable, but, as we shall presently see, the presentation of such motives to the Jews for such purposes is specially corroborated by the Roman historian Tacitus.

5. The statement of Josephus concerning the general difference of views between the Pharisees and Sadducees closely corresponds to the declarations of the New Testament. Josephus is more full, inasmuch as it was part of his purpose to describe those sects; whereas the sacred writer alludes to them only incidentally, and describes them only so far as necessary

---

* See Josephus's War, vi. 1, 4. quoted in Debt and Grace, page 336. We might have supposed it a blunder, though a very inexcusable one; but when the attention of Mr. Hudson was called to the error, he told the informant (a student of Chicago Theological Seminary) that it was corrected in a later edition. On procuring that later edition, we found that the *whole argument* and passage remained as before, with the slight difference, that, instead of "he says," it now reads, "he makes Titus say," — still holding Josephus responsible for the sentiment.

for explanation. The accounts are entirely harmonious.

6. It is proper to add, that, in general, the statements of Josephus on this and other kindred subjects are received by the great mass of historians and antiquarians; and indeed, in connection with the New Testament, they constitute a very large part of the material for the history of Jewish affairs in those times. To mention all the writers whose statements rest more or less extensively on the declarations of Josephus would be simply to cite the names of every writer in every department of literature who has had occasion to treat of that nation or that age. His general trustworthiness as a writer, not indeed free from mistakes arising from forgetfulness, inattention, and misinformation, yet, on the whole, well-informed and accurate, especially on topics where, as in the present case, he had the means of personal knowledge, is vindicated by the later investigations.

We conclude, then, that the attempt to overthrow the testimony of Josephus on this subject totally breaks down. It lacks the first element of a valid impeachment; and the decision to "dismiss Josephus as an unreliable witness" is a very serio-comic device to get rid of a fatal testimony.*

---

* We would refer to Dr. Traill's introductory essay on the personal character of Josephus for a valid though brief defense of his credibility as a writer, pages 14-25. It will be observed that the weightiest names cited by Mr. Hudson against him are *names of the past*. Traill well remarks, "A diligent use of the copious means placed at our disposal by those researches in Palestine which English, French, German, and American writers have effected, yields proof, various in its kind, and often very definite, entirely excluding as well the skepticism that had been admitted by some of the learned of the seventeenth century as the less erudite cavils of recent wri-

We pass to Tacitus the more readily in this connection, because his testimony bears directly on the same use of the doctrine of future rewards to encourage personal bravery and endurance to which Josephus refers. It is given also in connection with the same events; namely, the capture of Jerusalem by Titus. He was cotemporary with that transaction; and, in writing an account of it, he evidently had taken pains to inform himself concerning the Jewish nation. His honesty of intention is unquestioned, as well as his accuracy in stating such things as he had the means of investigating. From the nature of the case, being a *Roman* historian, he commits many errors in narrating the *past* history of the nation, as he did not have access to the Hebrew Scriptures, or other authentic information on that subject; but, in his delineation of their current habits and traits, his narrative is generally correct, and, in regard to marked and prominent facts, trustworthy.*

Tacitus writes thus of the Jews: "Infanticide is in every case a crime (*necare quemquam ex adgnatis flagitium*); and the souls of those slain in battle or by torture they believe to be eternal. Hence a desire for offspring, and a contempt of death. Dead bodies they bury rather than burn, after the custom of the Egyptians: they bestow the same care [as do the Egyptians],

---

ters. Beyond possibility of doubt, as may now be shown, Josephus was accurately and familiarly conversant with the things and with the places, as well as with the transactions, of which he speaks: quite certain it is that he was observant in his habits, and, in the main, correct in his statements" (p. 23, American edition).

* Mr. Hudson warmly commends the honesty of Tacitus (Debt and Grace, pp. 336, 337).

and hold the same belief; concerning the state of the dead [*de infernis*," the infernal regions, or their occupants. — See Freund's or Andrew's Lexicons]. Hist., v. 5.

Here the Roman historian testifies to the same general facts with Josephus. The desperate valor of the Jews in battle, and their invincible endurance of suffering and torture, were well known to him, and emphatically recorded by him (v. 14). Equally notorious was the fact, which he and Josephus alike recorded, that *this fierce bravery was sustained by the hopes of a future life*, and was stimulated by appeals to those hopes. The coincidence is striking.

But Tacitus does not leave the subject here. He proceeds to speak of their funeral customs, — burying, and not burning, wherein they resemble the Egyptians; and to this he adds, that they bestow the same care as do the Egyptians, and hold the same belief concerning the state of the dead or the infernal regions. What that belief is the reader will find exhibited in a previous chapter of this discussion. Its grand feature, as conclusively proved, was, that after death the soul enters on a protracted state of rewards or punishments. Tacitus thus fully confirms the statement of Josephus, that the Jews of that day held the doctrine of a twofold state of retribution after death; and corroborates even his special and repeated declaration, that they were sustained in battle and under punishment by appeals to that belief.

The mode in which Mr. Hudson deals with Tacitus is equally remarkable, perhaps, as his method with Josephus. He *entirely omits the latter part of the pas-*

sage comprising the statement of their belief concerning the state of the dead; and, quoting only the previous remark concerning those who die in battle or by torture,* he proceeds to say that "the language in this passage is peculiar, in that it clearly denotes the immortality of a class." If the writer had said what his argument requires, " the immortality of *only* a class," he would have elicited from Tacitus the preposterous statement that only those who die in battle or by torture live hereafter. That is to say, it does not follow, from the historian's mentioning the hopes held out to those who die in battle or torture, that all other persons were to fail of immortality: he evidently means simply that *special* promises of future blessing were held out to them, — assurances of pre-eminent reward, privilege, or exemption; while the question, how it would be with other parties, is met only in his fuller statement afterwards, which covers the whole ground. Indeed, the phraseology of Tacitus was perhaps purposely chosen to indicate the notion of *special* privilege in the other world. He does not employ the word "immortal" (*immortalis*), nor the term which denotes simply perpetual existence (*sempiternus*), but the peculiar word "eternal" (*æternus*), which (though frequently synonymous with immortal) is used to designate the mode of existence belonging to the gods, and had already, at that period of the Roman language, begun to be sometimes specially limited to what is divine.†

---

* His entire quotation is this: that among the Jews "infanticide is a crime, and the souls of those dying in battle or by torture are eternal: hence a love of offspring, and contempt of death." Why does he arrest the passage there?

† See Freund's or even Andrews's Latin Lexicon under the words *æter-*

There is therefore good reason to believe that Tacitus, who is remarkably precise in his use of language, by this carefully chosen word intended to designate special, and perhaps even divine prerogatives promised to the hero. At the very least, he testifies to the open fact that the daring of the brave among the Jews was preeminently sustained by the hope of future blessings;* while he testifies with equal distinctness that, besides such special expectations, the Jews held a general theory of the future world similar to that of the Egyptians. They believed in a future state of rewards and punishments.

The Jew Philo was born at Alexandria, in Egypt, a few years before Christ. His own views are admitted to be strongly tinged with Platonism. Still he has left numerous remarks which bear on the subject under discussion. His testimony is to the same effect: —

"Perhaps some one will say he [Cain] should have been put to death at once. This is a human mode of reasoning, fit for one who does not consider the great tribunal of all: for men look upon death as the extreme limit of all punishments; but, in view of the di-

---

nitas, æternus. Thus Cicero: "Deus beatus et æternus," Fin. 2, 27; and again (Nat. Deor. 1, 8), "Nihil quod ortum sit, æternum esse potest." Of course he means in the strictest use of the term; for he himself extends its application. Freund defines the word *æternus* to differ from *sempiternus* ("that which is perpetual, what exists as long as time endures, and keeps even pace with it") by denoting "that which is raised above all time, and can be measured only by eons." Of *æternitas* he says, "In the time of the emperors a title of the emperor, like *divinity, majesty*," etc. Pliny writes to Trajan, " Rogatus, Domine, a Nicensibus per *æternitatem tuam* salutemque ut," etc., Pliny Ep. 10, 87. The reader will remember that the emperors were already flattered with ascriptions of divine qualities.

* This term is a near approach to the New-Testament phrase, "eternal life."

vine tribunal, it is scarcely the beginning of them." *
"The constitution of man [say the Scriptures] was
compounded of an earthly substance and a divine
spirit; . . . so that, if man is mortal as to his visible
part, he is immortal as to the invisible. Wherefore we
may truly say that man stands upon the border-line of
a mortal and immortal nature, participant of each as
was needful, and that he was made at the same time
mortal and immortal; mortal as to his body, immortal
as to his mind."† "Death is twofold; one of the man,
the other of the soul. Death of the man is the separation of the soul from the body; but death of the soul
is the destruction of virtue and the assumption of vice.
. . . The one, as it were, conflicts with the other; for
the former is a separation of things conjoined, of body
and soul: the latter, a conjunction of both; the inferior,
the body, gaining the mastery over the superior, the
soul.‡ "But, to me and my friends, death with the
pious would be more acceptable than life with the impious; for those so dying immortal life receives, but those
so living eternal death awaits."§ The true proselyte
"receives the most fitting gift of a secure place in
heaven, such as one may not describe; but the repro-
bate of noble birth is dragged down to the lowest depths,
being cast into *tartarus* and deep darkness." ‖ "He
that is driven forth by God suffers eternal (*ἀίδιον*) banishment; for while one who is not yet firmly held by
vice, may, upon repentance, return to virtue, the native
land from which he roved, he who is seized and subju-
gated by great and incurable disorder must to all eter-

---

* Philo Judæus, ii. 421. † Ib. i. p. 32.
‡ Ib. i. p. 65.   § Ib. i. p. 233.   ‖ Ib. p. 433.

nity bear the dire penalties, immortally degraded to the place of the impious, that he may suffer unmixed and continual calamity." * These and many other utterances leave no doubt of the views which Philo represents, — the immortality of all souls, and an endless retribution of blessedness or suffering.

Perfectly coincident with these statements, and therefore fully corroborating them, are the brief allusions to the prevalent Jewish views found in the New Testament itself.

In Paul's defense of himself before Felix, he most distinctly declares the doctrine of a "resurrection of the dead, both of the just and unjust," to be held by him and his Jewish accusers in common : "And have hope toward God, which they themselves also allow, that there shall be a resurrection of the dead, both of the just and unjust" (Acts xxiv. 15).

Other passages, though less explicit than this concerning the future separate destiny of the wicked, yet involve the general doctrine of a future existence, and abundantly confirm the fuller statements of this passage and of Josephus. Thus, when the Sadducees came to try the Saviour with their puzzle concerning the resurrection, the question evidently assumes that the then common notion of a future life included the indiscriminate resurrection of all. The question takes for granted that the seven brethren and the one wife all alike participate, as matter of course, in the resurrection (Luke xx. 27–33).

So likewise in repeated instances in which the peculiar views of the Sadducees on this subject are spoken

---

* Ib. i. p. 139.

of in contrast to those of the Pharisees, the difference is never given as a difference only of degree, — the one as holding that a part only of the race will exist hereafter, and the other that none of them will continue, — but as a difference of kind; the one affirming, the other denying, a whole invisible world, a whole future existence. In the presence of the Sanhedrim (Acts xxiii. 6–8), " when Paul perceived that the one part were Sadducees, and the other Pharisees, he cried out in the council, Men and brethren, I am a Pharisee, the son of a Pharisee: of the hope and resurrection of the dead [not merely the righteous dead] I am called in question. And when he had so said, there arose a dissension between the Pharisees and the Sadducees: and the multitude was divided. For the Sadducees say that there is no resurrection, neither angel nor spirit: but the Pharisees confess both." Here Paul advances the unrestricted proposition of the resurrection of the dead; and the explanatory remarks of the sacred writer also state the dissent of the Sadducees in the same sweeping form. In the same manner, though more briefly, the Sadducees are mentioned by each of the evangelists, Matthew, Mark, and Luke (Matt. xxii. 23; Mark xii. 18; Luke xx. 27), as those " which deny that there is any resurrection."

How completely does Martha's reply to the Saviour (John xi. 24) assume the undoubted fact of a future existence: "I know that he shall rise again in the resurrection at the last day."

The undoubting hold which the doctrine of a continuance after death, and of a resurrection, had on the whole mass of the Jewish people, is well exhibited in the opinions entertained by the multitude concerning our Saviour. When he asked his disciples, "Whom do men say that I am?" they inform him of three or four different opinions (Matt. xvi. 14; Mark viii. 28; Luke ix. 19); and *every one of those opinions supposed him to be a deceased person re-appearing on earth.* Even Herod Antipas, the murderer of John, when he heard the fame of Jesus, "said unto his servants, This is John the Baptist; he is risen from the dead; and therefore mighty works do show forth themselves in him" (Matt. xiv. 2). It matters not for our present purpose that this future existence is mentioned in the form of the resurrection, the completed aspect of the future life. Enough that a belief in the continued existence of man, of all men, after death, appears clearly to have been the general belief of the Jews at the time of Christ. And the testimony as clearly shows that there was to be a resurrection both of the just and of the unjust, — a future existence both of happiness and of misery.

Other testimony might be added, as from the first and second books of Maccabees, and from the book of Enoch, the last of which is admitted by such men as Dr. Davidson, and Dillmann, the learned editor and translator of the book, to be singularly clear on the subject.* The Christian bishop Hippolytus, of the second century, reiterates all the assertions of Josephus so remarkably, though in different phraseology (Liber ix. 28–30), that he has been supposed either to follow Josephus, or the same authority from which he drew; but to avoid collateral discussions, we content ourselves with the testimony we have cited, which is authentic, clear, and to the point. *See Appendix, Note I.*

CHAPTER III.

NEW TESTAMENT TEACHINGS. — IMMORTALITY. — IMMEDIATE DESTINY.

WE have seen the indications that the Jews from ancient times held the belief of a future state of retribution. We have also seen, that, in the time of our Saviour, the prevalent opinion of the nation recognized that state as one of happiness or of suffering. *We find no trace of any denial of future suffering, except on the part of those who denied all future existence.*

The Saviour and his apostles were therefore not called upon to propound the doctrine of suffering hereafter with the formalities of a new and before unheard-of announcement. There was no pressing occasion for them to insist with peculiar prominence on the fact or the duration of that two-fold retribution, but rather on its application. It was natural for them, when they spoke of the subject, to dwell chiefly on the characters to which those rewards and punishments should be assigned. This is, in fact, the more common form in which these instructions are given; although they do at the same time very clearly state that the duration of that doom is eternal, and that it consists in holy blessedness on the one hand, and sin and misery on the other.

It was not the mission of Christ and his apostles to expatiate upon any abstract or naked doctrine of immortality, — an immortality considered irrespective of all its moral relations and tremendous issues. Inasmuch as no such meaningless immortality exists under the government of God, as it would be of no account whatever to man, and as these messengers came on an errand most intensely practical, they, in accordance with the universal custom of God's Word, speak simply and always of the great moral and practical aspects of that immortality. While, therefore, they abundantly assert the doctrine, — an immortality both for the good and for the evil, — it is always in the form of the *actual, concrete immortality* which those two classes will positively experience, rather than in propositions of some abstract unreal immortality which no one ever will experience, and which, as being shorn of all moral relations, is of no account. On such propositions they waste no breath.

Here, then, we readily dispose of an objection on which some have endeavored to place much stress. Mr. Hastings, with great industry, and with a liberal display of italics and capital letters, large and small, sets forth the number of times that the word "soul" occurs in the Scriptures, and triumphantly inquires why we never find this particular word (for he ingeniously avoids alluding to other words descriptive of the soul's *destiny*) coupled with the epithet "immortal," and the like, in such phrases as "immortal soul," "never-dying soul," "undying spirit."* Mr. Hudson employs a similar mode of argument: "But if the soul's immor-

---

* Pauline Theology, pp. 70, 71.

tality were so marvelously clear a postulate of human reason, it must be a most cherished sentiment, and must give rise to many common expressions, household words of natural theology. In fact, whenever and wherever this doctrine has obtained, it has created various modes of expression that reveal the sentiment. Why, then, are these expressions altogether avoided or ignored in the Bible? Why should the Holy Spirit, so ready to catch the language of the mortals who were to be taught the way of life, have failed to conform to their style of thought in this most important item of their own immortal nature? Why, if God has told men that they must enjoy or suffer for ever, has he never urged his invitation or his warning in the name of the immortality he has given them? Such a gift, surely, would be pre-eminently worthy of mention to those who think and say so much of their supposed possession of the boon." *

The question is, Why does not the Bible deal in such phrases as "the immortality of the soul?"—phrases of so frequent occurrence in human compositions. The answer is short and simple. It is not alone because the fact was admitted and might be assumed, but also because they were charged with messages of such tremendous import concerning the *character and conditions* of that endless existence, as quite throw into the background the abstract proposition of the soul's immortality. If they had been mere human teachers, very possibly they might have indulged in sentimental dissertations and romantic speculations on the greatness and the immortality of the human soul. But

---

* Debt and Grace, p. 165.

they came as divine teachers, to teach men concerning their present and eternal *relations to the government of God*, to proclaim endless holiness and well-being, or everlasting sin and woe, as pending on faith and repentance here. To them the naked question of immortality, aside from these relations and issues, was of no account at all,—no more than the life of an oyster. They therefore addressed themselves to their divine mission, and told men always of the *actual* immortality before them. They never tell men so little as the bald fact that they shall exist hereafter: they tell them a great deal more; they tell them abundantly *how* they shall exist. The remark is true in regard to the righteous as well as the wicked. Indeed, the objector is obliged to make this fatal admission in the statement of his objection : " Why, if God has told men that they must *enjoy* or suffer for ever, has he never urged his *invitation* or his warning in the name of the immortality he has given them ? " And yet the righteous are admitted to be immortal by special provision, if not by native gift.

Such is the Scripture mode of speech on this subject. It does not discourse of the immortal *being* or *existence* of either class of persons, nor say that they shall never cease *to be;* but it speaks of the everlasting *life* of the one class, the eternal weight of glory; their glory, honor, incorruptibility ($\dot{\alpha}\varphi\theta\alpha\rho\sigma i\alpha\nu$) ; their incorruptible crown; their inheritance incorruptible, undefiled, and that fadeth not away ; their shining as the stars for ever ; their state in which they shall hunger no more; neither thirst any more, where there shall be no more death, neither sorrow nor crying, nor any more pain. Precisely so, on the other hand, if there is no metaphysical statement concerning the "never-dying spirit," or the "eternal *existence*," of the wicked, there are the most positive and awful assertions of their everlasting *punishment*, their never-dying worm and unquenchable fire, their never receiving forgiveness in this world or the world to come, their eternal damnation, the smoke of their torment that ascendeth up for ever and ever, their shame and everlasting contempt, their departure into everlasting fire prepared for the devil and his angels, everlasting destruction from the presence of the Lord, their being destined to the blackness of darkness for ever, and receiving from God indignation and wrath, tribulation and anguish, at the day of judgment. It is therefore little more than a quibble to argue that the phrases "immortal," "never-dying," and the like, are not applied to the soul itself, when they are abundantly applied to its destiny and condition. "It matters not that the Bible does not know the *phrase* 'immortal soul,' when it so manifestly knows the *thing*." And, indeed, so perfectly in keeping with the whole practical method of God's Word is its entire abstinence from all utterance concerning the *mere* "immortality of the soul," that, had it been otherwise, very likely the present objectors might have been first to question the genuineness of the passages, and to insinuate that they were "evidently of foreign origin, of a philosophic cast, and, so to speak, un-Jewish," at least unscriptural.

The Scriptures, then, describe the actual fate and condition of both the righteous and the wicked, as they continue in conscious joy or woe for evermore.

The Scriptures affirm the conscious existence of both classes of men during the period after death and prior to the resurrection of the body.

It is a somewhat logical portion of the common doctrine of annihilation to deny the active and conscious existence of the dead prior to the resurrection. Many, if not most, of its advocates hold to an actual extinction of being, from which men are resuscitated only at the resurrection. The tendencies of a system which revolts from the idea of endless sufferings inflicted on the impenitent, naturally recoil also from admitting the continuance of those sufferings for an unknown time, continuing certainly in some cases many thousand years; while consistency requires, that, in denying the conscious activity of the wicked, that of the righteous should be also denied or questioned. The exclusive stress which the scheme lays upon the resurrection indicates the same felt necessity.

It is freely conceded and maintained by us that the Scriptures contemplate the entire consummation of human destiny as taking place when soul and body are re-united in a future world. The body, which shared the soul's probation, must also share its retribution. Towards that state of re-union most of the utterances of God's Word on this subject are directed, just as most of its declarations concerning Christ's kingdom view that kingdom, not in its progress and intermediate state, but in its thorough consummation. It lays a very marked stress on the resurrection and its sequel. Intent on the final issue, the retribution of the complete man, it says comparatively little upon the intermediate state of the soul previous to the resurrection of the body. Still, the Scriptures do speak, in our judgment, distinctly and emphatically upon the immediate doom of both classes of men on passing from this life. Such has been the clear and general understanding of the Christian Church. Out of the immense throng of Christian writers, however, it is easy to cite occasional instances of men who, pressed, as they supposed, by the prominence of the resurrection, and the imagined incompatibility of the public doom then to be pronounced with a previous retribution, have endeavored to explain away these teachings. Still the declarations of the Scriptures on this point are perfectly level to the common apprehension.

A considerable portion of the teachings already adduced from the Old Testament have a bearing on this subject. To those remarks the reader is referred. We proceed to show that the New Testament teaches the conscious activity and retribution of the soul on passing from the body.

First, in regard to the righteous. Here we find clear though brief declarations that cover every aspect of the subject, and show that to the believer the alternative condition is either to be in the body below or with the Lord above.

1. It is taught that the soul without the body *might* enjoy celestial glories and communications. In 2 Cor. xii. 1-4, Paul says, " I will come to visions and revelations of the Lord. I knew a man in Christ above fourteen years ago (whether in the body I can not tell, or whether out of the body I can not tell: God knoweth), such a one caught up to the third heaven. And I knew such a man (whether in the body or out of the

body, I can not tell: God knoweth), how that he was caught up into paradise, and heard unspeakable words, which it is not lawful for a man to utter." Here the apostle, while informing his readers that he was "caught up to the third heaven," "caught up into paradise," also twice solemnly reiterates the declaration, that, "whether in the body or out of the body," he can not tell. In his view, then, it was possible for such experiences of heaven to take place "out of the body;" and the very fact that he raises the suggestion, and repeats it so earnestly, shows that he judged it to be "out of the body." Alford remarks thus: "If 'in the body,' the idea would be that he was taken up bodily; if 'out of the body,' to which the *alternative manifestly inclines*, that his spirit was rapt from the body, and taken up disembodied;" but, whichever might be his decision between the two modes, he clearly affirms the possibility of a man's being taken to the third heaven, to paradise, and hearing unspeakable words there, while out of the body.

2. It is also taught in the New Testament that not only the soul of the Christian might, but that it *would*, enter and enjoy the presence of Christ at death; and that the continuance of its life here in the body actually delays its enjoyment of Christ's immediate presence in glory. "For to me to live is Christ, and to die is gain; but if I live in the flesh, this is the fruit of my labor: yet what I shall choose I wot not. For I am in a strait betwixt two [literally "the two"], having a desire to depart and to be with Christ, which is far better: nevertheless, to abide in the flesh is more needful for you" (Phil. i. 21–24).

In the previous context (verses 19, 20), the apostle declares that even the hostile preaching of his opponents "shall turn to my salvation;" "according to my earnest expectation, and my hope, that in nothing I shall be ashamed [or brought to shame], but that with all boldness, as always, so now also, Christ shall be magnified in my body, whether it be by life or by death." He knew so well that God would cause even the malice of foes to redound to his salvation, that he hoped to be perfectly undaunted in devoting his body, with all its powers, to the honor of Christ, whether it were to be "by a life" of labor, or "by a death" of martyrdom. "For to me to live is Christ, and to die is gain;" i.e., while I live, I live in Christ, and when I die, I go to live with him, as the thought is more fully evolved in the subsequent verses: "What I shall choose I wot not. For I am in a strait betwixt the two, having a desire to *depart and be with Christ* [the one alternative], which is far better: nevertheless, to abide in the flesh [the other alternative] is more needful for you. And having this confidence, I know that I shall abide and continue with you all for your furtherance and joy of faith." The passage clearly affirms, not only that his death would be to him a gain, and the better alternative, but that his continuing to live and labor for the Philippians was a detention from the immediate presence of Christ; the attractions of that presence being so strong as to put him in a great strait whether he should desire to live and labor, or to die and go home to his reward.

The only objection that deserves attention is this: That, though the period from death to the resurrection should be one of total insensibility, the apostle might properly speak of passing directly from death to heaven, because, " in respect of his own perceptions, the moment of his breathing his last in this world would be instantly succeeded by that of his waking in the presence of his Lord." * But this explanation wholly fails to meet the point. The apostle was perplexed between his earnest longing to be with Christ and his desire to stay longer here and do good to the churches. But, if death were succeeded by a long unconsciousness, a speedy death would bring him no sooner to Christ, and could hold out no inducement such as to place him in a strait. It was no alternative *betwixt* two. Let him have both privileges. They did not interfere in the slightest degree. Let him live Christ a hundred or eighteen hundred years, and then depart; he will be just as near the joys of Christ's presence then, and no nearer. The alternative that Paul makes between these two strong desires is entirely fatal to the attempted evasion.†

To the same effect is the passage in 2 Cor. v. 1–9: " For we know that if our earthly house of this tabernacle were dissolved, we have a building of God, a house not made with hands, eternal in the heavens. . . . Therefore we are always confident, knowing that, whilst

---

* Whately's Future State, p. 87.

† Ellis and Read make a characteristic and noticeable comment: " He was perplexed between the two, whether to choose life or to choose death; they were both equally indifferent to him " (p. 139). He must have been thus in the state of a worn-out man of the world, who has nothing to hope either in life or in death, — a sort of ancient Chesterfield.

Mr. Hudson's attempts on the passage hardly deserve attention, but may be found in a note in the Appendix.

we are at home in the body, we are absent from the Lord (for we walk by faith, not by sight): we are confident, I say, and willing rather to be absent from the body, and to be present with the Lord." Here are the same alternatives presented in double mode: To be at home in the body is to be absent from the Lord; and to be absent from the body is to be present with the Lord; and the latter was the thing which the apostle was "willing" to do. It is difficult to see how any honest interpretation can escape the meaning. Life in the flesh detains the Christian from Christ's immediate presence; and death introduces him there.

3. It is affirmed that the believer upon the death of the body actually does enter heavenly blessedness at once. The penitent thief on the cross "said unto Jesus, Lord, remember me when thou comest into thy kingdom. And Jesus said unto him, Verily, I say unto thee, To-day shalt thou be with me in paradise" (Luke xxiii. 42, 43.)

The meaning of this declaration, which has been the common apprehension of the Church, lies plainly on the face of it. To the prayer for a gracious remembrance at the future unknown coming of Christ in glory, "when thou comest in (*ἐν*) thy kingdom," — whenever that may be, — Christ replies with the promise of *immediate* blessedness, — "*to-day* with me in paradise." And this interpretation will sustain the most rigid examination, and repel all attempted evasions.

"Paradise" is mentioned in but two other passages of the New Testament. In 2 Cor. xii. 2, Paul first speaks of having been "caught up to the third heaven," and, in verse 4, repeats the statement thus: "He was caught up into paradise, and heard unspeakable words," where it is a place of blessed consciousness and communion with God. In Rev. ii. 7 occurs the promise unto the faithful: "To him that overcometh will I give to eat of the tree of life, which is in the midst of the paradise of God," — where paradise includes the joys which are elsewhere (Rev. xxii. 2, 14) described as the full fruition of God's immediate presence.* It was to be "with Christ." This confirms and fixes the general meaning of paradise. "To be with Christ," it will be remembered, was the end of Paul's own highest longing (Phil. i. 23). This was to take place, not at some distant vague future, but "to-day." That day, then, the dying penitent was to meet the dying Saviour beyond this world in conscious blessedness in the immediate presence of God.

That this passage declares precisely what it appears to signify — the presence of the crucified malefactor with Christ in paradise *on that very day* — is the united voice of modern critics and commentators. No modern commentator or editor of respectable scholarship is

---

* Such being the actual and indisputable New-Testament usage, the history of the word is of no special account. It is supposed to be foreign to the Hebrew or Greek; an Eastern Asiatic word employed to describe the parks and pleasure-grounds of oriental monarchs (Neh. ii. 8; Eccles. ii. 5), used also in the Septuagint of the Garden of Eden (Gen. ii. 8, 9, 10, 15, 16; iii. 1, 2, 8, 10, 23). Hence, like Zion and other words, it became elevated, and designated the blissful region filled with the presence of the Monarch of heaven. No questioning whether this was (in the present case) in or out of *hades* can evade that plain fact of the New Testament. It includes the region to which Paul was taken when caught up, while living, to the third heaven; it comprehends the region of future joy to all the redeemed of the Apocalypse at last; it comprises the place where Christ went when he prayed, "Father, into thy hands I commend my spirit."

known to defend a different view; and most commentators in strong terms denounce the futility of all attempts to tamper with the passage, or its plain meaning. So Bergel, Olshausen, Kuinoel, De Wette, Meyer, Alford, and numerous others of less commanding eminence. So such editors as Knapp, Hahn, Lachmann, Tischendorf.*

There have, however, been attempts to tamper with the passage, from the days of Marcion the heretic, who adopted the summary method of rejecting the whole verse. This method was much the easiest, as appears from the variety and awkwardness of the subterfuges employed by others. It was only open to one objection, that the verse is found in all manuscripts.

Ellis and Read † prepare the way for their exposition, by certain objections to the common interpretation. Among them the most noticeable are these: 1. That

---

* Ellis and Read (p. 161) make this deceptive statement: "In the margin, Griesbach puts the stop after 'to-day.'" The fact is that he did it in the margin because (bold as he was) he did not dare to do it in the text. He was a venturesome man, who never hesitated to introduce changes in the text when he saw what he deemed a good reason. Accordingly, he often unhesitatingly inserted words and phrases in the body of the text, and struck out others; he also indicated words that ought, in his opinion, probably, though not certainly, to be inserted or omitted; he specified what readings seemed to him of equal authority with those in the text, or perhaps preferable, those which seemed to him requiring to be added, though not without some doubt, and those which deserved further consideration. For these various methods of dealing with the text, he had twelve different signs to signify the state of the case. But there were certain other emendations which he sometimes chose to indicate in the margin, but to which he did not venture to commit his scholarship or his judgment by expressing any opinion whatever. The present case is of this last description. Griesbach does not venture to change the punctuation of the text, or even openly to question it. He throws an irresponsible suggestion into the margin.

† Pages 159–161.

paradise is "a location on the new earth; and how could either Christ or the thief be in paradise that day, when paradise does not yet actually exist?" To which a sufficient answer is found in Paul's statement in 2 Cor. xii. 4, that he himself had been already caught up into paradise. 2. "How could Christ be in paradise that very day he was crucified, when, on the third day after, he said to Mary, 'Touch me not, for I have not yet ascended to my Father'?" Answer: Christ himself makes it perfectly plain, when, in his dying prayer, he said, "Father, into thy hands I commend my *spirit*." His spirit was with God at death; his re-animated body did not ascend till forty days after its resurrection and re-union with his spirit on earth. 3. The soul of Christ, when he died, was "in a state of death;" then "how could any part of him, whether soul, body, or spirit, as a living thing, be with the living thief in paradise on that day, while both were dead?"—an inquiry that may have some force with those who believe that the whole spiritual being of the God-man was extinct, annihilated, during the interval between the dissolution and resurrection of his body. 4. The thief, it is said, did not die till the next day or the day after, therefore, "how could the thief, while hanging alive on the cross, and Christ, who was dead during the three remaining hours of that day, be in any other place than on the cross?" The assumption made simply on the ground of the *alleged* practice of not breaking the legs of the crucified till after the lighting of Sabbath candles, and this taking place not till "an hour and a quarter, or, according to some, till twenty-five hours, after the expiration of that day," would be characteristically bold in any case when adduced to settle a question of fact, but becomes idle in face of the direction (Deut. xxi. 22, 23) to take down the crucified on the same day, the declaration of Josephus (War, iv. 5, 2), that, in his day, it was the custom to take down and bury the crucified before sunset, and the special assertion of John (xix. 32) that the legs of the thieves were broken to insure their being taken away before the coming-on of the [Jewish] Sabbath, i.e. before night of the day of crucifixion.

The first evasion (proposed and apparently preferred by the same writer) is this: "The thief prayed, Lord, remember me in the day of thy coming.* And Jesus said unto him, Verily, I say unto you, this day (the day of my coming) shalt thou be with me in my kingdom." And on the next page he explains, that, by "this day, the day of my coming," is meant the day of "Christ's second coming," "to be remembered when Christ came, not when he went away," — a period in the then distant future. In other words (if we rightly understand an exposition sufficiently vague in the expression and connection), the real meaning is, "in *that* day thou shalt be with me in paradise." On this attempt only two remarks are called for. 1. The first step is the arbitrary change of the previous verse, destitute of all valid foundation.† 2. The second step is a still more violent change of meaning in the word "to-

---

* The reader will observe the change of the text. "when thou comest in thy kingdom," to "*in the day of thy coming.*"

† Among all the Greek manuscripts, the reading, "in the day of thy coming," is not known to have been found in more than one (Codex D), and that one remarkable for the capricious alterations which cause it to rank lowest of the five older manuscripts.

day" to make it really mean "*that* day," a distant future day; a signification of which the Greek word (σήμερον) no more admits than does the plain English word "to-day."

A second evasion (also suggested by the same writer), and perhaps the most common, is to connect thus: " Verily I say unto thee to-day, thou shalt be with me in paradise;" that is, I say it to-day.

The first and obvious suggestion is the absurdity of putting in his mouth the idle statement that he says a thing "to-day," when every thing that is said, is and must be uttered on the speaker's "to-day." To avoid this absurdity, Mr. Hudson endeavors to find a special emphasis for the word, thus: "I say unto thee, even this day, when all seems so unlikely, thou shalt be with me in paradise when I enter my kingdom." To this we reply,—

1. The mode of conception, "when all seems so unlikely," is entirely alien from our Lord's method of view and speech. When did he deem it needful, even in declaring his most stupendous future doings, to lower the Godlike certainty of his assurances by any such deprecatory remark as "strange as it may appear to you," or, "though it may seem so unlikely"? The Saviour had made much more astounding predictions than the simple promise that a penitent and forgiven sinner should join him in heaven, and deemed it needless to allude to the seeming difficulty of the case. It may be the method of a common man, struggling hopefully under difficulties, to say that, incredible as it may now appear, he shall still be able to redeem his promises. It was not the manner of the Saviour. 2. There

was no call for such an allusion. The penitent thief had no occasion for it. He expressed himself with the fullest confidence in Christ. He did not say, "Help me if thou ever hast the power;" but, "Lord, remember me when thou comest in thy kingdom." To have replied to him, "Improbable as it may seem, I will," would have been simply to suggest a doubt to a dying man who had no doubt before. It would have been as unsuitable to the state of mind in the one party, as it would have been out of character in the other. 3. This interpretation destroys the chief point and force of Christ's words, as a gracious reply. The petition was, "Remember me when thou comest in thy kingdom," the distant and unknown future. The answer assures him, not alone of a distant future remembrance, but of an immediate blessing, "*To-day* shalt thou be with me in paradise," as a sure pledge of all that he asks for the future. Our Lord grants even more than he asks,—he shall enter *to-day with Christ* on a state *which is itself the pledge and the intermediate introduction* of the whole grand consummation which was asked. The other explanation, so far as this word is concerned, wholly misses this point or any particular point. All reference to the actual request disappears, and that, too, notwithstanding the elaborate solemnity of a double assurance. 4. But a decisive objection is found in the collocation of the Greek. The representation is sometimes made, that, so far as the language is concerned, this is a simple question of punctuation; whether a comma shall be put before or after "to-day" (σήμερον). This is a mistake. It is a question of Greek collocation under emphasis. The Greek language does not involve the ambiguity which exists in the English in this respect. It is admitted on both sides that the σήμερον (to-day) is strongly emphatic. Indeed, this is the only justification which Mr. Hudson can find for his interpretation. Very well, then. As a strongly emphatic word, according to the usages of the Greek language, its position conclusively determines that it does not qualify the words, "I say," but the words, "thou shalt be with me;" the strongly emphatic word in any clause preceding the less emphatic. In the Greek, it occupies precisely the position to be the most emphatic word of the last clause; but if transferred to the first clause, to be the least emphatic of the whole. And, as both sides admit its highly emphatic character, the case is settled.*

On this attempt to join "to-day" with "I say unto thee," Alford strongly remarks, "Considering that it not only violates common sense, but destroys the force of our Lord's promise, it is surely something worse than silly."

But Mr. Hudson has, as usual, a second resort: "Or the term 'paradise' may denote the state of the saints in the under-world." This virtually concedes the point we argue. That "state" was to be attained "to-day." Either, then, it was to be a state of conscious well-being, or the promise of the Saviour entirely evaded the petition, and was itself both mean-

---

* The Greek now reads, 'Αμὴν λέγω σοι σήμερον μετ' ἐμοῦ ἔσῃ ἐν τῷ παραδείσῳ. Whereas, if the meaning were as Mr. Hudson and others claim, it should read, 'Αμὴν σήμερον σοι λέγω, μετ' ἐμοῦ ἐν τῷ παραδείσῳ. The only exception to the principle is when sometimes an emphatic word is reserved to the end of a clause, for the sake of some appended explanation or evolution, which is here not the case.

ingless and delusive. For, 1. To promise a man that he shall be to-day in a state either of entire extinction or of blank and indefinitely prolonged unconsciousness, was a singular boon to declare with such solemnity. 2. To describe an unconscious state as being "in paradise," a place which, even in its lowest physical meaning, was a garden of delight, and as "being with Christ," a phrase continually used to describe the highest blessedness of the saints in heaven (John xiv. 3; xvii. 24; 2 Cor. v. 8; 1 Thess. iv. 17; Phil. i. 23), would be preposterous. 3. To say, in answer to a petition to be remembered in glory, "I most solemnly declare unto thee I will this very day (or, on this day when it seems all so unlikely, I will) introduce thee into a state of extinction, impaired mental activity, or entire insensibility to last for some thousand years," — this would indeed be asking for bread, and receiving in the gravest form of mockery a stone. If paradise does denote even the state of the saints in the under-world, it is still *paradise*, and paradise with Christ.

Accordingly, such a writer as Archbishop Whately, disdains all these subterfuges, though inclining to advocate an intermediate state of unconsciousness, and plants himself chiefly on the position that "this case is a very peculiar case, and therefore can hardly be regarded as decisive as to what shall be the lot of other men." He argues that this man's faith was peculiar and pre-eminent, as was also the time of his death, occurring at the time of Christ's death, and attended with many miraculous circumstances. But that there was any thing in either of these facts to warrant the slightest belief, that, for these reasons, God in his single instance broke through the grand economy of his dealings with the pious dead, the archbishop does not and can not show. And the man who asserts this treatment to be different from that of other eminent saints is bound to prove his point.

Enough for the present that the penitent thief was that day received to blessedness. Let his case take its place with other evidences.

Almost equally decisive is the case of Stephen (Acts vii. 55–60). As the mob were about to rush upon him, "he, being full of the Holy Ghost, looked up steadfastly into heaven, and saw the glory of God, and Jesus standing on the right hand of God, and said, Behold, I see the heavens opened and the Son of man standing on the right hand of God." The mob immediately hurried him to the fatal spot, and there "they stoned Stephen, calling upon God, and saying, Lord Jesus, receive my spirit." Now, who can doubt what was the expectation of this man, "full of the Holy Ghost," who had just been looking straight into heaven, and seeing "Jesus standing on the right hand of God," when, immediately after, he addresses that same Jesus with his dying breath, and as his body falls, prays, "Lord Jesus, receive my *spirit*"? Can there be a reasonable doubt that he expected his spirit at once to join at God's right hand that Saviour on whom he had just been gazing, towards whom his spirit was even then yearning with ineffable love, and to whom he was speaking as one already in his presence?

The reader will not fail to observe that the language of Stephen is substantially the same with that addressed by the Saviour himself to the Father at the very moment when his divine spirit passed from its crucified body, "Father, into thy hands I commend my spirit" (Luke xxiii. 46). Stephen evidently expected to experience the same immediate condition which Christ expected. Whoever is prepared to believe that he who claimed to have shared the glories of the Father before he "became flesh," expected, when he laid down that flesh, to be for a time either extinct or unconscious, upon the utterance of these words, can also believe that such was the expectation of Stephen.*

4. The Scripture furthermore teaches that spirits of believers long since departed are living, and with God. "The spirits of just men made perfect" are enumerated in this sense unmistakably in Heb. xii. 23: "But

---

* In connection with this passage (Acts vii. 59), a singular piece of effrontery deserves mention, as showing the nourishment on which a large portion of the believers in annihilation are fed. It occurs in Ellis and Read's Bible vs. Tradition, *sixth edition*. The writer begins by saying, "The grammar of the text charges the saying, 'Lord Jesus, receive my spirit,' upon the wicked Jews, and afterwards records what Stephen did and said." The reader who will examine the Greek text will see at a glance the astounding impudence of the statement; for the Greek can by no possibility be so translated or interpreted.

But the writer proceeds: "We waive this, being willing to allow that the translators were fallible, and attribute both sayings to Stephen. *Dexai* [δέξαι] means the right, *hand* being understood; metaphorically it means assistance, aid, strength, courage, and is equal to the expression, 'Lord Jesus, strengthen my spirit,' or 'nerve me up to endurance.'" Here this writer apparently confounds even the spelling of the Greek words (δεξιά and δέξαι), and mistakes the adjective "right" for the verb "receive" in the imperative mode. The error is made additionally ludicrous by his attempt to translate a sentence, which, according to his text, would admit no translation or meaning. It is needless to add that the verb means "receive;" and that no instance can probably be found in the Greek language where it even approaches the meaning "strengthen." Ellis and Read's book is understood to be a favorite treatise with a certain class of annihilationists.

ye are come unto Mount Sion, and unto the city of the living God, the heavenly Jerusalem, and to an innumerable company of angels, to the general assembly and church of the first-born which are written in heaven, and to God the Judge of all, and to the spirits of just men made perfect, and to Jesus the Mediator of the new covenant, and to the blood of sprinkling, which speaketh better things than that of Abel."

The apostle is here enumerating the inviting and attractive features of the Christian's present connections in contrast to the terrors of the dispensation of law. They are associated with the heavenly Jerusalem and *all the holy*, viz. (to follow in the main the excellent exposition of Alford), the great host of angels, the *church* (on earth) of the first-born (i.e. heirs, see i. 14) who are destined to life, and have their names registered in the book of life above (see Luke x. 20), and with God himself the judge (and deliverer) of all his people, and with the perfected spirits of the righteous already ransomed and gathered round him, and with Jesus the great Mediator and atoning Saviour.

For the details of the exposition, we must refer the reader to the commentators (particularly Alford, who is very clear on this passage). Still the intelligent reader will see, in the first place, that the language itself— "the *spirits* of just men made perfect" or consummated, advanced to glory—requires this as the obvious meaning. The apostle speaks of the just, not in their complex nature, but of their spirits: just as in 1 Cor. ii. 11, where "the spirit of man which is in him" is specially designated and distinguished from the whole man; and in Luke viii. 55, where it is said of the dead maiden restored to life by Christ, that "her spirit came again." In 1 Pet. iii. 19 also, by general admission, "the spirits in prison" are the disembodied spirits in confinement. The same word (πνεῦμα) is a common word to designate those spirits that the Saviour cast out so often,—spirits that had no body of their own.

The word, then, is carefully chosen. But here we have the spirits of *the just;* and not only so, they are the just "made perfect" (τετελειωμένων). This is the word used by the same writer, ch. ii. 10 (comp. v. 9), to describe the advancement of Christ to glory,— "make the Captain of their salvation perfect through sufferings,"—and, as if to indicate clearly that it so signifies in the present instance, the very next words introduce that glorified "Mediator of the new covenant." Were we to translate the word "made sinless,"—which is contrary to usage, and to the fact that the apostle speaks not of the spirits, but of *the just,* as having attained this condition,—we still have a state of things belonging only to the other world.* Moreover, the completeness of enumeration clearly requires the interpretation here maintained. We have God and Christ, and the angels and *the church* of those who are written in the book of life, and, besides them, the *spirits* of the just men made perfect. Now, in what way can we un-

---

* The word τελειόω has for its broad and radical meaning to consummate, or make complete. In the passive voice (as here), to be consummated or completed, as, 1. a prophecy in its fulfillment (once only, John xix. 28). 2. a principle or power when it is fully developed or exhibited; e.g., strength, love (2 Cor. xii. 9; 1 John ii. 5, iv. 17; Jas. ii. 23). 3. persons, when fully attaining (1) to a goal in view, perhaps Luke xiii. 32; (2) to a character required (Phil. iii. 12); (3) to a condition in prospect (John xvii. 23)—particularly the condition of future glory (Heb. v. 9; vii. 28).

derstand this latter clause, except in the obvious and simple way? Accordingly, though there are some minor diversities of connection and interpretation, as, for example, on the question whether these spirits are those of the Old or the New Testament saints, or of both alike, nearly all respectable interpreters, from the Greek fathers to the present time, with one accord, agree that they are the disembodied souls of the righteous in heaven. Thus Calvin: "Holy souls, which, having put off the body, have left behind all the filth of the flesh," and now "live with God." Bengel: "Separated souls," who, "after their own death, are receiving the fruit of the consummation achieved by Christ's death and the righteousness thence arising." So Alford, De Wette, Ebrard, Huther, and a large number of the most eminent expositors quoted by them, and differing among themselves only on the point previously indicated,— whether these are the spirits of the Old-Testament or the New-Testament saints, or, as Alford and others understand, both together.

Similar is the teaching of Heb. vi. 12, "That ye be not slothful, but followers of them who, through faith and patience, inherit the promises. For when God made promise to Abraham," etc. Two questions arise: First, Who are the persons referred to as inheriting? Second, What is meant by "inherit the promises"? That the persons chiefly in view must be those believers who have passed from this life would appear, because (1) we can be exhorted to be followers [imitators] properly only of those who precede us; (2) none but those who have actually completed the life of fidelity, and gone to their reward, can be properly held up for the encouragement of Christians still struggling; (3) the "faith and patience" seem to be mentioned as accomplished facts; (4) the inheritance of the promises constitutes a difference between them and the still living Christians whom he addresses; (5) and the writer immediately proceeds to specify Abraham as an example in his mind. What is it to "inherit the promises"? "The promise," in the New Testament, very often means the thing promised, the fulfillment of the promise. Such, according to almost all interpreters, says De Wette, is the meaning here (see Gal. iii. 22; Acts i. 4; Luke xxiv. 49, etc.). To "inherit," in the New Testament commonly means to possess (by the firmest title). These persons of whom we are to be followers, including Abraham, are described as now inheriting the promises. The translation accurately expresses it, "who inherit the promises." The original Greek does not speak of men who inherited, or were to inherit, or who shall inherit, but (with the present tense of the participle denoting primarily, present, continuous action) "who inherit the promises" (τῶν κληρονομούντων).

Thus the most obvious meaning of the passage is an exhortation to imitate the faith and patience of Abraham and believers like him, enforced by the thought that they are now reaping the promised rewards of that faith and patience. The only plausible objection is, that, in Heb. xi. 39, it is said, "And these all, having obtained a good report through faith, received not the promise," etc. The objection is only specious. This last passage simply asserts, that, during their life here below, they did not receive the fulfillment of the promise, that is, of Christ. The promise of his coming and redemptive work was not fulfilled, as the next verse explains, till the times of the apostle, "God having provided some better thing for us."

Another passage, apparently announcing the immediate blessedness of the dying saint, is found in Rev. xiv. 13, "Write, Blessed are the dead which die in the Lord from henceforth: Yea, saith the Spirit, that they may rest from their labors; and their works do follow them" (literally follow with them). Some diversity of interpretation exists as to the connection in the first clause, — whether it means blessed from henceforth, or blessed those who die from henceforth. De Wette, indifferent to all theological aspects of the case, and viewing it merely as an acute scholar, understands it, "Blessed from now onward," and adds, "it would promise them immediate blessedness." The reason immediately rendered in the following clause certainly seems decisive, and at least asserts the fact by its own force: "Yea, that they may rest from their labors [κόπων wearisome, painful toils]; and their works do follow with them." Such was the blessedness of dying in Christ, — to rest from vexatious toils, and to have their works (i.e., by a common metonymy, the fruit or reward of their works) *accompanying* them when they die. This is not the description of a state of extinction or unconsciousness, but of active enjoyment. His works do not "follow with" a man lost to all consciousness.

To these passages some would add very positively Rev. vi. 9-11, though others object: "And, when he had opened the fifth seal, I saw under the altar the souls of them that were slain for the word of God, and for the testimony which they held: and they cried with a loud voice, saying, How long, O Lord holy and true, dost thou not judge and avenge our blood on them that dwell on the earth? And white robes were given unto every one of them; and it was said unto them that they should rest yet for a little season, until their fellow-servants also, and their brethren, that should be killed as they were, should be fulfilled." We certainly should be cautious in drawing doctrinal statements from a passage so highly figurative. We may freely admit that the location "under the altar" is symbolical, and that the prayer and the reply is dramatical. Still it remains that the souls, or disembodied spirits, of the holy martyrs are here distinctly recognized; that they are spoken of as having earnest desires for the consummation of their blessedness and of God's absolute reign; this, too, while their murderers still "dwell upon the earth;" as being meanwhile clad in "white robes" of purity and joy (see chap. iii. 4; vii. 13), and bid to rest (i.e., as some say, to restrain their petitions, or, as others, rest in blessedness — see xiv. 13) till their brethren are gathered with them. The "white robes" given to them of course are not literal garments; but they represent a fact: in the words of Alford, "the white robe, in this book, is the vestment of acknowledged and glorified righteousness in which the saints walk and reign with Christ," and indicates that individually they are blessed in glory with Christ, and waiting for their fellows to be fully complete."

The Scriptures, secondly, affirm the conscious existence of the wicked after death and previous to the judgment. The case may be considered as settled by that of the righteous, unless it can be positively shown from the Scriptures to the contrary. So far from this, however, the Scriptures, as we shall see directly, recognize the continued consciousness of the wicked after death and before the resurrection.

Judging by the fate of the fallen angels also, we should expect the continued existence of lost men until the judgment. For we are told (Jude 6) that "the angels which kept not their first estate, but left their own habitation, he hath reserved in everlasting chains under darkness unto the judgment of the great day;" and again (2 Pet. ii. 4), that "God spared not the angels that sinned, but cast them down to hell, and delivered them into chains of darkness to be reserved [being reserved] unto judgment." They, then, though cast down to hell, are still reserved in chains unto the judgment. Others of them apparently were indeed at liberty for a time to roam the world on their work of evil, but still looking forward to a time when they shall be ordered into the "abyss" (ἄβυσσον, Luke viii. 31), and to a "time" of "torment" (Matt. viii. 29).

In the same mode, and by similar phraseology, does the New Testament describe the immediate portion of the wicked. It describes the dying transgressor as passing to his peculiar place or abode, recognizes the disobedient of former times as in a state of imprisonment and consciousness, and speaks of the immediate fate of the dying sinner as at once in "hell" and "in torments," even while the living were on earth.

In Acts i. 25, we read, "That he may take part of

this ministry and apostleship from which Judas by transgression fell, that he might go to his own place." The statement implies a departure from the position to which he did not belong, at once to the place that properly belonged to him. Several diverse vagaries have been advanced as to this *place* to which Judas went; but the best modern scholarship seems to agree on that view which suggests itself at once to the common reader, and which the scholarly rationalist, De Wette, has expressed when he says it was his "merited place, his place of punishment in hell." So also Alford. So Meyer, "The context requires us to understand *gehenna*."

The passage, 1 Pet. iii. 18–20, bears still more distinctly on this subject, where we read of Christ "being put to death in the flesh, but quickened by the Spirit: by which also, he went and preached unto the spirits in prison, which some time [once] were disobedient, when once the long-suffering of God waited in the days of Noah, while the ark was a preparing, wherein few, that is eight souls, were saved by water."

In reference to this passage, there are some questions still unsettled, but with which we have no present concern. The points to which we call attention are somewhat generally conceded by the best modern scholarship. For the purposes of this argument, it is of no importance what was the nature of the preaching, nor perhaps, even, whether it was done by Christ in person, or by Noah the preacher of righteousness; although, if the more common view of later scholars be received, that it was by Christ in person, the case is more thoroughly decisive. It may be considered as admitted that the persons here spoken of are the disobedient of Noah's time. It is also settled that "in prison" means, what it seems to mean, in a place or state of imprisonment, penal confinement. The phrases "in prison" and "into prison" ($\dot{\varepsilon}\nu\ \varphi\upsilon\lambda\alpha\kappa\tilde{\eta}$ and $\varepsilon\iota\varsigma\ \varphi\upsilon\lambda\alpha\kappa\dot{\eta}\nu$) occur in the New Testament twenty-six times, invariably in this sense. The Greek word ($\varphi\upsilon\lambda\alpha\kappa\dot{\eta}$) prison is also used in Rom. xx. 7 to denote the bottomless pit (verse 3) in which Satan was to be confined.* And the parties thus in penal confinement, in the home of the lost, are the "*spirits*" (departed spirits, De Wette) of those once disobedient when the long-suffering of God waited in the time of Noah: the word is carefully chosen, and the statement clear. Here, then, the Scripture calls those who died impenitent in former days, "spirits in prison" or in penal confinement. If the preaching was through Noah, then they are spirits now in confinement; if by Christ in person, then they were in confinement when he went and preached to them, that is at the time of his death.

Another important passage is found in the account of the rich man and Lazarus (Luke xvi. 19–31). The entire passage should be carefully read in connection. The principal statements, however, are found in verses 22 and 23: "And it came to pass that the beggar died, and was carried by the angels into Abraham's bosom. The rich man also died, and was buried: and in hell he lifted up his eyes, being in torments, and seeth Abraham afar off, and Lazarus in his bosom."

On this passage, Universalists and annihilationists

---

* The Church fathers use the word for $\H{\alpha}\delta\eta\varsigma$, and the Syriac translates it *cheol* (De Wette).

alike have exhausted their ingenuity to evade the clear teachings which the plain reader of the Bible and the unprejudiced scholar equally find in the narrative.

The question whether this is a history or a parable, it is not necessary to discuss. In either mode, the Scripture teaches truth, — important and often vital truth. The chief difference is, that the one mode asserts what has occurred, the other " what does occur." Grant it to be a parable. The notion that a parable does not convey important and even definite truth, will be maintained by no intelligent reader of the Bible. Thus, for example, some of the most striking facts in regard to Christ's kingdom, its methods, progress, and relations, are conveyed in that remarkable group of parables, — the tares and wheat, the growing corn, the mustard-seed, the leaven, the hidden treasure, the costly pearl, the fisherman's net. Dr. Whately, while endeavoring to cut down this passage to the minimum of teaching, is obliged to say, "The only truth that is essential in a parable is the truth or *doctrine conveyed by it.*" * Mr. Hudson not only admits the same view, but is constrained to mention one doctrine that actually is taught in this passage: " We therefore freely say, that the parable, whatever it may or may not teach, assumes and implies *a judgment, or some kind of retribution after death.*" † Very well; and now the plain reader will say, " If it teaches any retribution after death, that is, if it, in fact, involve that truth at all, then it also involves with equal distinctness the statement, that that retribution is one of conscious joy or woe, and

---

* Future State, p. 56.   † Rich Man and Lazarus, p. 8.

commences at death." And such a sharp-sighted scholar and rationalist as De Wette perfectly accords with the view of the plain reader: "The rich man makes an idle, self-seeking use of his property, which may seem to correspond to the 'wasting' of verse 1; and the consequence is, that he, in return therefor (*anstatt*), reaches the place of torment (*Qual*) in the eternal furnace."

As various attempts have been made to transfer the plain meaning of this narrative to some "abolition of the Jewish priesthood," and what not, it is important for the reader to observe that the connection itself precludes such a perversion, and clearly fixes the reference to the subject of individual retribution after death for the use or abuse of the bounties of this life. Not only have scholars like Alford, De Wette, Olshausen, and others, pointed out the close connection of this passage with the earlier part of the chapter, the stewardship, but the reader may see for himself that one connected subject runs through the chapter,— the right or wrong use of riches, and the consequence hereafter. The chapter opens with the parable of the steward, who, being charged with wasting his lord's money, immediately set about so skillful (though unprincipled) an application of it, that he made friends for the hour of need, and that even his master admired his adroitness; closing with Christ's own injunction to his hearers so to use their riches in this life, that they themselves may be received into "everlasting habitations" (verse 9). The same exhortation and encouragement is repeated in verse 11. In verse 13, he warns them against the attempt to idolize wealth, to "serve God and Mammon." In verse 14, we are informed how the Pharisees, "who were covetous," derided him for these words; and, after three or four intermediate verses of general rebuke for their hypocritical pretenses, he proceeds to meet their derisive spirit, and crown his teaching with this terrible utterance on the abuse of riches. The context thus holds the passage fast to the theme of personal retribution after death. The offense of the rich man is not brought to sight except in connection with the previous warnings in regard to the use and abuse of riches.

Indeed, certain Universalist writers have attempted, by cutting off the connection between this passage and the previous part of the chapter, to deny that any moral quality is implied in the case of the rich epicure. The statement is not alone in conflict with the whole spirit of Christ's teachings as to the supreme folly of him who "layeth up treasure for himself, and is not rich towards God:" it is refuted by the previous full teachings of this same chapter, and the closing direction how to escape the place of woe by "repenting." "They have Moses and the prophets: let them hear them." In truth, there can be no mistaking the sketch of the rich man, as of a selfish sensualist, absorbed in pampering his own body, and leaving the poor and suffering Lazarus to such a living as the dogs pick up (see Matt. xv. 27), and to the tender mercies of the dogs themselves (verse 21). As the stress of the passage lay in its warning to the evil-doer, the moral character of the good Lazarus is barely indicated by his final reception to the companionship of Abraham, the father of the faithful; but our Saviour's explicit teachings as to that companionship, and who shall enjoy it, leave no doubt hanging over the case (see Matt. viii. 11; Luke xiii. 28, 29).

The passage, then, teaches, first (in Mr. Hudson's words), " some kind of retribution " to the wicked after death. The rich man "*died* and was buried; and in hell he lifted up his eyes, being in torments." *To die*, then, is not extinction: it is here the passage to a state of anguish. It teaches, further, that the retribution consists in conscious suffering. This fact lies all along the narrative as an emphatic portion of it. He lifted up his eyes in hell, being in torments: "I am tormented in this flame; thou art tormented; this place of torment." Mr. Hudson even admits this meaning of the language, remarking that " the torment of the rich man here described is not that of *gehenna*, but that of *hades*." * And the reader will not fail to observe, that the flame is here beyond all question the symbol, not of extinction, but of suffering: "I am tormented in this flame." The passage teaches, thirdly, that this suffering follows death at once. (1) This is the obvious connection of the transactions. The one person died, and was carried by the angels into Abraham's bosom: the other died, and was buried; and in hell he lifted up his eyes. (2) The suffering was taking place while probation was continuing on earth, and five brethren of the sufferer were still living. And if any one should insist that this is only dramatic costume, we add, that (3) The suffering is cotemporaneous with the joy of paradise; and the latter, as we have

---

* Debt and Grace, p. 210.

shown, commences at once. Indeed, it is not only admitted, but is strongly insisted on, by Mr. Hudson, that the representation in this passage "belongs to the intermediate state;" that is, to the *immediate* state of the dead previous to the resurrection of the body.*

This important passage, then, shows that the punishment of sin consists in continuous suffering, entered upon at death. Nowhere do the Scriptures imply any subsequent change of condition; but this very parable affirms that "there is a great gulf fixed" between the sinful and the holy, which, as Mr. Hudson admits, "fairly implies that the case of the rich man is hopeless." † He also says, "The rich man is there and 'in torments,' as if that were 'his own place;' while Lazarus is carried to Abraham's bosom, as if that were his proper home: *and this would be the just inference*, if the Scriptures told us nothing else concerning *hades*." ‡ This is admitting all we ask. This passage, as a whole, teaches these states of suffering and of joy to be the immediate and "proper homes" respectively of the wicked and the good. Let us also add, that, as the time thus elapsing prior to the resurrection of the body must in many cases be many thousand years, all arguments against the Scripture doctrine from the long duration of the penalty fall to the ground.

If it be asked, with what consistency, while we retain these teachings of the passage, we fail to receive literally the circumstances of dipping the tip of one's

---

* Debt and Grace, p. 210; Christ our Life, p. 131; Rich Man and Lazarus, p. 8.

† Rich Man and Lazarus, p. 8.

‡ Ib., p. 12. The word occurring in Luke xvi. 23 is *hades*, not *gehenna*. On this subject, see Appendix, note C.

finger in water and cooling the tongue, the flame, the lying in Abraham's bosom, the gulf, and even the oral communications between Abraham and the rich man, we reply, 1. The conditions of the narrative rule out a literal conception of these particulars by assigning it to time when the parties must have been disembodied spirits. They had died, and been buried; while the living were supposed to be still on earth. It was therefore subsequent to death, and prior to the resurrection. This fact determines the particulars to be figurative representations. 2. These modes of representation, figuratively employed, are common in the Scriptures. The joys of heaven are the marriage-supper of the Lamb; sitting down with Abraham; God feeding his saints, leading them to living fountains, wiping away their tears; drinking from the river of life. God himself, the bodiless Spirit, is constantly spoken of with fingers, mouth, and all the portions of the body. Any endeavor of Universalist or annihilationist to set aside the reference of these teachings to the spirit-world, because of their costume, must also annul most of the declarations concerning God and heaven. 3. Furthermore, this mode of representation is employed from necessity. We have no language, nor modes of conception, with which to speak of God and heaven and spiritual beings, except the language and conceptions drawn from earth and sense. The method is inevitable; and any argument founded upon it is, therefore, of no account.

There is, therefore, no reason for rejecting the obvious teaching of this passage, that the wicked pass from this world at once to a state of conscious suffering.

The reader will appreciate the case more readily on seeing some of the conflicting attempts of annihilationists to dispose of the passage, as well as some of their reluctant admissions.

The account of Lazarus and Dives has been as troublesome to annihilationists as to Universalists; and some of the former have borrowed the methods of the latter.

H. L. Hastings summarily sets aside the whole passage as incapable of teaching any thing: "Of course the parable of the Rich Man and Lazarus is not reckoned as teaching doctrine; for all the laws of criticism forbid that parables be made use of to teach doctrines." * Ellis and Read find, however, very decided doctrine: "In this parable, the Jewish priesthood, personated by the rich man, died, the priesthood being abolished; and while in *hades*, the dominion of death, he saw [so, then, death is not extinction of consciousness] the peculiar privileges of the Abrahamic covenant in the possession of the formerly despised Lazarus, who personated the Gentiles." † These writers prudently refrain from any remark on the phrases, "tormented in this flame," etc., except to say, that inasmuch as *hades*, in a large number of instances, denotes a "state of death, it would be strange indeed if in our text it should imply a state of life and torment;" and yet in that very state they make the rich man "see."

J. Blain finds still more abundant and curious doctrine. He sees rather the political than the ecclesiatical condition of the Jews described, but liberally al-

---
* Pauline Theology, p. 40.
† Bible vs. Tradition, p. 214.

lows a choice of either or both. He also, with curious inconsistency, finds protracted misery in the flames: "The rich man denoted the Jewish nation or the priesthood, or both combined. His death symbolized the death (destruction) of their political and ecclesitical state: torment in flames denoted or predicted the misery they would endure as a nation. It is a fact, that they have been in torment by persecution ever since they 'died' as a nation. Their looking to Abraham for relief may denote their relying on the law instead of on Christ, or grace through him. They have been 'buried' as to nationality and a priesthood. The poor man symbolized the Gentiles and publicans, who were looked upon as 'dogs' by the Jews, and lay at, or could only come to the 'gate' of the temple for 'crumbs' of light. 'Abraham's bosom' meant the gospel church; and when the Gentiles 'died,' or changed their former sickly state, they were not buried as were the Jews, but 'carried by angels' (messengers) into the gospel church. Peter and Paul were special 'angels' to thus transport them." * In this sad jumble, besides denying his own principle as to the office of the flames, the writer makes Abraham denote, first the law, and then the gospel church; while death at first denotes "destruction," and again the "changing of their former sickly state" for a sound one.

Mr. Edwin Burnham gets so far as to locate the scene apparently after death, and before the judgment; but he can see in it only "some transaction." "The parable of the Rich Man and Lazarus proves nothing

---

* Death not Life, p. 58.

to the point of eternal torment; for that parable refers to some transaction before the judgment." *

George Storrs discerns a little more than "some transaction" after death. He admits hypothetically that it teaches suffering: "Suppose the rich man to be actually in a conscious state after death, and in torment: it does not prove him immortal, or that his conscious suffering is to be eternal; for the advocates of the immortality of man admit that the state of the rich man spoken of was immediately after death, and before the day of judgment. Hence, whatever his state is now, it is not his proper punishment; that may be utter annihilation, for all there is in the text to prove the contrary: he has not yet passed the judgment. When he has, then comes the real punishment, and the Scriptures elsewhere must determine what it is. We have positive testimony that the wages of sin is death." † But the writer apparently admits, in these very sentences, the fact of conscious suffering "after death."

Dr. Whately finds retribution "very plainly" implied in this passage: "It seems to imply, indeed very plainly, that there is a future state of rewards and punishments, . . . and also that those who have been devoted to the good things and enjoyments of this world will have no share in those of the world to come, and will regret when it is too late their not having laid up for themselves treasure in heaven." ‡ This is certainly

---

* Anti-Eternal Torment, p. 5.

† Storrs's Six Sermons, p. 164. Mr. Storrs promises some fuller discussion; but this is all we find in two of his works.

‡ We reckon Dr. Whately in this connection because his entire mode of putting the case is to question the received doctrine.

a mild mode of interpreting the passage, but yields the principle.

Mr. Hudson is at first constrained to admit every thing we claim concerning the passage; and then, in one of his later treatises (the Rich Man and Lazarus), he retracts it all with his favorite prolepsis and "dramatic" element. He indeed strenuously asserts that the transaction is in *hades* rather than *gehenna*. He admits that it takes place after death, "in the intermediate state," and is a "retribution;" that it "implies that the rich man's case is hopeless;" that "the rich man is there and in 'torments,' as if that were 'his own place;'" while Lazarus is carried to Abraham's bosom, as if that were his proper home: and this would be the just inference if the Scriptures told us nothing else of *hades*." * Then, after spending four pages in elucidating the difference between *hades* and *gehenna*, he suddenly sets aside his whole discussion by one of his exegetical somersets, and declares that it really refers not to the intermediate state at all, but to the final judgment: "How then shall we explain the drapery which in Luke xxi. is thrown around the intermediate state, making it look so much like a world of retribution? I think there is an easy solution of this difficulty, without regard to the question of consciousness or unconsciousness in the disembodied soul. It is simply this: The final judgment is anticipated. This anticipation may be either actual in the expectant thoughts and feelings of the rich man and Lazarus; or it may be dramatic, transferred to the dead from the thoughts of the liv-

---

* Debt and Grace, p. 210; Christ our Life, p. 131; Rich Man and Lazarus, pp. 8, *seq*.

ing." * We care not to follow this tortuous course of exposition and argument, except to call attention to its admissions concerning the plain teaching of this whole passage.

H. H. Dobney unequivocally admits all that we claim: "Our Lord shows an ungodly man in a state of wretchedness after death. How long it would last is not intimated. It is true, there was no hope for him. He could not buoy himself up with the prospect of restoration. But whether that torment should endure for ever, or would ultimately destroy him, the parable does not intimate. It teaches a terrible and hopeless state for the wicked after death; and that is all." †

And that is all we are at present seeking to prove,— "a state of wretchedness after death," immediately consequent upon it; and whether we look at the plain aspect of the passage itself, at the discordant perversions of one class of annihilationists, or the reluctant admissions of another class, the case is a clear one.

The fact that the wicked are in a state of suffering after death, and prior to the judgment, is also clearly taught in 2 Pet. ii. 9 : "The Lord knoweth how to deliver the godly out of temptation, and to reserve the unjust under punishment unto the day of judgment." Such is the correct translation, rendered in the English version "to be punished." So Alford most decidedly, and Huther ; while Winer, who took the other view in the fifth edition of his grammar, seems to have abandoned it in the sixth. The Greek does not fairly

---

* Rich Man and Lazarus, p. 12.
* Dobney's Future Punishment, p. 239.

admit any other rendering.* Says Alford, "under punishment, not to be punished, but, as in verse 4, actually in a penal state, and thus awaiting their final punishment."

We think we have sufficiently maintained from Scripture the continued consciousness of both the righteous and the wicked after death, and previous to the resurrection of the body, — the one in conscious joy, the other in conscious suffering.

---

* Ἀδίκους δὲ εἰς ἡμέραν κρίσεως κολαζομένους τηρεῖν, literally " to reserve the ungodly, being punished, to the day of judgment."

CHAPTER IV.

NEW TESTAMENT TEACHINGS CONTINUED.—A RESURRECTION AND A JUDGMENT FOR THE WICKED.

THE souls of both the righteous and the wicked, it appears, enter at death upon a conscious state of happiness and of suffering respectively. The event called death, is to the wicked, not the termination of existence or of consciousness, but the beginning of conscious retributive suffering.

This does not prove, indeed, their eternal existence: it is not adduced for that purpose. But it does disprove one important position of the theory of annihilation. The dead, as we call them, still live. They experience a continued existence and activity beyond the grave,—an existence continued certainly to a very protracted extent. If continued till the resurrection, then it must be in many instances for some thousand years. Such a fact is of itself sufficient to invalidate the fundamental reasonings of annihilationists.

But the Scripture does not leave the subject thus: it makes further disclosures concerning their future history. The next step in these disclosures is the Scripture doctrine concerning the resurrection and the general judgment, and the formal sentence of retribution, in which the wicked as well as the good will appear.

It is the clear doctrine that full and final sentence of retribution takes place at the general judgment, that the judgment is preceded by a general resurrection of "all that are in their graves," and that this last event accompanies the second coming of our Lord with power and great glory.* The spirit then resumes the bodily form.

For those who read and submit to the plain teachings of God's word, it can not be necessary for me to argue at great length, that all men, the wicked as well as the good, are to be raised from the dead, and to stand in judgment before God. Still a brief sketch of those teachings may be in place.

And, first, of the judgment and retribution. It is ever a teaching of the Old Testament, though less minute than the New, that the wicked and the good alike shall stand before God in judgment. Such is especially the drift of the book of Ecclesiastes, as indicated, for example, in chap. iii. 16, 17, xi. 9, and conclusively summed up in chap. xii. 13, 14. The thought is more or less distinctly alluded to in numerous passages like Ps. i. 5, 6, although often in such a mode, that we can not say certainly that the *final* judgment is intended.

It was reserved for the New Testament to reveal the fact in its fullness, that "after death," at the "last day," the "day of judgment," when "the Son of man shall come in the clouds of heaven," all the dead alike shall stand before him to receive their sentence.

---

* The question, whether there is a literal and bodily "first resurrection" of the holy previous to the general resurrection of all the dead, is not material to the present discussion, and is therefore omitted. The simple fact of a universal resurrection is all that here concerns us.

Thus it is after death, not at death nor in death, that judgment and a *final* retribution come. "It is appointed unto men once to die, but after this the judgment" (Heb. ix. 27). "Be not afraid of them that kill the body, and after that have no more that they can do. But I will forewarn you whom ye shall fear: fear Him, which, after he hath killed, hath power to cast into hell; yea, I say unto you, fear him" (Luke xii. 4, 5).

The particular time is designated as the last day, the time when the Son of man shall come; and at that time the foes of Christ as well as his friends shall receive their sentence. "He that rejecteth me, and receiveth not my words, hath one that judgeth him: the word that I have spoken, the same shall judge him in the last day" (John xii. 48). "Or what shall a man give in exchange for his soul? For the Son of man shall come in the glory of his Father, with his angels; and then shall he reward every man according to his works" (Matt. xvi. 26, 27). "Whosoever shall confess me before men, him shall the Son of man also confess before the angels of God; but he that denieth me before men shall be denied before the angels of God" (Luke xii. 8, 9). See also Jude 13, and 2 Pet. iii. 7.

To this day of judgment are all transgressors reserved; and then shall they, as well as the righteous, receive their public sentence. "For if God spared not the angels that sinned, but cast them down to hell, and delivered them into chains of darkness, to be reserved unto judgment; . . . the Lord knoweth how to deliver the godly out of temptations, and to reserve the unjust unto the day of judgment to be [being] punished"

(2 Pet. ii. 4, 9). "And whosoever shall not receive you nor hear your words, when ye depart out of that house or city, shake off the dust of your feet. Verily I say unto you, it shall be more tolerable for the land of Sodom and Gomorrah in the day of judgment than for that city" (Matt. x. 14, 15). In like manner, the sentence of Chorazin, Bethsaida, Tyre, Sidon, Capernaum, Sodom, is referred to "the day of judgment" (Matt. xi. 20–23). "I say unto you, that every idle word that men shall speak, they shall give account thereof in the day of judgment. For by thy words thou shalt be justified, and by thy words thou shalt be condemned" (Matt. xii. 36, 37). "But now commandeth all men everywhere to repent; because he hath appointed a day, in the which he will judge the world in righteousness by that man whom he hath ordained" (Acts xvii. 30, 31). "For we must all appear before the judgment-seat of Christ, that every one may receive the things done in his body, according to that he hath done, whether it be good or bad" (2 Cor. v. 10, 11). The twofold retribution so fully described in the second chapter of Romans is referred to "the day when God shall judge the secrets of men by Jesus Christ" (verse 16); and it is said to the wicked, "But after thy hardness and impenitent heart treasurest [thou] up unto thyself wrath against the day of wrath and revelation of the righteous judgment of God." In 2 Tim. iv. 1, we read of "the Lord Jesus Christ, who shall judge the quick and the dead at his appearing and his kingdom." The solemn account of the judgment (Matt. xxv. 31–46), describing it as taking place "when the Son of man shall come in his glory, and all the holy angels with

him," also declares that " before him shall be gathered all nations," and represents the wicked as being present with the righteous to receive their final sentence. In 2 Thess. i. 5-10, the recompense, "tribulation," "taking vengeance," and punishment "with everlasting destruction from the presence of the Lord," is made cotemporaneous with the recompense of "rest" to believers; and both are assigned to the time "when the Lord Jesus shall be revealed from heaven with his mighty angels," — "when he shall come to be glorified in his saints."

It is needless to accumulate other proofs; for if these do not show that at the last day, the day of final judgment, the day of Christ's coming in glory, all the wicked as well as the good will stand before him in conscious activity to receive public sentence, nothing can show it.

The Scriptures also declare a general resurrection, in which the wicked as well as the good shall come forth from their graves preparatory to the judgment: "Marvel not at this: for the hour is coming, in the which all that are in the graves shall hear his voice, and shall come forth, — they that have done good, unto the resurrection of life; and they that have done evil, unto the resurrection of damnation" (John v. 28, 29). These are the words of Jesus Christ. They are uttered as the sequel of the statement, that "authority to execute judgment" is committed to the Son of man; and the whole as the grand climax of the great work which he was then performing on earth. They describe the resurrection of the wicked in the same terms with that of the righteous. To leave no room for doubting that the resurrection of the body is intended, he says, "They that are in the graves" [or tombs]. To anticipate a low modern cavil, that they shall be brought forth as dead persons or corpses, he declares "they shall hear his voice, and shall come forth." To cut off the allegation that a transient or momentary revivification is described, he announces it as only preliminary to the execution of judgment; and, in case of the wicked, it is here not even a resurrection of death, but of condemnation, "damnation." All attempts to pervert this passage from its plain meaning may be considered as now exploded. No respectable commentator, of whatever school, can probably now be found to lend his name to them.

The bodily resurrection of the wicked is also implied very fully and unquestionably in Christ's warning: "Fear not them which kill the body, but are not able to kill the soul; but rather fear him which is able to destroy both soul and body in hell" (Matt. x. 28). Paul asserts the same fact, "And have hope toward God, which they themselves also allow, that there shall be a resurrection of the dead, both of the just and unjust" (Acts xxiv. 15). Here he uses the same words to express the resurrection of the righteous and the wicked; and it will be observed that he testifies distinctly that this was alike his own belief and that of his Jewish opponents. This statement is in such terms as to admit no cavil. It is met, so far as we can learn, only by open denial. Thus to quote from one who, though an annihilationist, yet argues for the resurrection, and represents the reasoning of his associates, as follows: "It is said Paul *hoped* for the resurrection of the dead. Hope is made up of *desire* and expectation. Could Paul *desire* to see the wicked all in one vast company, weeping, wailing, crying for mercy, and mercy deaf to all their sorrows, anguish, and despair? Could he *desire* to listen to the curses and blasphemies, and witness the rolling sea of wickedness, that would pour forth from all the resurrected wicked in that day? Certainly not." * This matter may be left to be settled between these reasoners and the apostle.

The same fact is involved in the passage (Rev. xx. 11–15): " And I saw a great white throne, and him that sat on it, from whose face the earth and the heaven fled away; and there was found no place for them. And I saw the dead, small and great, stand before God; and the books were opened; and another book was opened, which is the book of life: and the dead were judged out of those things which were written in the books according to their works. And the sea gave up the dead which were in it; and death and hell [*hades*] delivered up the dead which were in them; and they were judged, every man according to their works. And death and hell [*hades*] were cast into the lake of fire. This is the second death. And whosoever was not found written in the book of life was cast into the lake of fire." Here the reader will observe, 1. The scene described is clearly the general judgment. Various circumstances fully identify it with that transaction as elsewhere described. 2. It is preceded by a universal resurrection of the body. It is " the dead, small and

---

* H. L. Hastings's Retribution, p. 143. Three other forms of denial are quoted by him from other advocates of annihilation, still more abrupt if possible; but no attempt to interpret away the language.

great;" those in "the sea," and those elsewhere in charge of "death and *hades*;"* men of diverse characters, to be judged, "every man according to their works." Not only the good were there, those whose names were in the book of life, but those who were "*not* found written in the book of life" were there also.

As the reader may like to know what objections are raised against such a passage by a portion of the annihilationists,—the more materialistic portion,—we annex them as stated by H. L. Hastings, who represents a different phase of the system.† It is alleged,—

1. The passage "is in Revelation, and Revelation is an obscure book." To which we need only say that, whatever may be the obscurity of any other portion of the book, *this* is a distinct account of the general judgment, fully confirmed and explained by abundant other passages of Scripture.

2. "The whole is a dramatic representation." But this statement when intended as a *denial* of the resurrection of the wicked, would cut up the whole doctrine of a future life; for this passage declares as clearly as any portion of the Scriptures, the great fact of a judgment and a just retribution. It is here stated just as distinctly concerning the wicked dead as concerning the good, that "they stand before God" to be judged and doomed.

3. "It is said that the *dead* stood before God, and

---

* "*Hades*" may be considered as the impersonation of the grave, the place of the dead; "death," already personified as riding on the pale horse, perhaps as the keeper or ruler of the realm. *All* the dead of the ocean and the land are there.

† Retribution, by H. L. Hastings, pp. 119, 120.

were judged, and so they were dead when they were judged; and hence they will never know any thing about the matter, nor undergo any further conscious punishment, but will simply be left alone in the grave where they are." We will not delay to dwell upon Christ's declaration, "They that are in their graves shall *hear the voice* of the Son of God, and shall come forth," nor upon the fact that "the dead" here includes *both classes alike;* for it is hardly supposable that a man who could descend to such egregious trifling with God's Word is to be satisfied, and have his quibbles silenced, by any forms of speech.

4. "Those found written in the book of life are made *alive,* but those who are not found written there do not *live* nor know nor suffer; but, if they are raised at all, they are simply so many lumps of clay, images, or carcasses, not raised 'to life,' but raised 'without any life.' " No reply is called for here. Waiving those other representations which describe the conscious state of the wicked at the judgment, any man who could allege that the Scriptures describe the judgment-scene as including the solemn mockery of summoning, by a vast miracle, millions of unconscious corpses before God to be tried, and sentenced, and executed with the forms of punishment, will not be likely to have his opinion changed by argument or Scripture.

5. "It is finally said that wicked men can not die a second time, and hence the 'second death' is a mere figure, which means no one knows what; because it is said that death and hell died the second death too, and there is no account of their having died a first death before." Here, again, we waive all other

discussion simply to remind the reader that the objection, in short, is just this: We deny the plainly asserted fact of a resurrection of the wicked, because we are puzzled as to the nature of the punishment described as following their resurrection and judgment.

The doctrine of a general resurrection of both classes of men is even declared in the Old Testament. "And at that time shall Michael stand up, the great prince which standeth for the children of thy people; and there shall be a time of trouble, such as never was since there was a nation even to that time; and at that time thy people shall be delivered, every one that shall be found written in the book. And many of them that sleep in the dust of the earth shall awake, some to everlasting life, and some to shame and everlasting contempt. And they that be wise shall shine as the brightness of the firmament; and they that turn many to righteousness, as the stars for ever and ever" (Dan. xii. 1–3). This passage appears to be a glance down to the "time of the end," which is specified in the verse following; and announces the resurrection of two classes of men, that "sleep in the dust of the earth," to two opposite destinies. On this point the sober class of modern scholars are apparently becoming agreed; e.g., Alford (on John v. 29), Stuart, Hävernick, Auberlen. Even such rationalists as Maurer and Hitzig, though endeavoring to refer it to an earlier period, admit the fact of a twofold resurrection to be here asserted; and "the book" (verse 1), to be the "book of life," "the list of the citizens of the Messianic kingdom" (Hitzig). The second verse would perhaps be more correctly translated, "multitudes of sleepers in the dust of the earth shall awake." * Those who, like Hitzig, insist on the partitive force of "many," limit the resurrection here spoken of to the Jewish nation. But even this narrowed application still leaves the parties divided into two opposite classes, the second of whom, in Hitzig's own words, " arise to judgment (John v. 29), awake to the punishment of eternal fire-torment (compare Isa. lxvi. 24 with Rev. xx. 14, 15), and become, by this their fate, an object of abhorrence." †

In view of the clear teachings of Scripture, especially the New Testament, concerning the resurrection and the judgment, Mr. H. L. Hastings, himself an annihilationist, warmly declares, "The same perverse logic which proves no resurrection of the wicked, proves no resurrection of any one, no pre-existence of Christ before his birth, no Holy Spirit but the Word, no baptism but the Spirit, no Lord's Supper, no future punishment, no second coming of Christ, no inspired revelation;" ‡ and another writer of the same school declares, "The method of interpreting Scripture on which this theory depends unsettles all faith in the Bible, and saps the foundations of Christianity." §

This fact, then, is settled. Not only do the wicked

---

* Stuart and others take the Hebrew רַבִּים as equivalent to the οἱ πολλοί of Rom. v. 15, 17, and meaning multitudes, the mass. Reference to other passages is hardly necessary if we carefully translate our text, which contains neither article nor relative corresponding to the English "them that." Very literally, it reads thus: "Manies [or multitudes] of sleeping [ones] of earth's dust shall arise."

† See note D, Appendix.

‡ H. L. Hastings's Retribution, p. 150.

§ Bible Examiner, quoted ib.

as well as the good consciously exist after the death of the body, but their history can be followed to the resurrection and the judgment-day.

Thus, after the dissolution and slumber of ages, by the grandest display of miraculous power which the world will have witnessed, acting instantaneously at every portion of the earth's surface, all human beings, the wicked as well as the good, will be re-instated in the full condition in which they wrought their works of holiness or sin. Why, now, this amazing preparation? Is this grandest of God's miracles, so far as the wicked are concerned, a mere abortive flourish? or is it the actual preparation for some proportionate result? The body had gone to dissolution. So also, according to these theorists, was the soul extinct, at least unconscious. The threatened death had done its work. The penalty had been fully executed. What more is required? "They are 'dead:' why not let them remain dead?" *

Such are the inquiries which are raised not alone by opposers of the theory, but are urged even by the more radical annihilationists. The latter class offer these plain inferences from the doctrine, in order to deny the Scripture doctrine of a resurrection of the wicked; and their more careful and conservative associates are exceedingly pressed with the difficulty. And meanwhile every thoughtful observer of God's revealed methods must feel the entire incongruity of such a stupendous miracle, wrought simply to do over again a thing already done; whereas, when viewed as the inauguration of such a retribution as the Scriptures

---

* H. L. Hastings's Retribution, p. 152.

are commonly understood to announce, the reason and propriety of the preparation require no showing.

How, now, do these writers deal with this miracle of the resurrection of all the wicked? how meet the difficulty of this mighty, but, on their showing, abortive preparation?

Mr. Hastings alone, of those whom we have consulted, fairly acknowledges the fact and the difficulty. He admits that he has no answer to give. He simply says, "Let us carry the question farther back. Why did God make the wicked to live at all? . . . If God has wisely allowed the wicked to exist for centuries in sin, blasphemy, and rebellion, certainly his wisdom will not further suffer serious impeachment, even though he should perpetuate [!] or restore their existence for another period sufficiently long for purposes of justice, judgment, and retribution." The statement, certainly, is valid; but it is valid to the extent of overthrowing all Mr. Hastings's objections to the *eternal* existence of the wicked, — the "perpetuation" of their lives. Accordingly, Mr. Hastings falls back upon the simple *fact* of the resurrection, disclaiming all power to render a reason or explanation. "The sum of the argument is, God will do as he pleases, purposes, and promises; nor can men, who 'are as grasshoppers before him,' stay his hand. Whether we can comprehend or explain it, whether we believe or doubt it, he will fulfill his word." * Assuredly there is no difficulty here in the fulfillment of God's promise, nor in understanding why the promise was made: the whole difficulty is with the human theory, which makes one of his most

---

* Retribution, p. 153.

solemn assurances, concerning one of the most remarkable transactions in the universe, so wholly futile.

Other writers positively deny that the wicked will be raised. Mr. Hastings testifies to the wide prevalence of this view. "Besides various publications teaching the doctrine referred to, one periodical has been largely devoted to its advocacy; and one or two weekly religious journals are edited by men, who, though forbidden by their positions to speak fully upon it, yet make no secret of their denial of the resurrection of the wicked, and inculcate it, either publicly or privately, as opportunity may be presented." * Edwin Burnham enumerates this as one of the views entertained on the destiny of the wicked: "When the wicked die in this world, they die soul and body, and will never be raised from the dead to all eternity; and this will be their final punishment." † Ellis and Read, in answer to the question, "Will the wicked dead be raised to life again?" declare it to be "quite certain that the resurrection of the wicked is not taught in the Old Testament;" ‡ and they carefully refrain from admitting that it is taught in the New.

Another resort is the doctrine already quoted, that the wicked dead are raised simply as dead men, corpses, or clods of inanimate earth, and in that condition are brought to judgment, and receive their sentence.

Closely akin to this last-mentioned evasion of the plain New-Testament teaching is Mr. Hudson's theory, which, as to conformity to the Scriptures, hovers per-

---

* Retribution, p. 155.
† Anti-eternal Torment, p. 1. See note p. 218.
‡ Bible vs. Tradition, p. 234.

haps half-way between the theory which denies a resurrection and that which admits the raising of a corpse to judgment. Mr. Hudson holds that the body makes an attempt to come to life, starts to do it, but can not quite succeed. His theory has already been cited; but we will here give it entire as a curiosity:—

"To endeavor after a philosophy of the resurrection, we may add a thought respecting that of the unjust. It is hard to believe that they are raised up by a miracle that ends in their destruction, or that accomplishes nothing but a judgment, which, in this view, must appear simply vindictive. If they have no immortality, why are their slumbers disturbed? But, if their resurrection is connected with the redemption by a law that finds illustration in analogous facts, this difficulty may be removed. Damaged seeds that are sown often exhaust their vitality, and perish in germination; and we have noted the fact, that of insects which pass through the chrysalis state to that of the psyche or butterfly, many, from injuries suffered in their original form, utterly perish in the transition. Now, the glad tidings of the redemption, quickening and invigorating the soul with new life, may so far repair the injury done it in the fall, that even the unbelieving, who derive many benefits therefrom in this life, may not altogether perish in the bodily death. Not to say that the average duration of life is greater for the gospel, it seems certain that life is of a higher type. Even bad men in Christendom are familiar with moral sentiments, great truths of humanity, which the heathenish intellect has not conceived. May not such truths, as food to the souls even of those who do not cleave to Him who is the Truth and the Life, cause death itself to be divided as the proper effect and token of the redemption? And, for judgment, it is as if the unjust, hearing the voice of God in the last call to life, should be putting on a glorious incorruption, and should perish in the act." *

And this is the resurrection, and "a philosophy of the resurrection"! The reader will please bear in mind that it purports to relieve the difficulty of a "*miracle;*" viz., the instantaneous resurrection, and restoration to life, of millions of dead and decomposed human frames. And he will observe, 1. The careful under-statement of the case, so as to miss the chief difficulty. The author calls it simply "a miracle that ends in their destruction;" whereas it would be, on his theory, a vast miracle of *construction* for *the sake of destruction* alone, — an unparalleled display of miraculous power in order to do over again a thing already done and finished; a re-creation of the body already destroyed, *solely* to annihilate it again. It is for the reflecting mind to consider whether God is wont to lavish miracles in such modes. 2. The confusion of things wholly different. Certain workings of natural law are cited as "analogous facts," analogous to an objectless *miracle*. The only analogous fact would be another equally objectless *miracle*. Let it be produced. 3. The noticeable inconsistency. (1) Mere superficial contact with "the glad tidings of the redemption" is here endowed with a preserving power over the body after death, — a preserving influence which the author's system distinctly restricts to a living faith. (2) The prolongation of "the average du-

---

* Debt and Grace, p. 264.

ration of life" *in this world;* though outward virtue and prudence without faith is also by implication quietly extended into the other world, and after the full infliction of the penalty of death on the body. (3) The alleged resurrection hovers uncertainly between a miracle and a natural phenomenon, with a strong tendency to the latter. 4. The entire degradation of the New Testament doctrine of the resurrection. It is reduced to a bad seed, sprouting, but failing to grow; a hurt insect, not quite able to pass from a chrysalis to a butterfly: "As if the unjust, hearing the voice of God in the last call to life, should be putting on a glorious incorruption, and *should perish in the act.*" In other words, he is never quite raised at all. And this is Mr. Hudson's "philosophy" of the Scripture doctrine, that "they that are in the graves shall hear his voice, and shall come forth; they that have done good, unto the resurrection of life, and they that have done evil, unto the resurrection of damnation;" that they "must all appear before the judgment-seat of Christ, that every one may receive the things done in his body according to that he hath done, whether it be good or bad." It would be simpler and fairer to deny the resurrection of the wicked outright; for the statement is equivalent to that.

This writer well exemplifies his own remark, that "it is hard to believe that they are raised up by a miracle that ends in their destruction." And the difficulty which this class of writers find on the subject indicates the great significance, in this connection, of the doctrine of the resurrection preceding the general judgment. That great event not only marks another distinct stage in the existence of man after death; it also fitly introduces, equally in the case of the wicked as of the good, the opening of another great epoch in their history.

---

* While these sheets are passing through the stereotyper's hands, we learn that Rev. Edwin Burnham, whom we have quoted in this and other chapters, has renounced his heresy, and is now an accredited Baptist minister. But his tract is still in circulation, and will be read by many who, like ourselves, will not have seen his refutation of his own arguments. The antidote will never neutralize the poison. There is therefore no occasion, were it now practicable, to withdraw our allusions to his annihilationist utterances. "The evil that men do lives after them." While answering his arguments, however, we give him personally the benefit of this notice; the statement resting on the authority of A. K. Potter, in "The Christian Era," of Boston, some time in March, 1866.

CHAPTER V.

NEW TESTAMENT TEACHINGS CONTINUED. — SHARING THE DOOM OF THE FALLEN ANGELS.

WE have traced the course of the wicked, by the light of the Scriptures, to the resurrection and the judgment. They hear the voice of the Son of God, and come forth from their graves; they appear in company with the righteous, before the judgment-seat, to receive their sentence.

Now, we find the Scriptures teaching that they shall have certain superhuman companions of their doom, and that the two classes shall share the same fate. It will form a strong link in the chain of evidence if we can ascertain what is the Scripture doctrine concerning the fate of those companions of theirs. We refer to the fallen angels, evil spirits. Here we shall find the utterance of Scripture clear and emphatic.

It is the Scripture doctrine, that wicked men share the same doom with the fallen spirits; and the doom of the fallen spirits is represented in the same Scriptures, not as annihilation, but as conscious existence, and endless continuance in suffering.

I. The unjust shall share the fate of the fallen angels. On this point, Matt. xxv. 41 is decisive. In that great representation of the general judgment, when the Son of man shall come in his glory, and all nations shall be gathered before him, after the King has addressed those on his right hand, "the righteous," with a welcome to the kingdom prepared for them from the foundation of the world, the narrative proceeds (verse 41), "Then shall he say also unto them on the left hand, Depart from me, ye cursed, into everlasting *fire, prepared for the devil and his angels;* for I was an hungered," etc. To the same effect the statements of Rev. xx. 10, 15. In the 10th verse, we learn that "the devil that deceived them was cast into the lake of fire and brimstone, where the beast and the false prophet are, and shall be tormented day and night for ever and ever." In the 15th verse, we learn, as the result of the judgment, when all the dead, small and great, stand before God, that "whosoever was not found written in the book of life was cast into the lake of fire."

The doom of the two parties is thus the same in kind. We might, perhaps, have drawn a strong presumptive argument from the fate of the fallen angels, to that of lost men, had there been no disclosure on the subject. We might have reasoned, that if it appeared that those beings, who fell before the fall of our first parents, were not, and were not to be, struck out of existence, but to be continued under the anger and vengeance of God, so also, most likely, it would be with human evil-doers. Certainly any rational argument to prove the extinction of sinners from the universe would be overthrown by finding that Satan and his companions were to continue in existence. But we are not left to inferences. The Word of God positively assigns the same final doom to wicked men as to evil spirits. What is that doom?

II. The fate of the fallen angels is not annihilation, but conscious existence, and endless continuance in suffering.

No doubt, many things in regard to the condition and history of the apostate angels remain in obscurity. Some things, however, are definitely revealed and settled. It is certain that their fall had taken place before our first parents were placed in the garden. It is certain, therefore, that Satan (and probably others of them) has existed in a state of the most vehement sinful activity for several thousand years already. It does not appear that any opportunity of recovery ever has been, or ever will be, offered to them. The contrary appears to be declared in 2 Pet. ii. 4: "For if God spared not the angels that sinned, but cast them down to hell, and delivered them into chains of darkness, to be reserved unto judgment," etc. Also Jude 6: "And the angels which kept not their first estate, but left their own habitation, he hath reserved in everlasting chains under darkness, unto the judgment of the great day." Meanwhile, by an arrangement and for reasons of which we have no explanation in the Bible, a portion at least of these hopelessly lost beings have been for a time suffered to leave their confinement, and mingle in the concerns of this world, where they are restlessly, malignantly, and powerfully active (Matt. xii. 43; 1 Pet. v. 8; Eph. vi. 12, etc.). We learn, furthermore, that the time is coming when Satan shall be bound "a thousand years," so that during the time "he should deceive the nations no more" (Rev.

xx. 2, 3); and after that, and before the judgment, "he must be loosed a little season," and shall again "go out to deceive the nations" (Rev. xx. 3, 7, 8). The details of this economy, so as to combine these representations, if we were able to find them, would be of no special account for our present purpose. It is, however, important to observe, in passing, that these beings thus reserved unto judgment, though not prisoners of hope, are in the full possession of their activities for thousands of years prior to the final overthrow.

What, now, is the final doom which the Scriptures assign to Satan? It is, in the plainest terms that language can furnish, torment, — endless torment. The closing statement concerning his fate is this: "And the devil that deceived them was cast into the lake of fire and brimstone, where the beast and the false prophet are, and [they] shall be tormented day and night for ever and ever" (Rev. xx. 10). The passage expressly and unequivocally declares three things, — suffering, incessant, eternal.

The Greek verb "tormented" ($\beta\alpha\sigma\alpha\nu\iota\sigma\theta\acute{\eta}\sigma o\nu\tau\alpha\iota$) occurs twelve times in the New Testament, with the *unvarying* meaning of harassed, pained, or tormented; excepting, for the present, its application to the lost. It is the word which describes the suffering of a woman in travail ("*pained* to be delivered," Rev. xii. 2); the suffering of severe sickness ("grievously tormented," Matt. viii. 6); the suffering by a terrible plague ("tormented five months," Rev. ix. 5); a suffering so great, that it is compared to the pain ["torment"] inflicted by the scorpion, and that the victims desired death.

It describes the mental suffering of just Lot among the wicked Sodomites, when that "just man *vexed* (ἐβασάνιζεν) his righteous soul with their unlawful deeds" (2 Pet. ii. 8); and the bodily exhaustion and mental anxiety of toiling weariness (Mark vi. 48), "*toiling*," harassed, or tormented, "in rowing." In Rev. xi. 10 ("the two prophets tormented them"), it describes the sufferings brought upon the earth by the prophets who had "power to shut the heaven that it rain not in the days of their prophecy, and have power over the waters to turn them to blood, and to smite the earth with all plagues." In Rev. xiv. 10, it describes the punishment of those who worship the beast: "He shall be tormented with fire and brimstone;" and in the next verse (11) the explanation is added, "They have no rest day nor night." In one instance only, it is by a strong figure applied to an inanimate object, a "ship *tossed* [tormented] with the waves" (Matt. xiv. 24), just as we in like manner should describe it as *racked* by the sea. In every other instance it is applied to the treatment of evil spirits, either as threatened by God in this instance, or as apprehended by themselves (Matt. viii. 29; Mark v. 7; Luke viii. 28).

Such being the case, the word "torment" (βασανίζω) being in every other instance, when applied to a living being, expressive of positive suffering, it would require a degree of hardihood on which all argument is lost to deny that meaning when it is found applied to the fate of lost spirits. Their fate is suffering.

Incessant suffering: "Shall be tormented day and night." The phrase "day and night" requires no explanation to the common reader. It asserts that the suffering is not a momentary pang, once felt and ended, but a constant, continuous woe. We need hardly sustain this meaning of the phrase by such references as 1 Thess. ii. 9, iii. 10, or remind the reader that it is employed (Rev. vii. 15) to describe the ceaselessness of the service of the ransomed martyrs in heaven.

Endless suffering: "For ever and ever," literally to the ages of the ages (εἰς τοὺς αἰῶνας τῶν αἰώνων). On this phrase, little need be said. It is the strongest form in which the idea of eternity is conveyed in the Bible. It is the most emphatic mode in which the duration of the life and glory of the righteous is expressed (Rev. xxii. 5), in which the continuance of God's glory is prayed for (Gal. i. 5, Eph. iii. 21, Phil. iv. 20, 1 Tim. i. 17, 2 Tim. iv. 18, Heb. xiii. 21, etc.), and in which the duration of God's or of Christ's own existence is asserted (Rev. i. 18, iv. 9, 10, x. 6, xv. 7).

How, now, do the advocates of annihilation dispose of this declaration? No two of them, apparently, can agree. It is worth while to take a glance at some of their methods.

Mr. Dobney, as usual, is the most candid. He seems to admit (pp. 227, 229) that "*the devil* shall be tormented day and night for ever," without denying the plain meaning of the language; but he argues (1) that "this text says nothing at all about sinners of the human race." Very true; but other texts already cited do say that they shall experience the same fate. Indeed, he finds himself obliged to meet the passage occurring five verses later in the same chapter (verse 15), which declares that "whosoever was not found written in the book of life was cast into the lake of fire,' — into the same lake of fire already mentioned. In view of this difficulty, he takes the ground (2), that, "because in the lake of fire the devil shall be tormented for ever, it does not necessarily follow that quite another race of intelligences cast into the same lake must *therefore* exist as long as he does, and endure the same torment:" "it may produce different effects; it *may* torment the one, and destroy the other." A man who can construct such an argument is certainly hard pressed; and a man who rests his belief of annihilation on such a basis is a bold man. The effect of being cast into the "furnace of fire" is elsewhere described as being, in the case of the wicked, "wailing, and gnashing of teeth." But (3) he maintains that, in verse 14 ("death and hell were cast into the lake of fire"), the punishment means extinction; therefore it may in verse 15. This, however, can not be shown. Death and *hades* being, as Alford well says, "the offspring of and bound up with sin," are viewed as alike "the enemies of God," and terrors of man. In God's victory over his foes, they, too, are overcome, and turned into the place of punishment. In verse 10, the beast and the false prophet (both, probably, impersonations) are included among the parties tormented for ever. It is only to the redeemed that there shall be no more death (xx. 4): to the lost it is nothing but death, — the second death. There is nothing inconsistent with other representations in the supposition that these enemies of God are here described as shut up with their victims, punished and punishing, in other forms to worry them for ever. If it were understood that they cease to be, this would come from the supposed necessity of the case, as mere personifications; and the difference between the fate of an impersonation and an actual living being would afford no ground for a similar conclusion in reference to the latter.

Mr. Blain says, among other things (1), that "the events here told are symbolic; and such prophetic language is hard to be understood, and is no proof of a doctrine when unsupported by other Scripture." In his exposition, however, almost the only thing which *he* finds hard to understand is that this very plain language can mean what it says. He proceeds (2): "Only earthly events are told in this chapter till we come to the 11th verse. 'Day and night' are, in *this* 'for ever,' (age): and they are not to be in the future world; 'for there shall be no night there.'" That is, he must affirm (*a*) that there are "two lakes of fire and brimstone" referred to in this chapter, within five verses,— one in this world, the other hereafter. And (*b*) the attempt to withdraw the scene from the future world on the strength of the phrase "day and night" would also withdraw "the great multitude" of the redeemed and glorified in heaven, "which no man could number," back to earth; for, while they are "before the throne of God," the next words declare that "they serve him *day and night*." The obvious fact is, that the language of time is almost necessarily transferred to the scenes of eternity; and the phrase "day and night" clearly bears its frequent meaning *continually*. The argument of Mr. Blain is worthy of the Universalists, with whom, we believe, it originated. But (3) he affirms that "the *literal* devil is not here meant." The Bible, he admits, "fully reveals a literal devil; but his name is only used figuratively in Rev. xii. and xx." If so, we can only say that the apostle has labored very hard and to very little purpose to make his own meaning plain; for he very particularly and emphatically describes him (verse 2), as " the dragon, that *old serpent*, which is *the Devil* and *Satan*."

Ellis and Read have a very marvelous criticism of the passage, containing the following statement: " The word *basinisthesontai* is the future tense plural of *basanos*,* a touch-stone to try metals, and means a trial, inquiry, or examination, to ascertain the genuineness or purity of any thing: hence, metaphorically, the word is used for an examination to obtain proof, to confirm any fact, torture employed to obtain evidence or extort truth, a proof given or obtained, a pledge," etc. After an equally luminous discussion of the phrase " for ever and ever," he concludes that " the verse will mean that whatever is symbolized by the beast and the false prophet and the dragon shall be tried till the end of the age." Most likely, to " ascertain their purity."

But the most amazing interpretation of all is that of Mr. Hudson, who, without deigning to offer a word of criticism or explanation on the phraseology, summarily converts this declaration of eternal torment into an assertion of final extinction. Hear him: " But why are they said to be ' tormented day and night, for ever and ever' ? This might be said of the beast and

---

* This is given exactly from the *sixth* edition of Bible *vs.* Tradition; the first Greek form misspelled, and the second confounding the noun βάσανος with the verb βασανίζω. The whole criticism is not an unfair specimen of the learning of the book. It is not probably a lapse, but the real measure of the learning.

the false prophet as impersonations, henceforth without power or worshipers. [Observe the admission.] Compare what is said of Babylon (chap. xviii. 7, 8, 19). But we think the language describes their utter and irrevocable destruction [annihilation], in a dramatic form, which is quite consistent with the general structure of the book."* Singularly dramatic! That "the language" which asserts, in the plainest, simplest form, suffering constant and eternal, should be summarily declared to assert the cessation of all suffering and all existence, — is there the instance of equal audacity on record?

One redeeming feature appears in these several arguments, — that no one of these four writers is willing to adopt the other's exposition.

But Mr. Hudson, after citing several "dramatic" passages, none of which has any relation whatever to this phraseology, leaves the passage for some general considerations on the destiny of Satan. "But will Satan actually cease from being? Is he, indeed, mortal? The prophecies all look that way. Our translators have indeed dealt somewhat tenderly with the great adversary in Gen. iii. 15, where the true sense is, that the seed of the woman shall *crush* the head of the serpent. The words in Heb. ii. 14, and 1 John iii. 8, express indeed the dispossession of Satan, rather than his final destruction. But that doom, in common with the destruction of every power hostile to God, is told in Daniel: 'I beheld then because of the voice of the great words which the horn spake: I

---

* Debt and Grace, p. 215. We find in Christ our Life a more protracted discussion; for which see Appendix, Note E.

beheld even till the beast was slain, and his body destroyed, and given to the burning flame. As concerning the rest of the beasts, they had their dominion taken away; yet their lives were prolonged for a season and a time' (vii. 11, 12). See also Matt. xxv. 41."

So, then, these "prophecies" which "*all* look that way," are reduced to two (Gen. iii. 15, and Dan. vii. 11, 12). In Genesis, the translators have shown no particular tenderness in the translation.* The word (שׁוּף) occurs in only three verses of the Old Testament; being used, however, four times, twice in the present passage. In three instances it cannot possibly mean annihilate, as will presently appear; and the one in question is the fourth. In this particular passage, it has been, perhaps, as well translated as was practicable. As the Hebrew uses the same word in both clauses, so the translators, — "*bruise* thy head, *bruise* his heel." To translate it "crush" would make no essential difference; for the second "crush" is evidently a biting of the heel by the serpent. Annihilation certainly does not lie in the *expression* "crush" or "bruise." The only other places where it is used are Job ix. 17, where a *living* and suffering man exclaims, "He *breaketh* me with a tempest;" and Ps. cxxxix. 11, "If I say, Surely the darkness shall *cover* (שׁוּף, fall upon, overwhelm) me, even the night shall be light about me," where it is again uttered of a person supposed to be still living. The reader will thus see that the attempt to find annihilation of Satan in the word "crush" is futile. If it should be persisted, that to bruise or crush *the head* is

---

* This sneer at "our tender translators" is repeated in Christ our Life, p. 146.

to inflict a fatal wound, we need only remind the reader that this language, as well as the whole curse on Satan, is applied to him under the likeness of a crawling serpent; and that, when such a figure is employed, this is the only mode of describing a complete victory over and subjugation of Satan, and is not in the slightest degree incompatible with the distinct statement, that "*the devil*" "shall be tormented day and night for ever."

The other prophecy cited as foretelling Satan's annihilation is in Dan. vii. 11, 12. But the reader who will examine the passage in its connection will look in vain for the slightest allusion to Satan, express or implied. The beasts there spoken of are four great human monarchies, or world-powers, repeatedly described in Daniel. The 11th verse probably refers to the fourth of these (so Hitzig), and the 12th to the preceding ones, which were perhaps, as dependent kingdoms, to be "prolonged for a season," after their dominant power was overthrown. But, whatever may be the meaning of the minor expressions, we know no respectable commentator who ventures to maintain that here is a reference to Satan, or indeed to any other "beasts" than those great worldly powers just described in the same chapter.

Mr. Hudson also adds, "See Matt. xxv. 41." But that passage speaks of "*eternal* fire prepared for the devil and his angels," and certainly offers no help in the effort to deny the eternity of the torments here described.

As these writers are fond of referring to the peculiar character of the book of Revelation in order to invalidate the force of its testimony, we may add, that passages in the Gospels fully corroborate the plain meaning of the text we have considered. In the remarkable narrative of the evil spirits and the herd of swine recorded by three evangelists (Matt. viii. 28–34, Mark v. 1–20, Luke viii. 26–34), the correspondence is very close. Each evangelist has retained the same strong word, "torment" ($\beta\alpha\sigma\alpha\nu\acute{\iota}\zeta\omega$), as expressing the punishment which the demons dreaded at the hands of Christ: "I adjure thee by God that thou torment me not" (Mark v. 7); "I beseech thee, torment me not" (Luke viii. 28). Matt. viii. 29 makes their meaning clear by giving an additional phrase, identifying this dreaded torment with their final punishment: "What have we to do with thee, Jesus, thou Son of God? Art thou come hither to torment us before the time?" Luke, by a further statement of the conversation, identifies the *place* of the torment as the "pit" or abyss where Satan is to be confined (Rev. xx. 1, 3), and whence the diabolical powers are let loose and come forth (Rev. xi. 7, xvii. 8). Thus Luke records (viii. 31): "And they besought him that he would not command them to depart into the abyss" ($\varepsilon\grave{\iota}\varsigma\ \tau\grave{\eta}\nu\ \check{\alpha}\beta\nu\sigma\sigma\omicron\nu\ \grave{\alpha}\pi\varepsilon\lambda\theta\varepsilon\tilde{\iota}\nu$). Many readers probably receive a wrong impression from the common version of the last few words; viz., "to go out into the deep," as though the request were that Christ would not send them into the waters of the lake. But the error is obvious in a moment; for, when the devils received permission to enter the swine, they actually impelled the herd directly into the lake. Besides, the request itself would seem unaccountably trivial. But the word translated "the deep" is decisive. It occurs in eight other instances in the New Testament. In one only of these cases is it applied to the region of the departed in general (Rom. x. 7): in every other instance it is the "pit," "the bottomless pit;" the latter phrase being a translation of the same one word. Thus Rev. ix. 1, 2: "To him was given the key of the bottomless pit; and he opened the bottomless pit, and there arose a smoke out of the pit, as the smoke of a great furnace." (The reader will remember the "furnace of fire," Matt. xiii. 42, 50; the "lake of fire and brimstone," Rev. xx. 10; and "the smoke of their torment," Rev. xiv. 11.) And again (ix. 11): "And they [the pests that came to "torment" the earth] had a king over them, which is the angel of the bottomless pit, whose name in the Hebrew tongue is Abaddon, but in the Greek tongue hath his name Apollyon." Again, Rev. xi. 7: "The beast" that kills the two witnesses "ascendeth out of the bottomless pit;" and "the beast" that carried the scarlet woman (Rev. xvii. 8) "shall ascend out of the bottomless pit, and go into perdition." And Rev. xx. 1, 3: The angel that had "the key of the bottomless pit" laid hold on Satan, and "cast him into the bottomless pit, and shut him up" for a thousand years.

Thus, then, the place where these evil spirits dreaded being sent to be tormented before their time was no other than "the pit," the home of Apollyon and the great diabolical powers that war against Christ, the abode in which Satan is to be confined for a thousand years previous to the millennium. On this point, there is, we believe, no diversity of opinion among expositors; indeed, the case admits of none. Thus says Alford:

"This word is sometimes used for *hades* in general, but more usually in Scripture for the abode of damned spirits. This last is certainly meant here; for the request is co-ordinate with the fear of torment expressed above."

The "pit," then, the home of Satan and the evil spirits, is a place of torment, not of extinction; where Satan can be bound a thousand years, and still come forth in all his power and malignity: and the lake of fire, whether precisely identical with it, or denoting "a further and more dreadful place of punishment" (as Alford suggests), is a place where they "shall be tormented day and night for ever and ever."

It is thus the Scripture doctrine, that Satan (in company with the evil spirits) shall experience eternal punishment, and that that punishment consists in suffering. It is the Scripture teaching also, that, at the last day, all the wicked shall experience the doom prepared for "the devil and his angels."

CHAPTER VI.

NEW TESTAMENT TEACHINGS CONTINUED. — DIRECT DECLARATIONS. — FUTURE PUNISHMENT CONSISTS IN SUFFERING.

THUS far we have traced in the New Testament teachings a continuous history of the soul after death. It passes at once to a state of conscious joy or sorrow. At the closing of this remedial dispensation, it is joined by the body, now roused from the sleep of ages, and in company with the whole human race, simultaneously clothed with flesh again by a miracle of inconceivable grandeur and extent, is summoned before God in preparation for a sentence still more formal and complete. The sentence assigns to the one class the eternal companionship of God and all holy beings; to the other, the society and the doom of the devil and his angels, — a doom elsewhere described as a perpetual and miserable existence.

But the New Testament does not leave the subject thus. It teaches in very express forms that the final doom of sin is, not insensibility and non-existence, but positive suffering, and that protracted and eternal. The attempt is continually made by annihilationists to forestall and rule out all this testimony by accumulated quotations concerning "death," "destruction," "perishing," and the like. But, as we have seen, these latter expressions have no such force. There is no collision between the two modes of statement: the one is only explanatory of the other. The passages which we are about to quote simply show what the Scriptures mean by death, perishing, and destruction. As, in the Bible, life is more than existence; so is death more than non-existence, and yet less. As, in this world, men often witness the ruin of a living man, which, as they say, is worse than death; so, in the other world, there is a destruction, which, by the confession of annihilationists themselves, is more terrible than extinction.

It is one of the commonest and simplest principles of interpretation, in secular as well as in sacred writings, to explain the briefer phraseology by the fuller descriptions of the same writers. To be saved by the grace of God, we find elsewhere includes the specific human acts of repentance and faith. To be justified by faith, without the works of the law, we learn does nevertheless comprise those very exercises of holy living which might at first seem to be excluded. The real meaning of the divine names applied to Christ is made absolutely certain by the fuller ascription of divine attributes, works, and worship. It is therefore both legitimate and indispensable to learn the force of the briefer terms of the Bible by the fuller statements which unfold them. Now, on the nature and duration of the punishment of the wicked, the Scriptures are consistent, uniform, and explicit.

I. First, The Scriptures, whenever they speak in detail, under a variety of forms, invariably describe future punishment as consisting in the infliction of suffering, and not in the arrest and cessation of it. Nowhere can the statement be found, that God's great and ultimate vengeance upon the sinner will consist in the final annulment of the woes that his sin has wrought. Everywhere, on the other hand, it is both implied and asserted that the penalty of sin is the letting loose of woe upon the transgressor's head. "There is no peace, saith my God, to the wicked."

Let the reader clearly mark the issue. Does the main stress and crowning stroke of divine punishment consist in the final extinction of the wicked, or in the tremendous pressure of suffering and anguish upon the sinning soul? The annihilationists maintain the former; the Scriptures, most abundantly and unequivocally, the latter.

1. This doctrine is contained in the assertion, that there are grades of punishment. The New Testament plainly declares that there shall be different degrees of penalty inflicted at the final judgment. "It shall be more tolerable for the land of Sodom and Gomorrah in the day of judgment than for that city" which should reject Christ's messengers (Matt. x. 15). "It shall be more tolerable for Tyre and Sidon at the day of judgment than for you," Chorazin and Bethsaida. "More tolerable for the land of Sodom in the day of judgment than for thee," Capernaum (Matt. xi. 22, 24). "And that servant which knew his Lord's will, and prepared not himself, neither did according to his will, shall be beaten with many stripes. But he that knew not, and did commit things worthy of stripes, shall be beaten with few stripes" (Luke xii. 47, 48). "Woe unto you, scribes and Pharisees, hypocrites! for ye devour widows' houses, and for a pretense make

long prayers: therefore ye shall receive the greater damnation" (Matt. xxiii. 14). In these and other passages, the Saviour clearly affirms diverse degrees of severity of punishment proportioned to the aggravation of guilt.

Mr. Dobney freely admits the fact. "Let it be admitted that there are, as we easily perceive there ought to be, degrees of punishment. . . . To the fact of degrees of guilt we must adhere; and then the consequence is inevitable." *

This teaching is entirely incompatible with the theory that extinction is the doom of sin. There are no degrees of extinction. Of a doom which consists in conscious suffering there can be greater or smaller inflictions; but of annihilation there can be neither more nor less; it is simply annihilation. It can neither be doubled nor halved, increased nor diminished. The Sodomite can be no less annihilated, the Capernaite no more, than the multitude of sinning Jews. The very announcement of degrees in the final penalty of sin, therefore, disproves the doctrine that extinction is the penalty.

Annihilationists have felt the force of the difficulty. To Mr. Dobney "it appears one of the very strongest of all objections" to his doctrine. The reply he makes is the following suggestion: "It is quite conceivable that the length of time which shall elapse ere the wicked utterly cease to be, and the degree of suffering by which the final dissolution shall be preceded and accompanied, may be exactly proportioned to their various deserts." Hudson more briefly says the same:

---

* Future Punishment, pp. 264, 265.

"The pangs of the second death may be the measure of the sins of life."* Hastings likewise: "It took some six hundred and thirty years to *execute* the 'death penalty' pronounced on Adam: how long it may require to execute the penalty of the 'second death' upon individual sinners, I do not pretend to say." †

Returning, now, to the fuller reply of Mr. Dobney, we find it to be this; viz., in proportion to the sinner's guilt, the longer he may be in dying, and the greater the attendant suffering. We think we can not mistake his idea of a *lingering* death. He evidently means the suffering is the more protracted and severe in proportion as the guilt is great. Mr. Hastings seems to indorse the view in the passage connected with what we have quoted.

Perhaps this is the best reply that the case admits. But, specious as it may at first sight appear, it is thoroughly suicidal. For (1), in supposing a protraction of suffering (and therefore of existence) in proportion to the aggravation of the guilt, the writer contradicts his own first principle by ascribing to *sin* the power to prolong existence. A degree of guilt immense and satanic might thus have the power to extend the existence beyond all conceivable limits. And as the sinful state continues even during the act of punishment, why, on the same principle, should not the successive degrees of ill-desert continue to protract the existence beyond each present infliction, till it becomes literally endless? How much less than this is involved in Mr. Hastings's admission, that "it took some six hundred and thirty years to execute the death-penalty pro-

---

* Debt and Grace, p. 400. † Retribution, p. 77.

nounced on Adam: how long it may require to execute the penalty of the second death upon individual sinners, I do not pretend to say"? Surely these words contain a marvelous modification of the original aspect of the system, which describes the penalty of sin as being utterly exterminated, literally cut off, burnt up, brought to an end, and the like. But (2) this reply abandons the fundamental principle of the system; namely, that the one grand penalty of sin is extinction. This is the one thing into which every form of Scripture threat is finally resolved: every thing means extinction. Much of the arguing of these writers requires, too, a rapid extinction. The whole analogy on which it turns fails them, except it be so understood. Thus all those phrases like "grinding to powder," "tearing in pieces," "cutting asunder," "burned up like chaff," if they could be validly used at all in the material sense in which annihilationists choose to take them, equally denote an *instantaneous* extinction. So these very writers elsewhere speak. Mr. Hastings asks, "What was the effect of casting bodies into this fire?" (the fire of Hinnom.) . . . "They were entirely and totally burned to ashes, *consumed, burnt up, devoured by fire*" (the Italics are his). "From *this* consideration, we should conclude that the future *gehenna of fire* would consume and destroy utterly every thing submitted to its flames."* Ellis and Read say, "The punishments that have taken place in *gehenna* [i.e., the Valley of Hinnom] destroyed life, and the torment was never protracted beyond a day: so the punishment that will take place in *gehenna* will destroy life in a

---

* Pauline Theology, p. 51.

limited period." Again: "We have now examined every passage where *gehenna* is named; and we find no expression indicating that the wicked will be kept alive in torment, but we do find a place where they will be miserably destroyed." Blain insists, with abundant reiteration, that "the fire that shall not be quenched" means "utter destruction." * Hudson, in speaking of these terms, "unquenchable fire," says, "Any mode of reasoning which would infer from them the immortality of the lost must assume the indestructibility of chaff, felled trees, and of the dry branches of a vine;" and he quotes a scholiast on Homer as explaining a similar phrase to mean "that which burns down quickly, or is quenched with difficulty."

Under all the forms of argument, indeed, the system puts forth this one prime fact, that the doom of sin is "destruction,"— meaning, thereby, annihilation. Mr. Hastings even prints in small capitals the word "sudden" in the passages that speak of "sudden destruction" coming upon the wicked; and, in the same connection, he lays down and earnestly maintains the proposition, that "punishment is not always in proportion to the pain endured," and that "the person punished may not endure torment at all." † He does indeed, elsewhere, and for another purpose, maintain that all the antecedent sufferings of Adam's life, for six hundred and thirty years, are included in the term "death." ‡ Yet, if there be any specialty in the system at all, it

---

* Bible *vs.* Tradition, pp. 84, 222, 226.
† Pauline Theology, pp. 59, 60.
‡ Retribution, p. 77. The reader will perceive the bearing of this admission on the system that elsewhere so narrows the meaning of the term "death."

consists in the pertinacious position, that extinction is the doom of sin. But here we have a sudden abandonment of the position, and a recourse to the common view, which locates punishment in suffering, — an abandonment so complete, that the extinction is but an incidental feature of the case, while the suffering inflicted is the chief thing; "the degree of suffering" being "*exactly* proportioned to their various deserts." Such is the dilemma in which annihilationists are involved in reply to the difficulty.

In truth, the Scriptures in this respect make the punishment of the wicked correspond to the happiness of the righteous. The righteous are represented as entering on a state of blessedness, varying in degree with their Christian fidelity and attainments, and differing as "one star differeth from another star in glory." The wicked enter on a state where their diverse degrees of guilt shall be met by diverse degrees of suffering.

2. The New Testament writers, in direct terms, constantly and chiefly represent the final doom of sin as a state of great suffering. This is the great emphatic fact which they put forth, the fore-front of their representation. It is described as a doom, terrific not merely in general, but specially terrific for its anguish. The utterances on this point are varied and abundant.

Thus the writer to the Hebrews describes it as far more terrible than that natural death which many annihilationists declare to be itself the only doom. "He that despised Moses' law died without mercy under two or three witnesses: of how much sorer punishment ($\chi\varepsilon i\rho o\nu o\varsigma\ \tau\iota\mu\omega\rho i\alpha\varsigma$, vengeance), suppose ye shall he be thought worthy who hath trodden under foot the Son of God? . . . It is a fearful thing to fall into the hands of the living God" (Heb. x. 28, 29, 31).

In Rom. ii. 5–9, Paul still more specifically defines the nature of that doom which makes it a fearful thing to fall into the hands of the living God, and informs us how the "wrath" treasured up "against the day of wrath" will express itself in the infliction of intense suffering: God will render "indignation and wrath, *tribulation and anguish*, upon every soul of man that doeth evil." In a subsequent verse (12th), he uses the word "perish" as the brief equivalent of these specific statements; just as in a previous verse the words "glory," "honor," "incorruptibility" ($ἀφθαρσία$), find their synonyme in the phrase "eternal life."

In 2 Thess. i. 6, again, he calls it tribulation: "Seeing it is a righteous thing with God to recompense tribulation to them that trouble you." This tribulation is the same thing which in verse 8 he phrases "in flaming fire taking vengeance on them that know not God;" and, in verse 9, being "punished with everlasting destruction from the presence of the Lord, and from the glory of his power." In the last quotation, the expression, "*from* the presence of the Lord," is understood by Alford, Lünemann, and others, as meaning "apart from" or "away from" the presence of the Lord. But, as the point is disputed, we need not insist upon it.

So our Saviour, after having pronounced his blessings (Luke vi. 21–23) on those that hunger now and weep now, and are hated and reproached, because they shall be filled and shall laugh, and whose "reward is great in heaven," proceeds (verses 24, 25) to pronounce a woe upon those whose only portion is in this life, because of the disconsolateness, destitution, mourning, and weeping hereafter: "But woe unto you that are rich! for ye have received your consolation. Woe unto you that are full! for ye shall hunger. Woe unto you that laugh now! for ye shall mourn and weep."

In the same strain, James (v. 1–6), anticipating the "*miseries*" of the ungodly rich in "the last days," at "the coming of the Lord" (verse 7), bids them weep and howl in the prospect, and warns them that those ill-gotten riches shall then prove a torture to them; "shall eat your flesh as it were fire;" where the reader will observe that fire is spoken of clearly as the agent of suffering: "Go to, now, ye rich men, weep and howl for your miseries that shall come upon you. . . . Your gold and silver is cankered; and the rust of them shall be a witness against you, and shall eat your flesh as it were fire. Ye have heaped treasure together for the last days," etc.

It is remarkable, how, under whatever image future punishment is set forth in the New Testament, the suffering of the state is almost invariably thrust forth as the grand feature of the case; sometimes even at the expense of perfect congruity in the representation. Is it a place of darkness, a furnace of fire, a debtor's prison, a banishment from the feast, a cutting-asunder, a lake of fire? The perpetual comment and incessant burden of the strain is the resultant woe. Let us look at the subject in detail.

In three several instances, our Saviour calls the state

or abode of those who are finally excluded from the kingdom of heaven "the outer darkness." In each instance, he adds the one fearful and emphatic description of that abode, that "there shall be weeping, and gnashing of teeth." Thus Matt. viii. 11, 12 : "And I say unto you, that many shall come from the east and the west, and shall sit down with Abraham and Isaac and Jacob in the kingdom of heaven : but the children of the kingdom shall be cast out into [the] outer darkness ; there [in that place, ἐκεῖ] shall be weeping, and gnashing of teeth." Again, in describing the intruding guest at the wedding-feast (Matt. xxii. 13): "Then said the king to the servants, Bind him hand and foot, and take him away, and cast him into [the] outer darkness ; there [in that place] shall be weeping, and gnashing of teeth." In declaring the doom of the unprofitable servant (Matt. xxv. 30) : "And cast ye the unprofitable servant into [the] outer darkness ; there [ἐκεῖ] shall be weeping, and gnashing of teeth." Such was our Saviour's sole and fearful comment on "the outer darkness." As this outer darkness unquestionably denotes the same thing with the "mist of darkness" in 2 Pet. ii. 17, and "the blackness of darkness," Jude 13, it certainly required no little hardihood in Mr. Hudson coolly to dismiss these phrases as simply synonymes of "non-existence," "blank nothingness." *

Twice the Saviour terms the condition of the lost a, or rather *the*, furnace of fire. But, though the image is just the opposite of the preceding, he describes the nature of the abode each time by the same sole and

---

* Debt and Grace, pp. 208, 209.

solemn characteristic, and in the same words: "There shall be wailing, and gnashing of teeth" (Matt. xiii. 40–42). "So shall it be at the end of this world. The Son of man shall send forth his angels, and they shall gather out of his kingdom all things that offend and them which do iniquity, and shall cast them into a [the τὴν] furnace of fire; there [ἐκεῖ] shall be wailing, and gnashing of teeth." Verses 49, 50: "So shall it be at the end of the world: the angels shall come forth and sever the wicked from among the just, and shall cast them into the furnace of fire; there shall be wailing, and gnashing of teeth." Certainly it requires some exegetical boldness to treat this repeated, deliberate, and solemn description — the sole summing-up of the whole state and condition — as a mere transient incident in the case. But we have not done with these expressions.

In Matt. xxiv. 50, 51, the Saviour describes their doom as having their "portion with the hypocrites," and adds the same sole characterizing remark: "The lord of that servant shall come in a day when he looketh not for him, and in an hour that he is not aware of, and shall cut him asunder [διχοτομήσει, cut him in two], and appoint him his portion with the hypocrites; there (ἐκεῖ) shall be weeping, and gnashing of teeth." Here "the hypocrites" have a portion, — of which the one characteristic is that it is a doom of suffering, — to which, in conjunction with them, the unfaithful servant is consigned, *after* an infliction ("cutting asunder"), which, according to annihilationist interpretation, would be extinction.

Yet once more (Luke xiii. 28) our Lord describes

the condition of those who are excluded from the kingdom of heaven by the same terse and solitary comment. He had been exhorting his hearers, "Strive to enter in at the strait gate," and warning them of the hopelessness of their longing desires when once the Master of the house hath risen up and hath shut to the door; and he proceeds: "There shall be weeping, and gnashing of teeth, when ye shall see Abraham and Isaac and Jacob and all the prophets in the kingdom of God, and you yourselves thrust out."

In another place, the Saviour represents the doom of the wicked under the form of an imprisonment in suffering, a delivering to "the tormentors." The parable of the merciless servant concludes thus (Matt. xviii. 34, 35): "And his lord was wroth, and delivered him to the tormentors till he should pay all that was due unto him. So likewise shall my heavenly Father do also unto you, if ye from your hearts forgive not every one his brother their trespasses." The word translated "tormentors" (βασανισταῖς) is correctly rendered. It designated torturers, officers who inflicted or superintended the process of bodily torture. The word, it is believed, has no other known use. Some commentators, and with them Robinson's Lexicon, have endeavored to soften the term to a simply synonyme for prison keeper, but without any authority.*

---

* On this whole subject of torture, see the article βάσανος in Smith's Dictionary of Antiquities. The writer sets out with the word βάσανος, which he defines as "the general term among the Athenians for the application of torture." It was sometimes employed in punishment, and was invariably used in examining slaves. "The parties interested either superintended the torture themselves, or chose certain persons for this purpose; hence called βασανισταί." Olshausen is constrained to admit the meaning

In like manner, as we have already seen previously, the lake of fire in which all classes of evil-doers shall have their part (Rev. xxi. 8) is the place of "torment for ever and ever" (Rev. xx. 10).

We are also assured (Rev. xiv. 9–11), " If any man worship the beast and his image, and receive his mark in his forehead or in his hand, the same shall drink of the wine of the wrath of God which is poured out without mixture into the cup of his indignation; and he shall be tormented with fire and brimstone in the presence of the holy angels, and in the presence of the Lamb. And the smoke of their torment ascendeth up for ever and ever, and they have no rest day nor night, who worship the beast and his image, and whosoever receiveth the mark of his name." Here the general statement of experiencing God's wrath becomes particularized into the definite infliction of terrific and endless suffering, and this made still more

---

of the word, though endeavoring to break its force. He renders it "the tormentors," and proceeds to say, " The βασανισταί, torturers are, according to the connection, the guardians of the prison, who also were certainly employed to inflict torture. There were, however, no special racks or tortures provided for debtors." Yes; but here was a *malignant* debtor, punished not for his debt, which would have been remitted, but for his malignity. Our Lord is representing a *moral* offense, — an offense against God; and, as usual, he *molds* the customs of men into such shapes as will express his higher principles. It was characteristic enough for Kuinoel, but unworthy of a commentator like Olshausen, to evade the acknowledged meaning of the language by such a remark. He might as well object to the teaching of the same parable concerning God's willingness to forgive, that there was no such custom among the Jews, Greeks, or Romans, as freely remitting a debt of ten thousand talents, — in truth, no such debts owed by servants to their masters; or, in the parable of the laborers hired for a penny a day, that there was no such usage as paying men equally for one hour as for a day's work. It is a paltry objection. Accordingly, Bengel, Meyer, Alford, adhere to the only known meaning of the word " tormentors," or torturers.

distinct by the statement that it is a suffering from which there is no interval of rest.

Messrs. Dobney, Ellis, and Hudson adopt the bold expedient of denying that this threat has any reference to the future world; the last-mentioned writer aiding himself by citing, in his "Debt and Grace," only the last one of the three verses, and, in his "Christ our Life," the last two. The passage, he remarks, " refers to the scenes of time, and not to the final judgment."

It would certainly be far easier to show that the Saviour's threat (Luke xii. 9), "He that denieth me before men shall be denied before the angels of God," refers to the scenes of time. No doubt the scenes and circumstances in which the offense is committed, are, *as in all cases* of sin threatened with future penalties, among the scenes of time. The *punishment* bears every mark of being the great final punishment, 1. When we consider the character of the offense, one of the greatest description. The beast is now generally conceded to be the persecuting sacerdotal power,— the fiercest form of antagonism to Christianity. To worship him, or to receive his mark, is, therefore, devoted adhesion to this fierce opposition. It is not merely to deny Christ before men, but to persecute him.* It is an offense committed, not by symbolical personages, but by individual offenders. Is there any thing in such an offense to justify or require our restraining the terrific

---

* It makes no difference whether we understand this sacerdotal power as both heathen and Christian (with Alford and Auberlen), or as simply heathen (with De Wette, Hengstenberg, Düsterdieck, Stuart, and others). The force of the argument will not be destroyed, even were we to adopt Mr. Hudson's explanation, that the sin is " the conduct of idolatrous people," though the interpretation is of the thinnest.

language of the threat from its full, tremendous sweep? 2. In the terms employed to describe the punishment, (*a*) it is eternal in duration, — "for ever and ever;" and that the eternity is one of *continuing suffering*, is proved by the subsequent statement, "they have no rest day nor night." (*b*) The words "tormented with fire and brimstone" manifestly refer to the same thing as having their "part in the lake which burneth with fire and brimstone, which is the second death." (*c*) The accumulation of the intensest expressions in fourfold mode, commencing with "the wine of the wrath of God, poured out without mixture into the cup of his indignation," is such as is nowhere surpassed, if equaled, in the Bible descriptions of future punishment. (*d*) The punishment is also clearly carried into the other world by the statement that it is "in the presence of the holy angels and of the Lamb." 3. In the marked correspondence of the passage to numerous others which evidently refer to the other world. Besides those which have been mentioned, we are at once reminded of such passages as the promise (Rev. iii. 5), "I will confess his name before my Father and before his angels;" of the general announcement of a final retribution (Matt. xvi. 27), "For the Son of man shall come in the glory of his Father, with his angels, and then shall he reward every man according to his works;" and of the combined promise and threat (Luke xii. 8, 9), "Whosoever shall confess me before men, him shall the Son of man also confess before the angels of God; but he that denieth me before men shall be denied before the angels of God." Also 2 Thess. i. 7, 8: "The Lord Jesus shall be revealed from heaven with his mighty angels, in flaming fire taking vengeance on them that know not God." In the intensity of its expressions concerning God's wrath, the passage also stands closely associated with those other passages concerning " the wrath to come," " the day of wrath," " the great day of his wrath," " the vessels of wrath: " those assertions, that " the wrath of God abideth on " those who do not believe in the Son ; that he will render " indignation and wrath, tribulation and anguish," in the day when he shall judge the world ; that " for these things the wrath of God cometh on the children of disobedience," and the like. In short, if this passage does not refer to the punishment of the future world, it would be hard to find one that can be shown to have that reference. Accordingly, scholarly commentators, rationalists included, almost without exception (such men, e.g., as Bengel, De Wette, Hengstenberg, Alford, Stuart, Düsterdieck, Graeber), have found this to be one of the clearest passages in the Bible on the subject of future suffering.

All these utterances are unequivocal: they depend on no inferences from ambiguous terms ; but, in the most direct and emphatic manner, they set forth the final doom of sin under the one great aspect of suffering, woe. In the present connection, we cite but one more passage, somewhat less explicit in word, and yet equally clear and significant in fact.

Mark ix. 42-48: " And whosoever shall offend one of these little ones which believe on me, it is better for him that a millstone were hanged about his neck, and he were cast into the sea. And if thy hand offend thee, cut it off: it is better for thee to enter into life maimed, than, having two hands, to go [depart ἀπελθεῖν] into hell [γέενναν], into the fire that never shall be quenched [ἄσβεστον unquenchable] (where their worm dieth not, and the fire is not quenched). And if thy foot offend thee, cut it off: it is better for thee to enter halt into life, than, having two feet, to be cast into hell (into the fire that never shall be quenched; where their worm dieth not, and the fire is not quenched). And if thine eye offend thee, pluck it out: it is better for thee to enter into the kingdom of God with one eye, than, having two eyes, to be cast into hell-fire; where their worm dieth not, and the fire is not quenched."

To avoid all complication with any doubtful reading, we have marked with parentheses, and propose not to make use of, certain portions of this passage which are wanting in some four or five out of seventeen uncial manuscripts, and which are dropped from the text by Tischendorf, though retained by Lachmann and Alford.*

Here, again, no evasion can hide from the reader the fact, that the grand representation involved is the horribleness of the condition into which the wicked must depart. First is the solemn warning, that it were far better to be drowned in the sea before committing the sin of misleading Christ's little ones. Then comes the

---

* Alford insists on retaining the text as in our version, and characterizes the omissions as corrections by the copyists, easily accounted for. The authorities are as follows: for retaining, uncial manuscripts A, D, E, F, G, H, K, M, S, U, V, X, T, most cursive manuscripts (a large number), most of the Latin versions before Jerome, the Vulgate, Gothic, Ethiopic, both Syriac versions, and others, Augustine, Irenæus; against it are only B, C, L, Δ, with cursives 1, 28, 118, 251, 255, 2 pe, one Latin version (out of some seventeen), the Coptic and Armenian, to which must now be added the Codex Sinaiticus.

admonition to sacrifice, at whatever cost of pain and loss, rather than encounter the doom in question. And, finally, we have an accumulation of images of woe and terror connected with the doom itself: it is *gehenna*, the *gehenna* of fire, the fire unquenchable, the deathless worm, and the fire that is not quenched.

The parallel passage in Matt. xviii. 8 has also "everlasting fire." Let now the reader bear in mind the Scripture's own corresponding phraseology, " tormented in this flame," " tormented with fire and brimstone for ever and ever," " shall eat your flesh as it were fire ; " let him observe the stress which is laid upon the interminableness here asserted in at least four different forms, — unquenchable, that is not quenched, everlasting, that never dies ; let him note the horror of the images employed in themselves, and their incompatibility except as they are *images* of horror, — unquenchable fire and undying worm ; let him observe how this accumulated terror is addressed in solemn warning to the individual sinner, as a doom which he is not only to behold, but to experience, — and he can not doubt the aim of the passage as a declaration of dreadful woe in the other world.

The cavils against this obvious meaning rise through all grades, from the lowest. As to the endlessness of the infliction, among other things, Mr. Dobney (page 208) suggests that the fire is called unquenchable, " not as absolutely and in itself inextinguishable, but relatively to the object cast into it ; " whereas Matthew expresses it in the parallel passage as " the everlasting fire" (τὸ πῦρ τὸ αἰώνιον). Ellis and Read have a ready device to meet this difficulty ; for, with their accustomed scholarship, they translate the latter phrase (p. 221), "the fire of the age." Not quite satisfied with this, they suggest (p. 222), that, "even supposing the original would bear this construction [namely, that of the common translation], it would only imply that the *instrument* of the punishment would be perpetual;" as though the Saviour had employed such reiterated and tremendous emphasis to establish in his solemn warning merely the proposition that a fire should burn on, and a worm live on, for ever. But here Mr. Hudson comes to the rescue: "It is not the immortality of the individual soul, but the *multitude* of those who finally perish, that challenges the unquenched fire and the unfailing worm" (Debt and Grace, p. 199). Without pausing to inquire into the consistency of the admission with some of his other arguings on the subject,* it is enough to say that this material conception is not only false to the original declaration, but just perverts the whole force of the passage from a terrific warning to the individual sinner into a general remark about the immense multitude of those who shall finally perish. To what purpose did the Saviour use that emphasis of threefold reiteration, "the unquenchable fire, the fire that is not quenched, the deathless worm"? Was it

---

* Three pages later (p. 202), this writer takes a different, and, it would seem, incompatible position. "The former (ἄσβεστος) describes the *fierceness* and all-consuming violence of the fire; the latter (αἰώνιος), its irreparable *effect*. The *eternal* fire is that which destroys utterly and for ever." Thus an eternal fire becomes the briefest fire conceivable. Mr. Hastings advances an interpretation of the unquenchable or unquenched fire equally characteristic. The result he reaches makes it one of a class of fires which "have not been *quenched*, but, having accomplished their end, have *ceased to burn*" (Pauline Theology, p. 52). And this equivocation we are to understand as exhausting the force of Christ's solemn declaration!

to describe as matter of information the number of the lost? or was it to bring home the terror of future punishment to the individual? To ask the question is to answer it. There could not be a grosser deviation from the intent of the utterance than Mr. Hudson has advanced. It is vain for him to say that his explanation brings home the terror of the scene to the individual: for his theory is that the individual is extinguished by the fierceness of the flame; he is not there as a spectator to witness it.

But a more specious objection is raised from the origin of the phraseology in question. It is alleged, truly, that the particular mode of expression is drawn from Isa. lxvi. 24; and it is maintained that "the words by their own force can prove no more in the one case than in the other. If they properly signify or imply immortality in the New Testament, they will do the same in the Old Testament" (Christ our Life, p. 97). The case is artfully stated; for we never decide the meaning of declarations merely by "the proper force of the words," but also by the scope, connection, and subject.

But to go into the details of the argument. It is said (p. 98): "As worms and fire utterly consume a dead body; so, if the antitype be true to the type, the two passages furnish the liveliest picture and the strongest proof of the utter extinction of the lost." Here is the main argument of the whole body of annihilationists on this subject. It is the fundamental principle of the system. And its unsoundness appears at once from the fact that *it necessarily cuts off the possibility* of imaging forth any other penal transaction than a transient one, and forcibly turns all such representations into images of extinction; for the reason that every process in a temporal world is temporary, and each process here that is most terrific and painful is *incidentally* the most short-lived. Dissolution most speedily attends it. The system thus insists on dragging every thing to this material standard, and lays down a principle which beforehand precludes our finding any threat of punishment consistent with immortality; whereas the Scriptures everywhere use and must use the *imperfect* types of this world to express the complete and perfect things of the other. As, on the one hand, a perishable city typifies a heavenly home, a passing inheritance in Palestine an endless possession of blessedness, and the pleasures of feasting, which so soon reach satiety and loathing, continually represent those joys that never pall; so, on the other hand, the abode, condition, sufferings, of the lost, are everywhere set forth in forms of horrors so intense, that, from the very constitution of things *here*, they are transient. But the Scriptures everywhere correct this incidental defect in the type by statements indicative of the eternity of the antitype; and these expressions of eternity the annihilationists continually overrule. They override them, and rule them out, on the ground that the figures connected with them, and which they endeavor to extend, have these incidental defects. The words are not permitted to perform the use for which they were designed, simply because they have such a use.

But to meet the objection directly. The original passage in Isa. lxvi. 24 is not a picture of annihilation, but of visible continuous horror. 1. Such is the comment of the passage itself. After announcing that these victims of God's vengeance shall lie without the city, to be viewed by its holy inhabitants, while "their worm shall not die, neither shall their fire be quenched," the next words are, "and they shall be an abhorring unto all flesh." 2. Such is the nature of the scene in which it is found: it describes a permanent state of things; it is laid in Messianic times; it is the holy mountain Jerusalem (verse 20) with "the new heavens and the new earth," and "a seed," which shall be equally permanent (verse 22). From month to month, and from Sabbath to Sabbath (a permanent arrangement), "shall all flesh come to worship before me, saith the Lord" (verse 23). In connection with this everlasting state of things, the next announcement is, "they [the inhabitants of this holy mountain] shall go forth [*non loco, sed contemplatione*, Calvin], and look upon the carcasses of the men that have transgressed against me; for their worm," etc. It is a sight coeval with the other facts and scenes of this Messianic state. 3. The phraseology itself conforms to the connection, and compels this view. What need of an eternal agency to perform a work of dissolution that Nature alone quickly accomplishes? A transient fire will soon reduce a body to ashes: the perishing worm is adequate to the work of speedy decay. But that "*their worm that shall not die*" can fairly signify here nothing short of an eternal corrosion; and that "*their fire shall not be quenched*" can signify in this connection no less than an endless combustion. The phraseology employed precisely conforms to the perpetuity of the scene of which it describes a part. 4. The interpretation of the Jews before Christ to this effect may be seen in the apocryphal books of Judith and Sirach. Thus (Judith xvi. 20, 21): "Woe be to the nation that riseth up against my people; for the Lord Almighty will take revenge upon them: in the day of judgment he will visit them; for he will give fire and worms into their flesh, that they may burn and may feel for ever" ($καύσονται$ $ἐν$ $αἰσθήσει$ $ἕως$ $αἰῶνος$, burn with feeling or in consciousness for ever). So, more briefly, Sirach vii. 19: "The vengeance on the flesh of the ungodly is fire and worms." 5. The ablest modern commentators, especially those who are untrammeled by any consideration but the meaning of the text, take this view without hesitation. Thus Knobel, one of the latest and keenest of the German rationalists: "The bodies of the fallen remain unburied for their punishment; and Jehovah will cause that they, still having feeling (Job xiv. 22), shall be incessantly and painfully eaten by worms, and that the fire by which he has slain them shall burn perpetually, and cause them lasting suffering." Maurer, also a rationalist, simply quotes as his interpretation the two before-cited passages from Judith and Sirach of the Apocrypha. Rosenmüller understands, that, like dead bodies, the living shall be continually eaten by worms. He adds, however, that others, as Vitringa and Gesenius, hold that, to the general figure drawn from the fires in the valley of the sons of Hinnom, "the prophet adds another figure," of dead bodies gradually eaten and devoured by worms; and to these dead bodies themselves, sensibility is attributed. Certainly, in this sense, the passage is by our Lord transferred to the punishment of the wicked condemned after death to eternal flames." Meyer, also, in his comment on the passage as it stands in Mark ix., fully sustains the view: "A figurative designation of most painful and endless hell-punishments (not merely pains of conscience) after Isa. lxvi. 24; compare Sirach vii. 19, Judith xvi. 21. Against the literal understanding of the worm and fire,-it is conclusive that they are, in fact, incompatible together."

The truth is, that the prophet, as in so many other instances, under the guidance of a higher power, rises to a remarkable and unheard-of conception, and employs language already fitted for the uses of the gospel; and the Saviour needs make no change in the phraseology to express thereby the endless sufferings of the lost. That the Saviour does so employ it, we have sufficiently shown. No tampering with the edges of the declaration can escape the emphasis of his repetition, — the use of the parallel word eternal, — and the point of his solemn warning addressed to the individual offender to escape such accumulated woe. Accordingly, the great body of commentators who have any standing as scholars or critics, whether orthodox or rationalist, have recognized the Saviour's utterance as a clear designation, in word at least, of endless sufferings.*

We cite one other passage, Matt. xxv. 46: "And these shall go away into everlasting punishment; but the righteous, into life eternal." In connection with this

---

* An attempt to sustain the annihilationist view by a passage of Eusebius in which πῦρ ἄσβεστος occurs twice, and by other citations, is examined in Note F, Appendix.

must be taken the previous verse (41st) : " Then shall he say also unto them on the left hand, Depart from me, ye cursed, into everlasting fire, prepared for the devil and his angels." That the punishment (κόλασις αἰώνιος) is suffering, not extinction, will appear in several ways. 1. We might properly appeal to the very idea of punishment. It is in some way, always, the infliction of suffering. Deprivation is suffering, while there is a living being to feel that suffering. Death is suffering, not alone in the pangs of decease, but in the extreme terror that it brings to the living in view both of those pains, and of the dread scenes that are to follow.* Even extinction, in so far as it would be punishment at all, would be so only in so far as the expectation of it, and the process, would be productive of suffering. 2. Classic usage sustains this fundamental idea. The verb to punish (κολάζω) is used throughout the classics in connection with the agencies of suffering. Thus, Passow give instances of only these connections: to punish with words, with blows, with death, with the severest vengeance (τιμωρίαις), to be punished by one's sins. And the noun κόλασις in Plutarch is synonymous with τιμωρία, — the two words being the two common words, if not the only ones, used to express the infliction of suffering for wrong-doing.†

---

* Mr. Hudson endeavors to conceal this important but palpable fact, and argues as though a case of punishment by death were a refutation of the idea of suffering. See Reviewers Reviewed, p. 32, etc.; Debt and Grace, p. 192.

† As to the reading, there is no variation. The conjectures to which Mr. Hudson devotes half a page, while as usual protesting that he will not " raise any question of the genuineness of the text," have no foundation whatever, and are now rejected by all respectable authorities as baseless.

19

3. New Testament usage favors the meaning. The only other use of the noun κόλασις occurs in 1 John ix. 18: "Because fear hath torment," κόλασιν.* Mr. Hudson's statement that "the translation of the word [here] by 'torment' is nearly, if not wholly, without parallel, and is unsupported by lexicographers," has a verbal correctness, and no more. The word "torment" is perhaps not used; but the idea of suffering inflicted — of chastisement — is supported by lexicographers, and is now defended in this particular passage by most of the latest and best scholars; and his attempt to substitute "restraint" is, so far as we know, without support either in form or in fact. Passow's only definition of the word, as applied to men, is "chastisement, punishment, by words or acts." Huther (in 1861) thus sums up the case: "The word κόλασις always has the signification, 'punishment.' This signification most interpreters firmly retain in the present instance, though they deviate from each other variously in the nearer determination of the thought. Thus Lücke explains, consciousness of punishment; De Wette paraphrases 'has,' by 'receives,' punishment; Düsterdieck, 'has already punishment, i.e. condemnation.' Ebrard translates κόλασις 'pain;' Lange, 'Fear is a painful feeling;' Besser, 'the pain of punishment'" (Strafpein): to which Huther himself accedes, explaining "the pain which one experiences in expectation of being punished by him whom he fears." So much for authorities on the meaning of the word in that passage. It occurs nowhere else in the New Testament. The verb

---

* For a further examination of κόλασις, see Note G, Appendix.

κολάζομαι is found only in Acts iv. 21 and 2 Pet. ii. 9; and in both cases has, by universal admission of commentators, it is believed, the sense of "punish." In both instances, very clearly in the former, it bears the aspect of the infliction of suffering.* 4. The connected phraseology employed is decisive. It is *everlasting* fire, *everlasting* punishment. Instantaneous punishment, overwhelming fire, might be consistent with annihilation; but the reiterated statement, that the process is eternal, agrees only with a punishment which consists in some form of suffering. The only mode of escape is in the hardihood which vacates the word "everlasting," in both instances, of its legitimate meaning (*as in all other cases of the kind*), and makes it signify something else, as final, irreversible. The strength of the case is increased by the additional fact, that precisely the same phraseology is used in the same breath to denote the duration of the happiness of the righteous: it is in both cases αιώνιος. Furthermore, both fates are *alike* described as states or permanent conditions "into" which the respective classes shall "depart" or "go away," — these shall go away into everlasting punishment; but the righteous, into life eternal. So verse 41, "Depart into everlasting fire." (So also Mark ix. 43: "It is better for thee to enter into life maimed, than, having two hands, to go [ἀπελθεῖν, go away] into hell." 5. An additional consideration,

---

* A characteristic specimen of Mr. Hudson's interpretation and argument is found in the following: "In Acts iv. 21, the verb κολάζω occurs and the context favors the sense of punishment *with a view to* 'restraint' and prohibition," i.e. to a resulting restraint; where he deliberately confounds the punishment with its expected result — two things as distinct as the discharge of a gun and the subsequent flight of a frightened bird.

absolutely conclusive, is the explanation which verse 41 furnishes. This everlasting punishment is "the everlasting fire [τὸ πῦρ τὸ αἰώνιον] prepared for the devil and his angels." But that everlasting fire, as we have already seen in our remarks on Rev. xx. 10, and Luke viii. 28, 31, is the "abyss," or bottomless pit, the place of "torment," the "lake of fire" where "they shall be tormented day and night for ever and ever." To a Universalist or annihilationist, this passage may offer no difficulty; but to most men it is final.

Perhaps it may be advisable to attend briefly to certain counter considerations alleged by the advocates of annihilation.

Some of them (e.g., Storrs, Blain, Hastings) have endeavored to maintain that the word κόλασις itself means annihilation; derived, as they suggest, from κολάζω, which has for a primary meaning to prune, curtail, dock: hence they say cutting off, or abscission, in their peculiar sense of extinction.* These widely circulated books are the foundation of the faith of a large portion of the annihilationists; but unfortunately for them, the word has no such meaning anywhere in the Greek language, as extinction, annihilation, or abscission in any such sense. Mr. Dobney and Mr. Hudson are wise enough to avoid the gross error. The latter shrewdly remarks, that, "in pruning, the tree is not cut off, only the branches;" and expressly admits that there is no proof that the word has the meaning claimed by his associates.†

---

* Storrs's Six Sermons, p. 59; Hastings's Pauline Theology, p. 59; Blain's Death not Life, p. 79.

† Debt and Grace, p. 190.

The latter writer, however, claims that non-existence is a state, and therefore may be "everlasting" (Christ our Life, p. 148). But this is only a play upon words. We may carelessly, and for want of language to talk about *nothing*, call non-existence a state; but it is in fact neither state, attribute, nor condition. It is blank nothingness,— a no-state, a no-condition. Of what would it be the state or condition? of the being who is non-existent? But the state of a nothing is what? Nothing,— no state at all. If non-existence is actually a state, then nothing has become something. How can we, except as we impose on ourselves, speak seriously of non-existence as actually an everlasting something; as having any duration at all, any measure. Out on such nonsense! The lapse of *time* after an extinction may be longer or shorter; but non-existence is neither longer nor shorter. There is no such thing as half nothing or twice nothing, or any multiple or extension of it. Annihilation is not an everlasting punishment: * it is a transient punishment, having no duration beyond the instant of infliction; although it may previously weigh upon the mind with dread. It avails nothing to quote careless admissions from able writers to the effect that final extinction is everlasting punishment. The very confusion in which, according to the quotation given, the younger Edwards involved himself, shows his error. He said, "Endless annihilation is an endless or infinite punishment," and "on

---

* It is apparently at the expense of consistency with himself that Mr. Hudson (Christ our Life, pp. 127, 148, etc.) maintains that "utter extinction" is "eternal punishment, an eternal state." For, in all his special interpretations of the Scripture word "eternal," the eternity is not one of duration, but of effect.

this basis, says Mr. Hudson, he builds an argument for eternal suffering, making free with infinitudes, as if a second might be added to the first." The statement is the sufficient refutation of the basis itself.*

But we are met with the same argument in another form; viz., that privation is punishment, and annihilation is eternal privation, and, therefore, eternal punishment. But there is no privation except as there is some person to be deprived, and no eternal privation except as there is eternally some being deprived. We deem it important to remark, in passing, that the punishment even of privation is a positive thing: it consists in the pain, mental or bodily, which that privation is fitted to produce and does produce. It is punishment because there is an existing person who feels it. The baffling of desires and hopes may be the keenest anguish. The privation exerts a positive and continuous effect. It is a punishment only on the condition and during the time that there is a conscious being to feel or to dread it. The souls which are not yet created are undergoing no punishment in not now possessing the pleasures of life. The soul that has ceased to be, *afterward* suffers no punishment in not possessing those pleasures. All the punishment there is takes place while there is some one in existence to be punished. There is no punishing further. To state the case clearly is to prove it. The punishment of anni-

---

* Two quotations on the same page (Christ our Life, p. 152) from Baxter, and Gordon Hall, declare annihilation to be a severer penalty than endless suffering; contrary to the fact, and contrary to Mr. Hudson's whole argument.

hilation considered as a privation is therefore transient: it continues so long as there is a person to feel or to shrink from that privation and no longer. To call the *punishment* of annihilation eternal is to impose on one's self with words. Annihilation is the end of punishment.

But it is thought by annihilationists to help their argument by insisting strongly that death is punishment. True, death is *suffering*, both in the process usually, and always in the anticipation. And the terrors felt by anticipation are not alone or chiefly the pains of the dying hour; but, as Shakspeare says, it is " the dread of something after death " which " makes us rather bear those ills we have, than fly to others that we know not of." Death is thus the most terrific of punishments; in this life, and all through life, it presses with great power upon the soul. And beyond this life it introduces, as we believe the Scripture teaches, to still sorer suffering, and becomes an " *everlasting* punishment; " otherwise it would be strictly a transient punishment. So annihilation, we grant, might be reckoned a punishment so far and so long as it causes pain and dread in the person who anticipates and should experience it; and no longer. But since there is strictly no such thing as eternal annihilation, that is, a non-existence that has an actual and eternal existence; since the annihilated being experiences no suffering beyond the moment of extinction, there is nothing in any of these suggestions to break the force of the Saviour's words, or to diminish the proof that the punishment here spoken of was a state of positive suffering.

Other passages, equally significant, should not be forgotten. Such are Matt. xxvi. 24, Mark xiv. 21: " Woe unto that man by whom the Son of man is betrayed! it had been good for that man if he had not been born." So terrible is the doom awaiting him, that he had better never have been born than encounter it. But annihilation would simply restore things as they were before he was born. " Be not afraid of them that kill the body, and after that have no more that they can do. But I will forewarn you whom ye shall fear: Fear him which after he hath killed hath power to cast into hell " (Luke xii. 4, 5). Physical death, then, is not worthy of consideration in comparison with the doom after death. " Fear not them which kill the body, but are not able to kill the soul: but rather fear him which is able to destroy [not now " kill "] both soul and body in hell; " the ruin of both soul and body in hell being so fearful a fate that physical death is not to be dreaded in the comparison. The same fearfulness of its suffering lies as the substratum of that gradation of penalties contained in Matt. v. 22, " Shall be in danger of the judgment — of the council — of hell-fire." *

---

* In this passage, all these grades of condemnation are clearly to be understood not as temporal penalties, but as transactions under the kingdom of Christ. The penalty in the previous verse (ἡ κρίσις, the judgment) is, of course, literally, that of the lowest Jewish court. But in the next verse, the Saviour proceeds to say how different it shall be in his kingdom, and *transfers* the κρίσις and συνέδριον to represent processes of condemnation in that kingdom. This is the clew to the interpretation. And the Saviour so puts it as to begin where the common standard ended, attaching to the slightest shade of sinful anger as heavy a condemnation as the Jew did to murder; so rising from severity to severity, and crowning the whole with hell-fire, as outstripping all that was was conceivable, and having no parallel in human

The future punishment spoken of in the Scriptures, clearly consists in intensity of suffering.

---

tribunals. The word *gehenna*, whatever its origin, so far as we can learn by careful examination, had in the Saviour's time *no other meaning than hell.* See Appendix, Note H.

CHAPTER VII.

NEW TESTAMENT TEACHINGS CONTINUED. — SUFFERING PROTRACTED AND ENDLESS.

WE have seen that the New Testament asserts future punishment to consist in suffering, and not in the cessation of suffering. Whenever it particularizes in regard to the doom of the wicked, it dwells with great and even exclusive emphasis on the terror and suffering of that doom. When, now, we furthermore find that punishment described as not only protracted, but endless and eternal, proceeding simultaneously with the blessedness of the righteous and co-eternal with it, nothing would seem to be lacking to the completeness of the proof. Such is the fact of the case. The declaration is made in various forms.

1. There are passages which involve the perpetuity of the infliction, although without the use of the word everlasting and the like. Thus the admonition (Matt. v. 25) given in allegoric form to become reconciled to the offended party, in order, as Meyer expresses it, "not to be cast into hell by God the Judge," closes with the solemn assurance, "Verily I say unto thee, thou shalt by no means come out thence till thou hast paid the uttermost farthing." In this is contained, as

the same commentator well remarks, the endlessness of the state of punishment, since the removal of the sin of him who is in *this φυλακή*, or prison, is an impossibility.

The same thought is conveyed at the close of the parable of the merciless debtor (Matt. xviii. 34, 35): "And his lord was wroth, and delivered him to the tormentors till he should pay all that was due unto him. So likewise shall my heavenly Father do also unto you," etc. As the payment of such a debt, whether the literal ten thousand talents of the parable, or the sinner's debt to God, is impossible, the delivering to the tormentors* till he should pay all, is an *endless* confinement in suffering. The comment is as old as Chrysostom, who says, "That is, perpetually; for he will never repay:" and it is perfectly obvious to the plainest reader.

Equally emphatic is the statement in Matt. xii. 31, 32: "The blasphemy against the Holy Ghost shall not be forgiven unto men.... Whosoever speaketh a word against the Holy Ghost, it shall not be forgiven him, neither in this world, neither in the world to come." The world to come requires no special explanation. Interpreters understand it in the obvious meaning: it designates the state of things after the coming of Christ and the judgment, onward. The two phrases, "this world" and "the world to come," cover the whole present and future. The Saviour not only first denies all

---

* On this word βασανιστάς, Meyer explains "the *torturers* to torture him, not merely to confine him. So Fritzsche and most commentators. The idea of βασανίζειν is essential as an image of the future βάσανος of *gehenna.*" So Alford, Bengel, etc.

future forgiveness to this kind of sin: he expands and explains his statement. By that expansion he assigns, by any fair interpretation of his words, a continued existence in the world to come as much as in this world, and declares that in that world, as in this, the sinner shall remain under the displeasure of God, never forgiven. De Wette admits, against his inclination, that the phrase ὁ αἰών μέλλων unquestionably covers eternity. He adds: " That, however, the eternity of hell-punishments is asserted in our text will be admitted by us only when we are compelled to take the declaration of Jesus with *verbal exactness*." Meyer says, " The eternity of the punishment here taught is not to be explained away."

2. There are passages which in set terms describe this punishment as endless, eternal, lasting for ever, or for ever and ever. Some of them have been alluded to already for another purpose. It is well, however, to see them together, in order to appreciate the boldness with which the annihilationists, like the Universalists, deprive them of their established meaning, *in all cases when they refer to punishment.*

In Matt. iii. 12 is described the searching work of Christ: " Whose fan is in his hand, and he will thoroughly purge his floor, and gather his wheat into the garner; but he will burn up the chaff with unquenchable fire." Here the perpetual vigor and force of the instrument is unmeaning except as describing the perpetuity of the punitive agency it exerts.*

In the passage quoted in the previous chapter (Mark

---

* See the fuller examination of this phrase, " unquenchable fire," elsewhere.

ix. 43–48), we have at least a threefold reiteration of the same mode of expression (after canceling those portions of the passage which some contend to be unsupported): "the unquenchable fire," "their worm dieth not," "their fire is not quenched." The reader will observe it is *their* worm that is deathless, indicating that not the general horror of the scene, but the special relation of these horrors to the occupants of *gehenna*, is in his mind when he describes it as endless.

In Matt. xxv. 41, the same fire is described as "everlasting;" and in verse 46 of the same chapter, the punishment again is "everlasting."

In Matt. xviii. 8, the same doom which in the following verse is called "hell-fire," is designated as the "everlasting fire."

The same phrase, "eternal fire," with the same signification, is found, Jude 7: "Even as Sodom and Gomorrha, and the cities about them, in like manner, giving themselves over to fornication, and going after strange flesh, are set forth for an example, suffering the vengeance of eternal fire."

Some of the annihilationists have, however, adopted the position of the Universalists, that the fire here spoken of had no reference to future punishment, but was simply the fire that destroyed those cities on earth. To the contrary, are (1), The usage of the phrase. In every other instance in the New Testament, the "eternal fire," "unquenchable fire," the "fire that burns for ever and ever," unquestionably refers to future punishment. Rampf well remarks that this designation is characteristic. (2), The connection. The last statement previous (verse 6) is concerning the sinning angels reserved in everlasting chains under darkness; and that statement is connected with this as a similar transaction, "even as," etc. The subsequent verses also (verse 14) bring to view the future punishment of transgressors, "wandering stars to whom is reserved the blackness of darkness for ever." The representation of final punishment alone meets the writer's scope. (3), The most scholarly interpreters, even though differing in details, are agreed on this feature, that a fire outlasting the sudden destruction of those cities, an eternal fire, is meant. They understand that there is an allusion to the natural phenomena around the Dead Sea as still bearing witness to ("setting forth") the continued vengeance of God on those cities, whose very mode of temporal overthrow — "fire and brimstone" — became one of the images or types under which the eternal punishment of those wicked people is represented in God's Word. There is a slight difference in the connection to which they refer the words "eternal fire." Some (as De Wette, Alford, Brückner) connect as in our translation. De Wette, who takes the lowest view, understands a reference to the belief expressed, for instance, by Philo Judæus (ii. 21, 142), that the fire in which those cities were overthrown still continues to burn under the earth, eternally, and that they still suffer a "punishment of eternal fire." Brückner maintains a double sense in πυρὸς αἰωνίου, including in one expression "the duration and type, or figure of the punishment." Others (as Bengel, Huther, Rampf) connect thus: "are set forth suffering vengeance, an example [rather type or typical example] of eternal fire." The Greek admits this reading perhaps more easily than the other. The translation sufficiently indicates the view of its advocates, which is very ably maintained by Rampf, one of the latest and most exhaustive commentators on this epistle.* But, whatever the mode of minor interpretation, these eminent expositors are agreed that the text refers unquestionably to the fire that is strictly eternal, of which that earthly fire is here regarded as a symbol.

To Bloomfield's similar exposition, that this doom was a faint type of the punishment inflicted by God in the next world, Mr. Hudson rejoins : " Very true : a fire that utterly consumes is a ' faint type ' of a destruction ever going on and ever incomplete." †

The sneer is pointless. That fire utterly consumed (*annihilated*, he means) nothing. The sinners themselves were but hurried to another severer doom ; while the annihilationist can not have the poor satisfaction of saying, that even the material scenes in which they lived, though ruined and transformed, ceased absolutely to exist. The appropriateness of the type consists in the irresistible, terrific, and agonizing nature

---

* " In representing the punishment itself and its significance, Jude admirably chose πρόκεινται instead of simple εἰσί. In the Dead Sea *lies*, ' is set forth,' the punishment of those cities before our eyes. At a sight of that Salt Sea, the fearful picture of the punishment which those cities underwent rises anew, living, as it were, before the human spirit. He views it as present. Suffering now, as they did, so terrible a punishment in fire-rain. δίκην ὑπέχουσαι, they are δεῖγμα πυρὸς αἰωνίου. This picture of the impure cities overwhelmed with fire is a living typical reference (Hinweis, index) to that other mysterious fire, which by the designation αἰώνιον (Matt. xviii. 8, xxv. 41) or ἄσβεστον (Mark ix. 43), is thoroughly characterized as that of hell."— Rampf's Brief Judæ *in loco.*

† Christ our Life, p. 110.

of the punishment, and its supernatural character as a direct and visible chastisement "from the Lord out of heaven;" and in the permanence of its marks. (4), The symbolic use of that scene to represent the punishment of the lost is clearly sustained by various passages in Revelation; the lake of fire (xx. 14); the lake of fire burning with brimstone (xxi. 8); fire came down from God out of heaven; the lake of fire and brimstone, where they shall be tormented for ever and ever (xx. 9, 10); perhaps also xiv. 10, 11, and xix. 3. The connection of the phraseology in these passages with the overthrow of Sodom and Gomorrha is not only admitted but maintained by Mr. Hudson.*

The passage, then, refers distinctly to the future punishment of sinners, which is here termed eternal.

In 2 Thess. i. 9, the punishment inflicted by the Lord Jesus, in flaming fire taking vengeance, is called an "everlasting destruction."

In Jude 6, certain fallen angels are declared to be reserved in everlasting chains unto the judgment of the great day. The word "everlasting" here employed ($\check{\alpha}\delta\iota o\varsigma$) is used but once besides in the New Testament (Rom. i. 20), and is there applied to the power of God,—"the eternal power and Godhead." As wicked men are to share the doom of Satan and his angels, this designation equally applies to their term of punishment,—as lasting as the attributes of God.

Mark iii. 29 expresses the fact in a twofold form, with reiteration: "But he that shall blaspheme against the Holy Ghost hath never forgiveness [literally hath not forgiveness to eternity $\epsilon i\varsigma$ $\tau o \nu$ $\alpha i \tilde{\omega} \rho \alpha$], but is in danger

---

* Debt and Grace, pp. 212, 243.

of [subject to] eternal condemnation;" i.e., the condemnation of God will rest upon him eternally; he will be for ever in the state of condemnation, in which indeed, the wicked already are (see John iii. 18). Such is the meaning according to the received text. But modern critics adopt a different reading of the Greek. Instead of *condemnation* (κρίσεως) they read *sin* (ἁμαρτήματος); "shall be subject to eternal sin," and its attendant guilt. The passage so amended contains the remarkable statement, that the wicked shall remain for ever sinful and for ever unforgiven. The manuscript authority on which this reading rests is such that Griesbach favored it, Lachmann and Tischendorf adopt it in their critical editions, and Alford and Meyer unhesitatingly accept it.*

Heb. vi. 1, 2: "Not laying again the foundation of repentance from dead works, and of faith toward God, of the doctrine of baptisms and of laying on of hands, and of resurrection of the dead, and of eternal judgment" [κρίματος αἰωνίου, eternal retribution]. The last phrase has, by some commentators, been held to be the κρίμα of the wicked only; but the majority of good commentators are now agreed to take it as referring to the just

---

* The authorities for it are manuscripts B, L, Δ, Cod. Sin. 28, 33, 2 pe; for ἁμαρτίας (sin) C¹, D, 13, 69, 346, Athanasius, Pseudo-Athanasius; the Latin versions (delicti, *sin*, except f.) Vulgate, Coptic, Gothic, Armenian, Saxon versions, Cyprian and Augustine. For κρίσεως, A, C², E, F, G, H, K, M, S, U, V, Γ, the cursives generally, both Syriac versions and others; while three cursive manuscripts read κολασέως, with the Arabic versions. Thus it appears, that, of the five oldest manuscripts, four, comprising the very oldest and best of all, read "sin" (ἁμαρτήματος or ἁμαρτίας), supported by nearly all the older versions. Tregelles coincides with Lachmann and Tischendorf.

and unjust alike, guided rather by the scope than by the more common application of κρίμα. Either interpretation bears on our argument, the latter even more decidedly than the former; for in one case the reward of the wicked is called eternal, in the other it is spoken of as co-eternal with that of the righteous.*

In Jude 13, certain evil-doers are spoken of as "wandering stars, to whom is reserved the blackness of darkness for ever" εἰς τὸν αἰῶνα. The reader will remember "the outer darkness" (Matt. viii. 12, etc.), where is weeping, and gnashing of teeth.

The same expression is found in 2 Pet. ii. 17, though with a change of the preceding figure: "These are wells without water, clouds that are carried about with a tempest, to whom the mist of darkness is reserved for ever," εἰς τὸν αἰῶνα.

In Rev. xiv. 11, the duration is expressed by the accumulated expression for ever and ever: The smoke of their torment ascendeth up for ever and ever, εἰς αἰῶνας αἰώνων.

The last-mentioned expression occurs also in Rev. xix. 3: "And her smoke rose up [rises up, ἀναβαίνει] for ever and ever, εἰς τοὺς αἰῶνας τῶν αἰώνων. It is objected, however, that this, being uttered concern-

---

* The words κρίσις and κρίμα by derivation would primarily denote, one the judicial process, the other the judicial sentence. They should apply indifferently to a favorable or an unfavorable case. But, as the judging of a sinful race is chiefly a condemning, the words are more commonly used in the adverse sense. In the New Testament also, not only is the distinctive use of the two terms frequently overlooked, but each of them often includes, together with the judicial process or sentence, the award itself. See instances in Robinson's New Testament Lexicon, under the words. Such is undoubtedly the case here. It is here almost precisely like our word "retribution."

ing Babylon, is merely a statement of its entire final demolition; and hence the eternity is merely an eternity of effect, — finality. But the reader will remember it is not a literal city, but *spiritual* Babylon (perhaps Pagan and chiefly Papal Rome), which is here described under this figure, and in the previous chapter, as a woman; the two representations being identified in xvii. 18. "If the woman," says Alford, [and we add, if the city], "represents merely the stonewalls and houses of the city, what need is there of 'mystery' on her brow? what appropriateness in the use of all the Scripture imagery, long familiar to God's people, of spiritual fornication?" The city, in its essential meaning, can not be even an abstraction, but the actual persons on whom God charged (xviii. 24) the "blood of prophets and of saints." This mingling of the underlying meaning with the figure of the representation appears not only in the circumstances alluded to, but also in the very description of the overthrow (verses 9, 10); where her "burning" is, in the same breath, identified with her "torment," thus: "Shall see the smoke of her burning, standing afar off for fear of her *torment*" (βασανισμοῦ). The smoke was therefore the same which is elsewhere called "the smoke of torment," the mark of suffering; and it rises up for ever and ever. Observe that the phrase "of her burning" is omitted in this closing statement, as though purposely to drop all connection with a literal conflagration, and to make the expression broad enough to be, in the words of Alford, a designation "of hell in general." *

---

* As this is not a material but a spiritual city, and the overthrow must

In Rev. xx. 10, the punishment of the devil, the beast, and the false prophet, is described as eternal suffering: "They shall be tormented day and night for ever and ever," εἰς τοὺς αἰῶνας τῶν αἰώνων.

of course, be in keeping, the whole representation, though borrowed from material transactions of the Old Testament, is raised into an entirely different plane, like the paradise, Zion, temple, sacrifice, etc., of the New Testament. Appeals, therefore, to such descriptions as Isa. xxxiv. 9, 10, do not settle the meaning of this. No doubt the language there employed to describe the overthrow of Idumea is the basis, and only the basis, of the present prophecy,— as the valley of the sons of Hinnom furnished the earthly image, and therefore one designation, of hell. Many commentators, however, have really missed the full force of the original passage in Isaiah, which describes, not merely a complete and final overthrow, but one whose marks and fearful tokens shall exist and display themselves through the ages, — therefore a fitting image of a ruin whose continuance is eternal; as much so as the nature of the case admits. The 9th and 10th verses read thus: "And the streams thereof shall be turned into pitch, and the dust thereof into brimstone, and the land thereof shall become burning pitch. It shall not be quenched night nor day: the smoke thereof shall go up for ever; from generation to generation it shall lie waste: none shall pass through it for ever." Knobel, in the last edition of his commentary (1861), thus explains the phenomena which perhaps the passage describes: "By volcanic revolution, the waters of the streams are changed to pitch (asphaltum), and the plains to brimstone; fire kindles upon the land, and makes it a burning pool of pitch. This prophecy readily occurred to the author, since in similar mode had the neighboring Valley of Siddim once been overwhelmed; and the nature of Idumea was similar to that of the valley. Hot springs are found there; modern travellers have found sulphur-springs (Burckhardt's Syria, pp. 731, 741), and volcanic cones with beds of lava (Ritter, Erdkunde xiv. p. 1045, xv. p. 769); Edrise even relates that the soil consists of pitch (Rosenm. Analecta Arab. iii. p. 4). Other Arabic writers give accounts of frightful fires in the earth, and outbursts of flame from it, which have been found in the State of Hedjaz, in the neighborhood of Medina (Seetzen, Correspondence, Feb. 1813, Burckhardt's Arabia, p. 547). Verse 10 is thus interpreted by Knobel: "The volcanic fire burns uninterrupted, and for ever smoke ascends from the burning land, as for a long time in the Vale of Siddim (Gen. xix. 28). Eden becomes an unoccupied desert. The fourfold designation of eternity, during which the desolation shall endure, intensifies the positiveness of the prophecy, and indicates deep displeasure." The reader will take notice that *a land exists* to suffer this lasting desolation.

Thus it will be seen that the endless duration of that punishment is asserted (1) in very numerous instances; (2) by all the forms of phraseology by which eternity is expressed in the Greek language; (3) by the same terms, equally varied and equally strong, by which the duration of the existence, attributes, glory, and worship of God, are described. One of the terms, indeed, (ἀΐδιος,) is used but twice in the New Testament: in one case it is applied to the punishment of the wicked, in the other to the nature of God.

Now, the terms which are translated "everlasting," "eternal," "for ever," "for ever and ever," and the other forms of expression by which this thought is expressed, are just as direct and simple in the Greek as in the English language. *They signify precisely the same thing, and are used in precisely the same way,* in these two languages. Much parade of learning has been made in regard to these terms. The unquestionable fact is, that they mean the same in the Bible that they do in common life, and are used in the same way; for the Bible uses the language and idioms of common life. Now, in common life, these terms are occasionally employed, no doubt, with some latitude; and yet every one knows that the real meaning of those terms is endless duration, and that meaning is not abrogated by occasional instances of careless use.

The attempt is made to set aside this testimony in two modes. First, certain writers endeavor to embarrass the question in the same mode with the Universalists, by alleging that these terms are often used for limited duration. So Blain, pages 86 and onward; and Hastings, Pauline Theology, pages 61. etc.; Ellis and Read, pages 264, etc.* Thus the Aaronitic priesthood is appointed to be an everlasting priesthood (Ex. xl. 15); the covenant with Abraham was an everlasting covenant, and the land of Canaan was an everlasting inheritance (Gen. xvii. 7, 8, etc.); certain servants were to serve their masters for ever (Ex. xxi. 6); Joshua directed that twelve stones from the Jordan should be a memorial for ever (Josh. iv. 7); and we read of the everlasting mountains (Hab. iii. 6), and the everlasting doors of Zion (Ps. xxiv. 7).†

This whole matter is easily disposed of to the perfect satisfaction of every man who is willing to be satisfied, or who will, in this matter, abide by the same principles that unhesitatingly govern him in all other interpretations.

1. The general and essential meaning and use of the words and phrases in question is clear. They mean

---

* A mass of ignorant confusion, found in the latter writers, on pp. 267, etc., where the idiomatic phrase εἰς τὸν αἰῶνα is confounded with other uses of αἰών entirely distinct, we do not refer to. To a person familiar with the Greek language, it is transparent and contemptible. To a person not acquainted with the language, its folly can not well be set forth. We refer only to the words and phrases properly translated "eternal."

† In the eagerness to find such passages, some singular errors are committed. Hastings and Ellis and Read cite, as their first instance, Jonah ii. 6, "The earth with her bars was about me for ever." This "for ever," say the latter writers, only embraced a period of three days and three nights. A total misapprehension. The passage is a part of what Jonah *thought and said of himself* while in the belly of the monster, which then seemed to him the sure passage to death; or, as he expresses it, the "belly of *sheol*." The translation of Henderson better brings out the sense: "As for the earth, her bars are shut upon me for ever." De Wette: "shut behind me for ever." The meaning is, he felt that he was for ever shut out from the land of the living. So Henderson, Gesenius, Rosenmüller, Hitzig. This, of course, without help from God; for he still trusted that God would deliver him from his fears, as intimated in the close of the verse.

eternity, — the same in English as in Greek and Hebrew. The fact is not affected by occasional instances in either language where impassioned utterance or popular phraseology may apply them without rigid exactness; where a speaker may call that eternal of which he can see no end, confounding the indefinite with the infinite; or where no termination is contemplated, even though as matter of fact it may speedily come. The meaning of the terms remains the same, notwithstanding the overstrained and careless use; and, in calm and well-considered utterances, not the slightest doubt attaches to the meanings. Thus men speak popularly of an eternal disgrace, an everlasting strife, an endless conflict; and every deed of real estate, though the sober language of a law-form, conveys the property to the purchaser, "his heirs and assigns *for ever*." The disgrace may be forgotten, the strife may cease, and the estate, for want of heirs or testament, may soon escheat to the state, without impairing the well-settled and legitimate meaning of those words in the English language. Precisely so in the Greek and Hebrew.

2. A careful analysis will show that many of the alleged deviations are more apparent than real; that the *language* employed has, in the intent of him who employs it, the usual signification: but he deliberately overlooks certain limitations, or suppresses certain implied conditions, or does not contemplate certain *facts*, which interfere with that intent. The Hebrew poet, with the same flight of imagination with which he endows the mountains with life and motion, also prolongs their age from an indefinite to an infinite duration. The gates of Zion, as the house of the eternal God, he chooses also

to invest with eternity by a poetic license.* The monument of stones was, in Joshua's actual intent, probably a memorial for ever: he contemplated no removal or destruction of it. As matter of fact it was destroyed, we know not when; but for that removal he made no provision, either in his plan or in his language. He did not prophesy that it would remain for ever, but directed that, so far as he and they could effect it, it should be perpetual. Precisely so do we understand the modern law conveyance to him, " his heirs and assigns *for ever:* " it indicates the intent of the grantor, a perpetual grant, never by him to be resumed but for aught of his interference, and so far as he can make it, to continue for ever. This condition is suppressed in the utterance; but, as soon as it is applied, the *language* appears in its usual meaning, whatever may be the resulting *fact*. The same is the meaning of the legislation, "He shall be a servant for ever." The party renounces his right, ever in all coming time, to claim his freedom, and, if his earthly life were to last so long, remains a servant for ever. The condition is suppressed, and makes the language seem to have a limited meaning; whereas it is only an intensive way of making a command or a prohibition. It is a perpetual ordinance. Even so modern and so precise a document as the Constitution of the United States, in one in-

---

* Let us be understood. When the Psalmist declares that Lebanon and Hermon skip like a young unicorn, that deep calleth unto deep, that the sea saw and fled, etc., we are not to maintain that the words " skip," " call," " sea," have lost their usual meaning, but simply that the poet, by a vivid and obvious stroke of imagination, chooses to attribute to those objects these living acts. So with the everlasting mountains. There were no such thing as poetic imagination if this principle were ruled out.

stance of special emphasis, rises from the level of a simple prohibition to incorporate the language of perpetuity : " No religious test shall *ever* be required as a qualification to any office or public trust under the United States." Now, suppose the Constitution were changed by a three-fourths vote of the States, or even violated in practice, would that affect the meaning of the original *language* as it came from the pen of Jefferson? Not at all. To this same intensive utterance of legislation and legal conveyance, which naturally sweeps on *without any limitation* whatever, we might refer the appointment of an everlasting priesthood, the everlasting covenant, and the inheritance for ever; or perhaps we are to view this class of arrangements and appointments as called everlasting, because they are the germ of what became perpetual in the gospel dispensation, being in the New Testament directly or typically identified with its own perpetual arrangements, e.g., the promise to Abraham.* These instances, therefore,

---

* This last view is not peculiar to English theologians and expositors. Von Gerlach remarks thus on Gen. xvii. 7, 8: "God makes with Abraham and his posterity an everlasting covenant; since this covenant of grace was the first germ of the new covenant in Jesus Christ. . . . The eternal possession stands in the first instance in contrast to the present temporary abode of Abraham in Canaan. Yet at the same time is this land, which God promised as an inheritance to Abraham and his seed, the visible pledge, the germ and prophetic type, of the new world which belongs to the church of the Lord: it is therefore called emphatically 'an eternal possession.' The same holds good of all the divine ordinances, which, in the Old Testament, are declared to be everlasting ordinances; and yet, in the New Testament, are in the letter abrogated, while in the spirit they have been fulfilled. So it is with circumcision, the passover, the priesthood, etc." Delitzsch says of the covenant of circumcision, " The circumcised man was to know himself as a member of a race-and-people union, with whom God has formed an everlasting covenant on the basis of promises which have the salvation of man for their contents, and whose offspring form a genealogical chain extending

when carefully considered, prove mostly, if not wholly, to be no exceptions in the intent of the speaker and the meaning of the language: the expressions are actually, and we may say deliberately, broader than the literal fact; (1) by a poetic embellishment, capable of no misunderstanding; (2) by the onward sweep of legislation, purposely intensifying into an everlasting bond; (3) by the designed and foretold absorption of a temporary, symbolic, or representative arrangement into an eternal economy, — as the Abrahamic covenant, the Aaronitic priesthood, the kingdom of David.

3. The alleged exceptional instances are all of them from the Old Testament, with its more highly poetic style and symbolic utterances. Not an instance is alleged from the New Testament. With these it is attempted to overthrow the deliberate and repeated declarations of Christ.

4. The alleged exceptions are adduced, not to show occasional exceptions in the absolute range of the words, but to destroy that meaning *in one entire class of cases singled out* for the purpose; and in that alone, — a proceeding, as matter of criticism and argument, quite intolerable.

5. The class of cases which it is thus proposed to isolate and exterminate is (1) numerous and varied in phraseology; (2) it comprises all the ordinary forms

---

forth to Jesus Christ, the salvation of the world." In the same strain, Hengstenberg writes ("The Jews and the Christian Church"): "According to the constant teachings of the Old and New Testaments, there is but one church of God, one Israel, one house under two administrations from the days of Abraham till the end of the world." Commentators are somewhat agreed that the everlasting kingdom of David became everlasting only in the reign of the Great Anointed of whom he was the type and precursor.

of designating eternity known to the New Testament, or to the Greek language; (3) it embraces all the terms which designate the eternity of God, of his attributes and glory,—one term ($ἀίδιος$) which is used in the New Testament elsewhere of God only; (4) it includes the same terms which — as will presently appear — designate the eternity of future happiness; (5) it in some cases, in the same text, applies the term alike to both retributions, so that objectors are driven to the monstrous inconsistency of arbitrarily assigning two infinitely different meanings to the same word in the same sentence, uttered in precisely the same way on the same general subject; and (6) it is supported, besides, by other modes of speech into which these terms do not enter.

Accordingly, the more intelligent advocates of annihilation deliberately abandon this defense as untenable, although previously calling attention to it for the sake of such effect as it may produce on some minds. Thus Mr. Dobney, after devoting three pages to show that these terms are often used in a limited sense, closes by declaring, "It is by no means or in any degree on the foregoing remarks that I would rest the answer to the argument derived from our present text (Matt. xxv. 46). I consent, with all my heart, to waive them here: I do waive them altogether, and rest the case entirely, so far as this text is concerned, on my next reply, to which I rather invite attention. Let it be cheerfully granted, then, that the word everlasting must, in each part of this text, be understood in its largest, widest sense, as denoting absolute eternity." *

---

* Future Punishment, p. 312.

Mr. Hudson, though repeatedly and somewhat prominently protruding this argument of a limited meaning of the terms (Christ our Life, pp. 120, 123, 132; Debt and Grace, pp. 210, 188), yet expressly disclaims his reliance upon it as his fundamental position, and even complains of one reviewer for failing to recognize the fact.*

Well they may do so. For however desirous to gain, as usual, the benefit of such suggestions in minds where they would have weight, they are too well aware of the impossibility of maintaining the position, and especially of its entire incompatibility with the objection on which they choose to stake the issue. A man can not well say much of the limited meaning of "eternal," etc., when his main position is, that it does mean eternity of effect. Still these writers certainly take all possible advantage of both the two opposite defenses, while they professedly abandon the former.

The second evasion, and the one on which annihilationism chooses to stake its attempt to turn these Scripture declarations, is this: the words do signify eternity absolute, finality, irreversibleness, or, as they choose to term it, eternity, not of process, but of effect. Punishment, they say, may consist in suffering or it may consist in extinction. Extinction may be called *eternal* punishment, because it is a punishment of which the effect continues for ever; that is, it is a final or irreversible extinction. In this mode they would dispose of the most troublesome passages, such as Matt. xviii. 8; xxv. 41, 46; 2 Thess. i. 9; Jude 13; 2 Pet. ii. 17, etc.

---

* Reviewers Reviewed, p. 12, and passages there cited from Christ our Life, pp. 4, 122, and Debt and Grace, p. 160.

The question at issue, then, is this: Do the words "eternal" and the like, when applied to the punishment of the wicked, entirely lose their fundamental meaning of *duration* (infinite, or at least indefinite), and convey only the notion of *final?* This is, in substance, the proposition of annihilationists.* It is the only real question. For the phrase "eternity of effect," as we shall presently see, is merely a disguising of the question, and actually disappears from the interpretation. Annihilation has, from the nature of the case, no duration beyond the moment when it takes place; neither has it any *effect* of which duration can be predicated; for its effect is non-existence, nothing. It is simply final; and such is the prevailing phrase by which, in Mr. Hudson's argument, it is expressed. Now, have these words, expressive of eternal duration, so completely changed as to lose the very notion of duration?

(1.) The attempt to break down, *in reference to one entire subject,* and that only, the well-settled and fundamental meaning of a class of words, by citing a few alleged exceptions out of several hundred instances in which the phrases occur, is at once a strange procedure. It would be natural, and in accordance both with common and Scriptural use, that a set of words employed in the New Testament more than a hundred times, and in the Old Testament about four hundred, should be occasionally used with some latitude.† Still,

---

* "These are examples in which the word 'eternal' denotes *finality,* rather than the endless continuance of the subject to which it is applied." Christ our Life, p. 118.

† In the New Testament, the adjective αἰώνως occurs sixty-six times,

if there is one idea that is fundamental in this whole class of cases, it is that of protracted duration, infinite, or at least indefinite.* Now this phraseology is that which is used to describe the duration of God's existence, glory, attributes, word, and worship; of Christ, his kingdom, his priesthood, his praise; it is applied to the future condition of the saints, and to the future condition of the wicked. Out of all these classes of topics, the last is singled out for an earnest endeavor to set aside the fundamental meaning of the terms: a few alleged exceptions are cited, and their whole force concentrated upon this one topic.

(2.) The looseness of the criticism is equally noticeable. The words αἰώνιος, etc., in these critics' hands, seem capable of any meaning at pleasure; and the last remnants of the original meaning, and indeed of any settled meaning, disappear under their manipulations. Thus they commence with attempts to prove the meaning, "eternity of effect;" in other words, "eternal," when applied to any process, does not describe the duration of that process to which the term is applied, but of something else, viz., its effect. But, as the process of annihilation actually leaves no existing result or effect, it becomes too palpably absurd to describe the re-

---

and the phrase εἰσ τὸν αἰῶνα, or its equivalent, some fifty-eight. In the Septuagint, αἰώνιος is found ninety-two times; and the noun αἰών, in some of its forms, three hundred and eight times.

* So essential is this meaning, that the notion of duration, of the onflow of time, seems inseparable from the root-word αἰών, and appears prominent in all instances of its use in the New Testament besides the particular phrases above referred to. Thus says Ellicott (Eph. i. 21): "With regard to the meaning of αἰών, it may be observed, that, in all passages where it occurs, a *temporal* notion is more or less apparent."

sulting nothing as eternal. Thus it became necessary to substitute the word "final" for eternal. Again, it is "irreversible;" an irreversible judgment (Heb. vi. 2). And, again, it is "critical or decisive." An "eternal victory" (a phrase cited from Wetstein) "plainly means a *decisive* victory," says Mr. Hudson. Now the word is further metamorphosed into "mortal, fatal." For, in the next sentence, the same writer proceeds: "In Mark iii. 29, the guilt is aptly called αἰώνιον, because decisive of one's destiny, mortal, fatal." Two pages later we are informed that the phrase "eternal chains" (δεσμοῖς ἀϊδίοις, Jude 6) is equivalent to the phrase δέσμοι ἄῤῥηκτοι, "chains that can not be broken." * Is this criticism and interpretation? Or is it inexcusably loose and random babbling? What can not be proved by such a style of argument, abandoning, as it does, every vestige of the legitimate meaning of words, until "eternal" becomes successively "final," "irreversible," "decisive," "mortal," "fatal," and equivalent to the phrase "that can not be broken." †

(3.) The alleged meaning entirely lacks support from New Testament usage. No instance can be adduced from the New Testament Greek in which these terms have lost their proper idea of protracted duration, and acquired that of mere "finality," or even "eternity of effect." Every instance can be most legitimately explained in accordance with the common meaning of the terms.

---

* The above quotation may be found on pp. 116, 118, 120, of Christ our Life.

† These processes are the *necessary* result of the exigency. It would not answer to render Mark iii. 29 *final* sin, nor Jude 6 *final* chains; for even that rendering would involve eternity. So final must give place to "mortal" and ἄῤῥηκτος.

The cases cited or alluded to by Mr. Hudson as proof passages, are Heb. v. 9, vi. 2, ix. 12, xiii. 20; Philem. 15; Rev. xvi. 6.

Following these texts in order, we read (Heb. v. 9), "And being made perfect, he became the author of *eternal* salvation unto all that obey him." It is claimed that eternal must here lose its ordinary meaning "if the word 'salvation' be taken in its strict sense of deliverance," i.e., a transient act of deliverance. But this is not the necessary nor ordinary use of the word, which is a very broad word, and designates, in the widest sense, the whole remedial work of Christ, from its inception (Luke xix. 10) to its fullest consummation in glory (1 Pet. i. 9), as may be seen by glancing over an English Concordance. The word "eternal" applies to it in its simple, ordinary sense. So De Wette: "eternal salvation; by all means is it so, continuing on in eternity, see Heb. vii. 25." Bengel: "it flows on for ever."

The phrase "eternal judgment" (κρίματος αἰωνίου, Heb. vi. 2) is claimed as a proof text; and Tholuck, with two or three others, is quoted as explaining it to be that "of which the *consequences* continue for ever." If this idea lay in the word "eternal," in this instance, it certainly would not go far to sustain its application *where there are no consequences* to continue, as in case of annihilation. But it is sheer confusion to force into the word *eternal* a meaning which is lodged only *in the other word* (κρίμα), judgment, retribution. This word "judgment" (κρίμα) is quite often used in the New Testament so as to include with the sentence *the punishment which it involves*. It can not be otherwise understood in Mark xii. 40 : "These shall receive greater damnation" (κρίμα), that is, clearly, condemnation to a severer punishment. This signification of the word is not only manifest in itself,—it is assigned to the word in Robinson's New Testament Lexicon, as a frequent meaning, of which, among others, the following are manifest instances: Luke xx. 47, xxiii. 40, xxiv. 20; Jas. iii. 1; Rev. xvii. 1, xviii. 20.* Thus in Mark xii. 40, Alexander properly translates κρίμα "righteous retribution," which, "in this case, of course means condemnation, judgment, or execution." Alford translates the same word, in Rom. xiii. 2, "punishment." Olshausen and Rückert (on Gal. v. 10) both defend this meaning as a frequent one. Bloomfield renders it "punishment" in the same passage. In the present passage, therefore, there is not the slightest evidence of any other meaning in the word αἰώνιος than eternal. Whether the κρίμα, or judgment, include the sentence and award of both the righteous and the wicked, or only of the latter, it is simply an "eternal retribution."

The phrase "eternal redemption" (Heb. ix. 12) does not offer support to any deflection of the word eternal from its ordinary meaning. Redemption (λύτρωσις) is defined in Robinson's Lexicon as "deliverance from sin and its consequences." This deliverance is, in the strictest sense, eternal. The grace of God, through Christ, will keep the believer for ever holy and for ever

---

* Robinson cites eight other instances, not quite so indubitable. Yet the careful Ellicott, while not accepting the meaning of punishment or condemnation as found in the word itself in some of these latter instances, adds (on Gal. v. 10), "The idea of punishment or condemnation is conveyed by and to be deduced from the *context*."

exempt from the punishment he deserves. "Eternally valid," says De Wette. "Eternal," says Bengel, "not for a day or a year only." Huther explains, "Of indestructible efficacy, in contrast to the offerings of the priests, which must be renewed each year." The deliverance is viewed as a permanent state, or if an act, then an act itself involving an efficacy and result: which efficacy is here described as eternal,— not 'final,' but enduring for ever. Whatever idea of *effect* is here involved lies obviously in the redemption, not in the word eternal. The force applied to the latter word is a needless confusion.

The case is similar with the phrase, "the blood of the everlasting covenant" (Heb. xiii. 20). The writers who adduce this as an instance of finality or eternity of effect would have us conceive of the "covenant" as comprising only a momentary or transient transaction, the mere act of arrangement; whereas, by a mental process as old and as constant as human speech, it comprises rather the contents of that covenant than the outward form of making it. We constantly say that such a treaty or compromise or truce lasted so many years or days; meaning, of course, not the process of making it, but things involved in it,— the peace or other terms covenanted by it. Precisely so here. The covenant is eternal; that is, the obligations (and blessings) included are never to be terminated or superseded. The explanation is as old as Theodoret, who says, "lest any one should suppose that this covenant will be terminated by another, he properly calls it endless, ἀτελεύτητον;" and Alford and Huther accept the exposition. De Wette says, "it is eternal, inasmuch as the deliverance (v. 9, ix. 12) and the inheritance (ix. 15) are eternal, and the kingdom of Christ (xii. 28) is enduring."

Another cited instance is Philem. 15: "For perhaps he therefore departed for a season that thou shouldest receive him forever" (αἰώνιον). All appearance of mere finality vanishes from the word when the English translation is conformed to the Greek, viz., "that thou shouldest *have* or possess him fully for ever.* Here the transient and uncertain ownership of a slave is contrasted with the eternal possession and enjoyment of "a brother beloved." Chrysostom's explanation, "not only in the present time, but also in that which is to come," or for ever, is adopted by DeWette, Meyer, Wiesinger [Olshausen]. "In this life, and in heaven," says Bengel.

One other New Testament phrase remains: "The everlasting gospel" (Rev. xiv. 6). It "certainly is not to be for ever preached," says Mr. Hudson. No; nor does the passage speak of the everlasting *preaching* of the gospel, but of the gospel itself, — its principles and truths. "Eternal truths of the gospel," is Stuart's explanation. "We have a commentary," says Hengstenberg, "in Matt. xxiv 35: 'Heaven and earth shall pass away, but my words shall not pass away.' God's Word, his threatenings and promises, are eternal and unchangeable, even as he himself is eternal and unchangeable, and because he is so." † Here is no other than the common meaning of eternal.

---

* "Have him for good," is Robinson's translation of ἀπέχῃς. "Possess him fully, entirely." Alford. The latter is the phraseology of Wiesinger, De Wette, Meyer.

† But for other procedures, we might be surprised to find Mr. Hudson,

Not a passage in the New Testament sustains the attempt to convert eternal into final. Equally unsuccessful is the appeal to "*equivalent*" instances in the Old Testament; that is, to cases where the adverb for ever (לָעַד) is employed in connection with a verb. Some of the instances at first seem plausible; but a closer examination shows that they are made up either of cases where there is an implied state or condition of things which is eternal, or of cases in which the finality is directly stated in the verb or noun, not in the word eternal. Instances of the first class are these: "Thou prevailest for ever against him;" i.e., with a superiority that lasts for ever. "Cast us not off for ever;" i.e., with a perpetual separation from thee. "Is his mercy clean gone for ever? doth his promise fail for evermore?" an everlasting withholding of mercy from the suffering. "So shall [should] I be delivered for ever from my judge;" a state of perpetual exemption from further inflictions of judgment. Instances of the second class: "Destructions are come to a perpetual end" [Hebrew, "to an end for ever"];* "It

---

without qualification, claiming Poole and Barnes on this passage, "as Poole and Barnes remark, it is so called for its blessed and eternal effects." Whereas Mr. Barnes remarks thus: "The gospel is here called eternal (*a*) because its great truths have always existed, or it is conformed to eternal truth; (*b*) because it will for ever remain unchanged, not being liable to fluctuation like the opinions held by men; (*c*) because its effects will be everlasting, in the redemption of the soul and the joys of heaven." All that Poole, in his annotations, says on the subject is this: "It is called the everlasting gospel, either with reference to the time past, as much as to say, the old gospel; or to the time to come, it being that doctrine of salvation besides which there neither is nor ever shall be revealed any other while this world endureth."

   * We waive any question of the true translation of this doubtful passage (Ps. ix. 6), and for the argument assume the English version to be right.

ceaseth for ever." Here the finality is contained and explicitly asserted in the words "end" and "ceaseth;" and the condition in which certain subjects are thereby placed is pronounced perpetual, viz.; in the one case a perpetual powerlessness to destroy (according to the most obvious interpretation); in the other, the soul's eternal inability of redemption. The dullest intellect can not fail to see the difference between an "*everlasting*" punishment, and a punishment "that comes to a perpetual end," or a punishment "that ceaseth for ever." Yet it is the aim of Mr. Hudson's laborious attempts to show that these utterly different expressions mean the same thing!

Several other passages are quoted: e.g., "They perish for ever" (Job iv. 20, etc.); "Thou hast put out their name for ever and ever" (Ps. ix. 5); "God shall likewise destroy thee for ever" (Ps. lii. 5). In these and other similar passages, the evident reference (as indicated in the context) is to a removal from this earth and its scenes. Thus in the last quoted passage, "God shall likewise destroy thee for ever: he shall take thee away and pluck thee out of thy dwelling-place, and root thee out of the land of the living." In all these instances, there is an express or implied allusion to the continuance of the scenes themselves, from which the party is to be eternally separated and separate; the same thought which is elsewhere often expressed (Ps. ciii. 16, etc.), "The place thereof shall know it no more." The idea of duration still lies in the word: it actually involves the continuance of one, if not both, of the objects thus related to each other.

It is true, an arrangement that is eternal is *also* final,

decisive, critical, ἀρρητος: yes, and it is solemn and momentous too, and must be joyous or sad, and a good many other things; but the *word* " eternal " does not mean all these. And the result of all the cases cited is, that no instance can be produced which can not be explained by the ordinary meaning of eternal, or which requires us to deprive the word of its fundamental notion of duration, infinite or indefinite.

(4.) Again: the attempt to change the meaning of eternal, so as to remove its ordinary signification of duration from all threat of punishment, breaks down on individual passages. In several instances, both forms of evasion, whether called finality or eternity of effect, are cut off as completely as is possible by the specification of a *process*, not of a result, and by statements that the process *goes on consecutively* for ever. In the passage already quoted (Rev. xiv. 11), the punishment is "*torment* for ever and ever," and " they have no rest day nor night." So also, in the same lake of fire in which all the wicked have their part, the devil, the beast, and the false prophet, are " tormented day and night for ever and ever " (Rev. xx. 10). No finality or eternity of effect can cover these statements. In Jude 6, the sinning angels are in perpetual *imprisonment*, " reserved in everlasting chains under darkness, unto the judgment of the great day ;" and, in verse 13, the same " blackness of darkness," apparently, is the doom of wicked men. In Mark iii. 29 (according to the amended reading), it is a state of eternal sin. Sometimes the endless duration of the infliction is described by language in which the word " eternal " does not occur. Thus in Matt. v. 25, 26, it is an imprisonment from which there is no deliverance till the utmost farthing is paid; and in Matt. xviii. 34, it is being "delivered to the tormentors till he should pay all that was due." And again, in Mark ix. 48, it is the fire that is not quenched, and the worm that never dies.* Many if not all these forms of statement are wholly incompatible with any other than the ordinary application of the words denoting eternity.

(5.) This attempt to find only finality in the terms describing future punishment is disproved by the nature of that punishment. As we have already shown at large, the New Testament constantly insists upon the woe of the doom, the anguish endured. As the punishment consists in suffering, there is not only no necessity, but no excuse, for the attempt to disturb the well-settled meaning of the language which ascribes to it positive duration in the same terms and connection in which eternal duration is ascribed to the blessedness of the righteous.

We may add, that this and all other attempts to evade the doctrine of eternal punishment by tampering with particular words and phrases is cut off by the consideration we are about to mention.

3. That the suffering of the wicked is eternal, is proved by the repeated declarations which describe it as co-existent and co-eternal with the blessedness of the righteous.

---

* Blain sagely remarks (and Hastings advances the same view), with small capitals, "It is the fire, not the sinner or his woe, that is said to be everlasting." So we suppose we are to understand that it is the "chains," and not the prisoner, who is to be everlasting (Jude 6); and in much the same way Mr. Hudson would teach that the "punishments" may be everlasting, but not the culprit.

(1.) It is described in general, as going on simultaneously. In Luke xiii. 24–30, the Saviour warns his hearers to "Strive to enter in at the strait gate," with the assurance that many will seek to enter in, and will not be able. He represents the master of the house as at length rising up, shutting the door, refusing them admittance. They "*begin* to stand without and to knock," and he bids them "*depart from me*, all ye workers of iniquity." Christ then proceeds to describe them as still viewing with anguish the joys of heaven from which they are excluded. "There shall be weeping, and gnashing of teeth, when ye shall see Abraham and Isaac and Jacob and all the prophets in the kingdom of God, and you yourselves thrust out."

The same representation, somewhat less minute, occurs in Matt. viii. 11, 12: "Many shall come from the east and west, and shall sit down with Abraham and Isaac and Jacob in the kingdom of heaven, but the children of the kingdom shall be cast out into [the] outer darkness; there shall be weeping, and gnashing of teeth." An important aspect of this threat is obscured in the common version (as we have before remarked) by so slight an omission as that of the article "the" in "the outer darkness." Both in this passage and in chap. xxii. 13, and xxv. 30, the original Greek designates it as "*the* outer darkness." Now, the shorter expression, "*outer* darkness," would resist the attempt to convert "darkness" into annihilation; inasmuch as it is darkness outer, or outside of the kingdom of heaven. But when it is spoken of as "*the* outer darkness," or the darkness without (τὸ σκότος τὸ ἐξώτερον), it can signify nothing else than the state of darkness and gloom which exists outside of that region of holy blessedness; and this meaning is further made certain by the explanation, in each of these passages, "there [in that place] shall be weeping, and gnashing of teeth." Here, again, the sitting-down with Abraham in the kingdom, and the weeping, and gnashing of teeth, in the state of outer darkness, are simultaneous; just as, in Luke xvi. 20, 25, the happiness in Abraham's bosom and the torment in hell are described as cotemporaneous.

In one of the passages just alluded to (Matt. xxv. 30), the representation is similar. When the lord of the kingdom reckons with his servants, the two faithful ones are welcomed with the invitation, "Enter thou into the joy of thy lord;" and the unprofitable servant is cast "into the outer darkness; there shall be weeping, and gnashing of teeth." The joy and the sorrow are clearly spoken of as co-existent conditions, in which the two parties were to dwell simultaneously; while the one enters into the joy of his lord, the other is in the outer darkness, where is weeping, and gnashing of teeth.

Perfectly clear and coincident with these texts is Rev. xxii. 14, 15: "Blessed are they that do his commandments, that they may have right to the tree of life, and may enter in through the gates into the city. For without are dogs and sorcerers and whoremongers and murderers and idolaters, and whosoever loveth and maketh a lie." Here the final condition of the impure and wicked is described as their being without, or outside of the heavenly city, within which the holy are admitted. It is the same state of exclusion from the heavenly kingdom which is elsewhere described as the outer darkness.

The same idea of *exclusion* is contained in the parable of the wise and the foolish virgins, in the same chapter. When the wise had entered with the bridegroom, "the door was shut." The foolish remain without.

Equally in point is Christ's representation (Matt. vii. 21-23) that the two alternatives, "in that day," are an entrance into the kingdom of heaven, or a separation from the presence of Christ: "Then will I profess unto them, I never knew you; Depart from me, ye that work iniquity."

In Matt. xxiv. 48-51, this separation is described as a companionship with hypocrites, and a participation in their woeful lot, — "shall appoint him his portion with the hypocrites; there shall be weeping, and gnashing of teeth." (The reader will observe that the same phrase, "to have a part or portion with one," is used in John xiii. 8, to describe the connection of believers with Christ, as sharing his destiny.)

The companionship in the state of exclusion and woe is still further indicated in Rev. xxi. 7, 8, where, on the one hand, "he that overcometh shall inherit all things, and I will be his God, and he shall be my son;" and on the other, "the fearful and unbelieving and the abominable and murderers and whoremongers and sorcerers and idolaters and all liars *shall have their part* in the lake which burneth with fire and brimstone" — the place of "torment." Here the same phrase describes participation in woe, which in the previous chapter describes the participation of the holy in the well-being of the first resurrection: "Blessed and holy is he that hath part in the first resurrection."

The Scripture thus plainly describes a condition of separation hereafter from Christ and the holy, of exclusion from the joys of heaven, and companionship with the wicked in their woes, which exists and continues while the holy are in heaven.

(2.) The punishment of the wicked is described as co-eternal with the well-being of the righteous.

In Matt. xxv., the co-eternity of the two destinies is twice implied or asserted. First, in his address, the Judge (verses 34, 41) says to the righteous, "Come, ye blessed of my Father, inherit the kingdom prepared for you from the foundation of the world," — that kingdom which is everywhere described as an "everlasting kingdom," — and to the wicked, "Depart from me, ye cursed, into everlasting fire prepared for the devil and his angels." The two parties enter at the same time on two opposite destinies, — the one of which is universally declared eternal (though here it is only implied); and the other, the punishment of the wicked, is, in express terms, pronounced "everlasting." Secondly, in the conclusion of the narrative, both destinies are alike described as states or conditions on which the two parties simultaneously enter, and both are alike pronounced eternal: "And these shall go away into everlasting punishment; but the righteous, into life eternal." Let three points in this passage be noted: (1) that no more in the one case than in the other is the retribution a transient act or process *to* which ($\pi\rho\acute{o}s$) the parties go, but a something *into* which ($\epsilon\acute{i}s$) they both enter *alike;* *
(2) that no more in the one case than in the other have

---

* "Go away into," says Blain, innocently, p. 77, "adds darkness to the text." He would read "go away *to.*"

we a right to depart from the true meaning of eternal (αἰώνιον), as designating everlasting continuance; (3) that the repeated application of the term, in the same connection, to the punishment of the wicked, as well as its use side by side with its application to the happiness of the righteous, gives it an emphasis which no sophistry can evade.

In Rev. xiv. 10, the torment of the wicked, which in the following verse (11th) is declared to proceed day and night for ever and ever, is asserted to take place in the presence (i.e. in the sight) of the holy angels and the Lamb: "And he shall be tormented with fire and brimstone in the presence of the holy angels, and in the presence of the Lamb." The word translated "in the presence of" (ἐνώπιον) is very frequently used in the New Testament to signify simply "in sight of," and is here so translated by Alford, Hengstenberg, Stuart, Huther, and others, sustained by Luke xvi. 23, ff.* The final separation between the righteous and the wicked, which the Scripture everywhere insists upon, manifestly requires this translation here. Still, the phraseology of the received version would be equally apposite to the argument. In either case, the holy angels, and the Lamb in heaven, are represented as spectators of the incessant and eternal punishment of the wicked. The two eternal conditions proceed cotemporaneously.

Dan. xii. 2 also describes in the same utterance the "life" of the righteous and the "shame" of the wicked, by the same epithet "everlasting." It can not with-

---

* Stuart finds the additional thought, that it is with their approbation.

out violence be understood otherwise than as declaring them to be equally, and in the same sense, everlasting.

The passage, 2 Thess. i. 7–11, involves the same view. Here the general statement (verses 6, 7), that God will recompense to the one class " tribulation," and to the other " rest," is followed by the particular assertion (verse 7), that this shall take place when the Lord Jesus shall be revealed from heaven with his mighty angels; at which time the one class " shall be punished with everlasting destruction from [away from] the presence of God and the glory of his power," and at the same time he shall " be glorified in his saints." Some have indeed held that the word " from " ($\dot{\alpha}\pi\acute{o}$) simply denotes the source from which the punishment proceeds. But this thought has already been fully set forth in verses 7 and 8: " The Lord Jesus revealed in flaming fire taking vengeance; " and, on this interpretation, the 9th verse would be a mere repetition without the slightest addition, except the eternity of the punishment. For this good reason, Alford, Bloomfield, Lünemann, and many other able interpreters (Beza, Schott, Koppe, Michaelis, Piscator, Schmidt, Krause), maintain the meaning " away from," " separate from." In any case, the *eternity* of the punishment is strongly set forth as a retribution commencing side by side with the rest and glory of the righteous.

CHAPTER VIII.

TENDENCIES AND AFFINITIES OF THE SYSTEM OF ANNIHILATION.

WE have now considered the system which teaches the annihilation of the wicked, and, we trust, have refuted it. We have shown negatively that its arguments are baseless, and positively that the Scriptures abundantly contradict it.

Light is often cast upon a system by observing its effect upon its adherents. The present system is too recent, and too limited in its acceptation, to show its full moral bearing. Many of its advocates, moreover, are professedly religious men, who have been led to its adoption, no doubt, by their shrinking from the severity of the Scripture doctrine. In such hands, the moral drift of the doctrine may be slow in showing itself. So was it with Universalism in the hands of John Murray; so with Unitarianism in the days of Channing and Worcester; but both these systems have their history.

Let the present system find its way into general acceptance, let bad men but have the additional encouragement of a doctrine that closes their responsibility, and the result is not difficult to foresee. Bad men have always had a hankering after the doctrine. When they could not persuade themselves of the future happiness of the wicked, they have most earnestly coveted annihilation as the next best gift. It is well known what use the ancient Epicureans made of their denial of immortality. *Ede, lude, bibe,* was the maxim, — "eat, drink, and be merry." We know also how those reckless men who once filled Paris with debauchery and blood inscribed over the entrance of all the public cemeteries, "Death is an eternal sleep." We have Paul's own commentary on the moral result of a denial of the resurrection: "If the dead rise not, let us eat and drink; for to-morrow we die." *

Even Mr. Hastings, one of the ablest advocates of the annihilation of the wicked, enters his solemn protest against the doctrine of no resurrection for the wicked, on the ground of its moral effects. "The results of that opinion [in France] are matter of history; and, though the idea of a resurrection of the just to life and glory changes essentially the fate of the believer, it makes little difference with the prospects of the ungodly. A mother, after her youthful daughter had been associated with a preacher who taught this doctrine, told me how *they* drew inferences of impunity in sin and security in impenitence which *they* could mention and act upon, though *he* might not be affected by them. I myself have been met with the same objection when I have sought to warn unconverted men to repent, and turn to God; 'if we die, and that is the last of us, it is no great loss.'" † If such is the moral influence of the doctrine of no resurrection, what must

---

* 1 Cor. xv. 32: "This connection of the clauses is the one maintained by Bengel, Meyer, De Wette, Alford, and others.

† Retribution, p. 155.

be the effect of the doctrine of resurrection only to annihilation? What is the essential difference? The testimony is important from such a source.

We might well hope, that, in the midst of a Christian community, these results of open vice would be slow to show themselves; perhaps would never appear. More likely, the chief influence would be a recklessness of the restraints of religion.

But there are certain tendencies and affinities of the whole system which do very distinctly betray themselves thus early in the writings of its advocates.

1. Rationalism: a tendency to disparage the authority and override the teachings of God's Word. Foremost in this respect, both in objectionableness and in adroitness, stands Mr. Hudson. It lies in his writings, not in gross and offensive, but in guarded and yet determined forms. His first and larger volume (Debt and Grace) is an attempt to *settle* the whole question on purely rational grounds. There is a brief examination of Scripture, necessitated by the nature of the case, occupying one-seventh of the volume. But the conclusion is established before reaching the Scriptures; and established on such principles as would give them no opportunity to testify against him, or as would seemingly *question their authority, and join the skeptic, if they did*. What is the true meaning of such passages as the following in his preliminary argument? He is speaking of the influence of the belief of eternal suffering on " the victim of abused power " in this world, who, he affirms, " can hardly know what faith is."

" Tell him of an eternity in which men of the most opposite conditions in this life may, in various degrees, suffer together, and that will not give him faith. As for himself, he feels sure that his present sufferings can not be the beginning of endless pains. Persuade him thus, and, however good you may say God is, your theology will be to him a divine despotism, and his faith is prostrate." *

Again : " Better no God than an evil God. Hence every theology which imposes evil as an eternal necessity,† or introduces it as a divine plan, tends to the denial of the moral quality of sin and of a personal divine Being. Total darkness is preferred to the baleful light. Better no sun frowning with lurid glare, than that the green earth, with myriads of people, should be scorched with deathless heat. A law of Nature, an impersonal and unthinking God, inextricably enveloped in the folds of matter, and only to be discovered as the no-God, would be the most grateful religion to such a woe-worn world.

" But men are not wont to rest in the doctrine of eternal evil, until it is proven past all gainsaying ; and the belief of a personal God is almost as natural as the disbelief of eternal evil. Hence the assertion of eternal suffering as a revealed doctrine tends not so directly to atheism, as to a rejection of the Bible for some form of deism. Of this skepticism, the Earl of Shaftesbury, the eloquent defender of the doctrine of divine providence, is an example. . . .

" It will not do here to say that skeptics are bad men, rejecting the Scriptures not so much because they are

---

* Debt and Grace, p. 62.
† " The doctrine of eternal sin and misery, as the result of evil in time, logically involves the eternal necessity of evil." p. 27.

supposed to reveal an *eternal* punishment, as because they do teach a *future* punishment. True it is that fallen man dislikes a God of justice. But when Christians overlook the difference between finite and infinite punishment, or rather between infinite loss and endless pain, they may, instead of removing a stumbling-block, only give new occasion of offense. Thinking men are loth to hear of a God who can not punish at all, but he must punish eternally." *

We fail to comprehend the bearing of these declarations, if they do not mean very emphatically to say that it is better to discard a revelation than to receive one containing the hated doctrine; and that nothing can or ought to make men submit to receive it. To the same purport is cited, as part of the argument, though not formally indorsed in word, a lengthened quotation, justifying John Foster in doubting that doctrine, though admitting that the Word of God is formidably strong against him. It begins: "If John Foster, or any man, deliberately and honestly conceive it irreconcilable with infinite love that God should condemn the wicked to everlasting punishment, we see not how he can accept the fact without blasphemy. If a man's reason, gazing earnestly and reverently, with lively consciousness of its own faint and glimmering vision, and full of thoughts of the compass and weight of infinite love guiding infinite power, is yet unable, we say, not to justify, but to believe in, the possible justice of eternal torments, we see not how he can accept the doctrine." † Here the reader will perceive the naked position, that no testimony, not even of God,

---
* Debt and Grace, p. 64.   † Debt and Grace, p. 56.

can bind a man to accept *the fact,* against his own judgment of what infinite love requires,—a sentiment that loses none of its rationalism nor objectionableness, though cited from such an author as Bayne.*

In the same tone, Mr. Hudson informs us, page 157, "that there can be no triumph of faith, if evil is unconquerable; and it is unconquerable if its extirpation would impair the welfare of the world, or bedim the glory of God." And, on page 157, we learn, that, "if our doctrine of evil be true, *it gives us a valid* THEISM."

The author's attention having been called by one of his reviewers to the insignificant place occupied by the scriptural discussion in his larger work,† he issued the smaller volume, entitled "Christ our Life." The opening sentence of this volume is highly significant. It reads thus, the Italics being ours : —

"The present essay is an enlarged form of a single chapter of a previous work, and is designed to meet the convenience *of those who rely for their views of future life upon the reading and interpretation of the Scriptures.*" ‡

The closing paragraph of the preface opens with the following significant hint : —

"For the reasons thus indicated, the writer doubts if an exclusively Scriptural argument will prove satisfactory to very many, however clearly it may appear to be made out." §

---

* The bold citation, however, does not present Bayne's full view of the case, nor do him justice.
† See preface to Christ our Life, p. 1.
‡ Ib. p. 3. § Ib. p. 4.

In this latter volume, when the author arrives at the troublesome texts of the Apocalypse, he prepares the way by a page and a half of statements affecting the canonical claims of the book. Of course, he professes, as always, to be above taking any advantage of the fact: "We say at the outset, that we are not going to deny the canonical character of the Apocalypse." Yet in the next sentence the motive leaks out: "But when a reviewer, as cited above, page 71, plants a chief corner-stone of argument in that book, it is proper that the reader should know the facts of which biblical critics are generally aware."* Yet Mr. Hudson reaches an important conclusion, — that the Apocalypse is one of the disputed books, and should not "be alleged as affording alone sufficient proof of any doctrine." And, lest this *caveat* should be ineffectual, he makes the additional suggestion : " Yet, if any one fears there must be a loose or a strained interpretation of the Scriptures somewhere, the Apocalypse is the book of all others which forbids a rigid interpretation." † Of course, with such a preparation, it is easy to make the phrase,

---

* Christ our Life, p. 136.

† Christ our Life, pp. 137, 138. It is entirely unsuitable to enter at large on the question of authorship within these limits; a question that occupies 60 pages of Davidson's Introduction. And it seems to us little less than criminal to throw out doubts for controversial purposes in the futile style of Mr. Hudson's allusions, where the subject is neither argued nor even intelligently presented. We merely say that the historical or traditional evidence is decided in favor of the authorship by John the Apostle: the only doubts raised have been founded on the style and contents. Such men as Davidson and Alford are satisfied. Alford, while admitting some difficulties in the style, not fully accounted for, yet speaks thus of the external evidence: " It is of the highest and most satisfactory kind. It was unanimous in very early times. It came from those who knew and had heard the apostle himself. *It only begins to be impugned by those who had doctrinal*

"tormented day and night for ever," describe "utter and irreversible destruction [annihilation] in a dramatic form."

Mr. Hudson has himself borne important testimony to the determined mode in which many of his coadjutors ride over the Scriptures. In speaking of those annihilationists who deny that the spirit is an immaterial substance, he admits that their theory involves the difficulty of making the wicked wholly die twice, and of teaching a second execution of the penalty of the law. And he adds, "This difficulty, with another to be named hereafter, *has led many to deny that the 'resurrection of the unjust' signifies their being made alive.*" *

Ellis and Read are still more outspoken. "We have elsewhere shown that the Scriptures teach plainly, unequivocally, repeatedly, and in the most forcible and varied language, that the fearful doom of the impenitent sinner is death, in the sense of privation of life, extinction of being; and therefore *there is no amount of the clearest testimony which could possibly teach the opposite doctrine.* It might indeed teach, were it to be found, that all the testimony was contradictory and unworthy of credit; and, teaching yea and nay of the same doctrine, *we might be fully justified in rending our Bibles to pieces, and scattering them to the winds of heaven, as unworthy of the slightest regard.* But, blessed be God, the Scriptures do not teach yea and

---

objections to the book. The doubt was taken up by more reasonable men on internal and critical grounds. But no real substantive counter claimant was ever produced."— Alford's Gr. Test. Prolegomena to the Apoc. § 117.

* Debt and Grace, p. 247.

nay of the same doctrine."* The spirit and meaning of the above remarks (the first portion of the Italics being so indicated by the author) are not mitigated by the assumption of the last sentence.

Mr. Blain is not behind his compeers: "When all other reasons fail to make this doctrine look consistent, it is said, 'We must believe what we can not comprehend.' This argument is consistent where God's moral character is not involved, as in the belief of his omnipresence, creating power, etc.; but *it is sin to believe a doctrine which impeaches his attributes.* While some other revealed doctrines are above our reason, none contradict it, *none injure his moral character, but this.*" † It is unnecessary to take advantage of the inadvertent admission that this is a revealed doctrine. Enough that the writer precludes all testimony on the subject by the distinct assertion, that this doctrine is so repugnant to God's moral character, that it would be a sin to believe it.

Mr. Hastings is equally decided: "The doctrine of eternal anguish and torture of the lost is in itself so utterly opposed to our natural conceptions of God, as revealed in the Bible, that it staggers the faith of the most devout; *how, then, can it be received by the unbelieving?*" ‡

Mr. Burnham remarks, in terms worthy of Theodore Parker, "The doctrine of eternal torment represents our loving God as an implacable tyrant." Again: after an enumeration of particulars which he declares to be involved in the doctrine, he inquires: "Is it possi-

---

* Bible vs. Tradition, p. 175.   † Death not Life, p. 116.
‡ Pauline Theology, p. 76.

ble that any human being can practically believe such a horrible collection of revolting absurdities to be the truth sent us by a loving and merciful God?"*

The tendency of these and many more like utterances is plain. The question is a question of *fact:* What will God do with the wicked? These writers declare the doctrine to be so incredible, that a communication purporting to come from God himself can not prove it. Indeed, as already intimated, a very considerable portion of the sect have taken the advance step of denying *any resurrection* of the wicked, in direct contradiction of Christ and of Paul.

2. A second tendency of these writers is a marked sympathy with and concession to the Universalist and the infidel.

We do not refer to the methods of dealing with Scripture texts, although the level of Blain's and Ellis and Read's exposition is certainly lower than the average of Universalist interpretation, and not a few even of Mr. Hudson's modes remind us, for magnanimity, of Hosea Ballou, sen., and of Thomas Whittemore.

We refer to the general modes of argument, the positions taken in regard to doctrine, expressions of sympathy for Universalists and infidels, and open declarations that they have the best of the argument as against the common theology, and that even they are justifiable in rejecting a volume which should contain such a doctrine as the majority of Christians in all ages have held to be in the Bible.

(1.) General methods of argument employed by the

---

* Anti-eternal Torment, p. 8.

two classes are substantially the same. There is the same dogged and invincible repudiation of a teaching which certainly lies on the face of the Bible, loading it with epithets of scorn and malignity.

Thus Mr. Hudson, as we have seen (page 338), calls it "a divine despotism." And on page 50 of his Debt and Grace, after a quotation from Dr. Cheever, setting forth in somewhat vivid terms the death which follows sin, he inquires, "What more could the adversary do or desire if he were God?" Mr. Burnham calls the God who is author of the doctrine, "an implacable tyrant." Ellis and Read speak of the teaching as "this most horrible doctrine, which is so derogatory to the character of God, and conflicts so terribly with every principle of justice and humanity which God has implanted in the human mind."* Mr. Blain calls it "the horrid doctrine of endless torment," "the slander of the Almighty." † He declares, that to show God to be "just and good" is impossible for all those "who hold to endless suffering for a failure *in the short and poor probation man has on earth;*" also that the reasons given to justify the doctrine "all outrage reason and common sense;" ‡ and, as we have seen, that "it is a sin to believe a doctrine which impeaches God's moral character," as this doctrine does. Much more of this kind of language and reasoning is found in this writer. Mr. Hastings, after pronouncing it a doctrine "which staggers the faith of the most devout," and inquiring, "how, then, can it be received by the unbeliev-

---

* Bible vs. Tradition, p. 276.
† Death not Life, preface, vii–ix.
‡ Death not Life, preface, p. iv, and p. 116.

ing?" proceeds to call it "the most terrific blasphemy, the most audacious and unmitigated libel, ever uttered against a God of love."* Then follow two pages in the old Universalist or rather skeptical strain:—

"Can it be possible, that while the Lord was passing by on Sinai, and thus proclaiming his goodness, there were, somewhere in the caverns of hell, thousands and thousands of wretched beings lifting their eyes in hopeless and never-ending anguish? . . . God loved the world; he gave his Son to die for them: and while darkness gathered over the land, while the earth shook and the rocks rent, while Jesus bowed and died, a token of God's good-will to man, can it be true that unnumbered myriads of spirits were lost, were wailing, and blaspheming God," etc.

The interpretation which finds the doctrine in the Bible, is, according to Mr. Hastings, a "false and horrible interpretation."

This method of appeal, not always nor often in such intemperate language, constitutes a very considerable staple in the annihilationist's argument. Indeed, its inherent incredibility, as cruel and derogatory to God, forms, under whatever disguises, the whole drift and strength of the system. Even the respectable and cautious Dobney drops such open statements as the following:—

"I thank God, who righteously requires the *love* of

---

* This utterance is not relieved by the faint admission preceding: "We say, first decide from the Bible whether the doctrine of eternal torment be true, and then, if we find no such thing is there taught, reject and oppose it as the most terrific blasphemy," etc. For the whole strain of argument before and after is, that such a thing *can not be* believed concerning a God of love; and he indorses the language which he ascribes to Bishop Newton, "Imagine it you may, but you can never seriously believe it." — p. 76.

my whole heart, that, in his blessed revelation, there is nothing akin to what I find in human books to make my religion one of terror rather than of reverent affection; reversing the apostle's declaration, and making perfect horror to cast out love.

"Speaking in the belief that the popular doctrine is not taught in Scripture, I do not hesitate to affirm, that any thing more perfectly adapted to harden men's hearts against God, and hinder them from beginning to think aright of him, could not have been contrived." *

Open scoffers at the Bible have said few fiercer things of its teachings. This style of argument is familiar to them, and has been one of their standing methods.

(2.) Not less significant are the numerous direct concessions to the Universalist and the infidel, which abound in the advocates of annihilation. They constantly admit that Universalists and infidels have the advantage on this subject, and are not blameworthy for rejecting such a doctrine at whatever cost.

Mr. Storrs writes as follows: "I am glad in my heart if I can approach one step toward Universalists without sacrificing truth: for I hope thereby to gain some, and save them alive, by removing out of their hands their main argument for universal salvation; viz., that 'the idea of the eternal consciousness of innumerable human beings in indescribable torments is irreconcilable with the perfections of God, and that, therefore, all will be saved.' The hearer, seeing no other view of the subject but eternal sin and suffering, or Universalism, takes hold of the latter. Every one who has had any thing to do with Universalists knows that this is

---

* Dobney on Future Punishment, pp. 133, 158.

their main fort, and here it is they always wish to meet their opposers; and their converts are made more from the exhibition of the horribleness of the punishment which their opposers say is to be inflicted on the wicked than any other and all other arguments they use." *

Again : " To talk of a soul always dying and never dead, or of a death that never dies, is such an absurdity, that I wonder how it was ever believed by any man who thinks for himself. A doctrine that involves such a palpable contradiction is not to be promulgated for truth, unless we wish to bring discredit upon revelation itself; and I can not divest myself of the conviction which I have so often expressed, that the theory I oppose has driven many thinking men into infidelity." †

Says Mr. Hastings, " Hence many minds reject revelation entirely, because it teaches, as they suppose, a doctrine so utterly repugnant to common sense and Divine Goodness. . . . We urge in justification of our course, that the doctrine of eternal torture of wicked men does contradict the apprehension, the experience, and the reasoning of mankind ; and, God helping us, we will, by a diligent and faithful examination of the original records, dismiss it from the Christian system, thus taking away both the scoff and the stumbling-block of the infidel and the rationalist." ‡

Mr. Blain is very full and varied in his expressions to the same effect. In his preface (page 8), he lays down this sweeping proposition for the benefit of the whole class of skeptics : " It is a sad fact, too, that more *millions* of Universalists, and, what is far worse, of infi-

---

* Six Sermons, p. 118. † Six Sermons, p. 119.
‡ Pauline Theology, pp. 76, 77.

dels, deists, and atheists, have been made by the popular doctrine than of real saints. The church, too, has been crowded with stony-ground hearers by it." On page 21, he informs us of one of his motives in advocating his system. After a quotation from Saurin, that "this threatening is a mortal poison, diffusing itself into every period of life, and making life itself bitter" to the wicked, Mr. Blain remarks, "I wish to remove such bitterness." On the next page (22d), he gives his vote for the Universalists as against the "Orthodox:" "The fact is, and Universalists see it, if the wicked are immortal, their doctrine is true." On page 70, he lays down the proposition, "that orthodox churches on this subject are equal to the Catholics, and much worse than the Universalists, in quoting a few isolated texts, and neglecting to examine their connections." One chapter of his book (pp. 104-111) is devoted to a deliberate attempt to show, that, in the argument between Universalism and Orthodoxy, the former has greatly the advantage; in which the following passages, sufficiently brief for quotation, show the drift of the whole:—

"A Universalist tract is in circulation, containing a hundred texts for their views. I have examined them, and find some fifty, which, when combined, afford much stronger proof for the restoration of all men than do the texts for endless woe when combined in like manner."* "The fact is plain to all who investigate as the greatness of the subject demands, that if all men are immortal, and these texts are figurative [i.e., the texts on which annihilationists rely], restorationists

---

* Death not Life, p. 105.

have the truth."* "The Church of God, while aiming to do good and save men, by erring, has wronged the Universalists — has made them such — has persecuted them for errors into which she had driven them. . . . It is slander to charge them, as many do, with throwing away the Bible (some are led to it) as an ultimate guide: they generally reverence it as the grand charter of their hopes for a future world. In this we agree. We owe them a vast debt, and should make sacrifices to pay it." †

Mr. Dobney declares, "Would we seek the *rationale* of infidelity, it might to a considerable extent be found in this, that religious men, having for the most part misapprehended the truth of Scripture on this point, have unconsciously, and with the best intentions, presented the God of revelation in such a light, that his creatures whom he would fain have addressed through them, and won to himself, have been scared at the terrific aspect." ‡ "And right joyous are we to throw down this buttress of infidelity which Orthodoxy has assisted to build, and to compel the unhappy opposer of Christianity to an unwonted silence, while the majestic voice is heard from the everlasting throne, 'Are not my ways just and equal, saith the Lord." §

3. Another affinity of the system already rapidly developing is materialism. We might have anticipated that a disposition so strongly marked, to materialize the utterances of the Bible, would naturally issue in a doctrine of materialism. But it is not necessary to draw inferences. Facts are already at hand.

---

* Death not Life, p. 107.   † Ib., p. 109.
‡ Future Punishment, p. 258.   § Ib., p. 278.

Mr. Storrs openly repudiates not merely the fact, but the conceivableness, of spiritual existence as distinct from matter: "If it is said [of the soul] it is a spiritual substance, I ask what kind of substance is that, if it is not matter? *I can not conceive, and I do not see how it is possible to conceive, of substance without matter* in some form, it may be exceedingly refined. I regard the phrase 'immaterial' as one which properly belong to *things which are not;* a sound without sense or meaning; a mere cloak to hide the nakedness of the theory of an immortal soul in man." [*]

Ellis and Read are very copious in the same direction. Their joint volume argues two main propositions, of which the first (covering 120 pages of discussion) is thus laid down: "First, We shall prove from the Bible the *corporeal being* and mortality of the soul, and the nature of the spirit of man; which spirit, not *being a living entity*, is neither mortal nor immortal." [†] Distinguishing the soul from the spirit (as indicated in the above extract), they proceed to say that the one is simply corporeal, nay, is the corporeal being; the other a kind of chemical or electrical agent that gives it activity. The gist of their dissertation on the soul is fairly given in the following brief but decisive extracts: "We say the true meaning of soul is a creature that lives by breathing." [‡] "Words can not make it more plain than do these texts, that the whole man is a soul, and *is corporeal*." [§] "A soul, in Scripture phraseology, means an animal or creature or life; a breathing creature, originally designed to live by

---

[*] Six Sermons, p. 29. [†] Bible vs. Tradition, p. 13.
[‡] Ib., p. 15. [§] Ib., p. 18.

breathing, whether such creature be living or dead." *
"A dead body is a dead soul, and a dead soul is a dead
body."† But does not some higher doctrine emerge in
connection with the spirit? No: the spirit is nothing
but the principle of bodily life. It is the same in animals as in men, and the superiority of men is due only
to their superior organization. The following extracts
fairly represent the doctrine. In answer to the question, "What is spirit?" these writers say it "primarily
signifies wind, air, breath; but it is sometimes used to
signify a principle having some relation to electricity,
diffused through the atmosphere, which is the principle
that stimulates the organs of men and plants into activity, and which is used by the animals themselves to
control their motions." ‡ "The resurrected Saviour
and the angels are tangible beings." § "This principle of life or spirit is not the air nor the breath, but is
contained in the air and the breath. . . . Life, then, is
not an abstract principle, but is an effect of this spirit
operating alike upon all organized beings. . . . Man
has no abstract essence within him which gives to him
any pre-eminence over the living souls of other animals. They all live, yea, the souls of all live, in common, by breathing the breath of life, because this
breath contains the spirit, the sustaining principle of
all lives. Man's superiority is derived from his superior organization." ‖ "The spirit of man, then, is not a
living entity; and, though no creature can live without
it, it is not alive itself." ¶ Ellis and Read, on page 108,
recapitulate their positions thus: "That [the spirit of

---

* Bible vs. Tradition, p. 32. † Id., p. 80. ‡ Ib., p. 84.
§ Ib., p. 85.   ‖ Ib., p. 86.   ¶ Ib., p. 87.

man] is primarily a principle of life contained in the breath; secondly, that the container is put for the contained, that it is the breath; thirdly, that as none of the results of animal life can take place without the animating principle, so the various tempers and faculties of mind are called spirit. But, spirit though it be, the cause of life is not life itself; and, although a subtle agent, it can not manifest any of the powers of life in an abstracted state. But, with the spirit, an organized breathing frame is enabled by God to manifest the energies of life. It is therefore the *flesh that lives:* the *body lives*, and the spirit does not live at all." * " We hope that enough has been said to convince every man that man has no spirit that can have a separate conscious existence." † " So we argue, that as the body without the spirit is dead, so the spirit without the body is dead also." ‡

The chief difficulty is to arrest our quotations; page after page being filled with such gross utterances, and they professedly founded on the Scriptures.

Mr. Blain is equally emphatic. He ridicules the preachers who have raised against him the cry of materialism, and " repeated the old story, that man has a soul, or spirit, which is a simple substance, indivisible, immaterial, uncompounded, and, so, indestructible. I ask, Why undertake to describe what they know nothing about, and of which all other men are equally ignorant?" § " Surely we have not come in contact with the substance of a so-called soul, any more than with men in the moon. It seems to me that the crucible

---

* Bible vs. Tradition, p. 109. † Ib., p. 112. ‡ Ib., p. 113.
§ Death not Life, p. 33.

by which men try the quality or essence of the soul must be something like what they say the soul itself is, — immaterial, not tangible to the five senses, nor yet to our mental vision: I have never seen the thing." * "The Bible tells us plainly that man and beast are made of the same material, 'dust,' and that both have the 'same breath;'" that they both die alike: but mark, a resurrection is not told for both." † "The fact is, the existence of a spirit, or soul, as an entity within us, is only inferred from a few uncertain texts, which can be easily explained another way; while numerous plain texts and the sense of the Bible are against it. Where does the book of Nature or the book of God tell what soul or man is made of, except in the earth-wide and heaven-broad declaration, 'Dust thou art?' Echo answers, 'Where?'" ‡

Mr. Hudson is constrained to admit § that "the prevalence of a materialist philosophy has frequently attended the doctrine" which he maintains; and, while he distinctly disavows and opposes that view, he also deems it necessary to make the following *quasi* apology for it: "We freely grant, nay, in behalf of materialists whose piety and devoutness is unquestionable, we insist, that speculative materialism is not to be for itself condemned." ‖ Perhaps not: what is there to be condemned "*of itself*," except the intents of the heart? But is not a practical materialism so openly gross as we have indicated above to be condemned both for its causes and its pernicious tendencies? When religious teachers professing Christianity publicly pro-

---

* Death not Life, p. 36. † Ib., p. 39. ‡ Ib., p. 42.
§ Debt and Grace, p. 243. ‖ Ib., p. 246.

claim that a man differs from a brute only in " his superior organization," and that the end of a man and the end of a brute are precisely alike, is there nothing to be condemned in such a doctrine? When men deny the conceivableness of "substance without matter," and even go so far as to aver that when the Scripture says, " God is a Spirit," and the like expressions, " the nature of God is not clearly determined by any of these expressions," * is there nothing to be condemned in it? and when, pushed by the emergencies of their own system, they go so far as deliberately to deny the resurrection of the unjust, what are the merit and meaning and influence of such a system?

Yet this is apparently the popular form of the doctrine. The book of Ellis and Read had long ago reached its sixth edition, and the circulation of Storrs's Six Sermons was claimed at twenty-five thousand copies (though mostly gratuitous) in 1855. Mr. Hastings deprecates the rapid spread of the view which denies any resurrection to the wicked, and Mr. Hudson cautiously implies the fact. The adherents of the doctrine in the North-west, so far as we have been informed, hold it mostly in this shape. We, indeed, have no doubt that this result is only a natural growth of the system; that the low and gross modes of interpretation on which the whole system rests will naturally end in this view. But no matter for our theory: such is the sad fact.

4. A fourth tendency of this system is to sensualism. We have not had opportunity to gather up, nor has there been time to develop, the fruits of this

---

* Ellis and Read, p. 86.

tendency: too many adherents of the system were trained among the sanctities of evangelical truth and life. But what is there to prevent a doctrine of rewards as gross as that of punishments? Why should they who talk of a literal grinding to powder, and burning to ashes, and recognize no other soul or spirit than the life of the body, stop short of a kind of Mohammedan paradise? Why are they not in a state of readiness to receive a heavenly city of literal gold and precious stones, with streams and trees and luscious fruits, and feasting with Abraham, and drinking new wine with the Saviour in his kingdom? Why not even extract the doctrine of "free-love" in heaven out of Matt. xxii. 30, especially as Mr. Hudson could easily furnish many German and some English opinions to prove that a literal fornication between the angels and human females is taught in Gen. vi. 2, and Jude 6, 7?

Accordingly, we learn that already this influence is unfolding itself. A writer in The *Independent* of Aug. 10, 1865 (Rev. Pharcellus Church, D.D.), informs us that he has encountered the doctrine in this gross form, except the "free-love" element: "In a remote settlement of the West" (in the State of Michigan), he found a body of men who hold that "the wicked are annihilated, their bodies being literally burnt up in the fires of the final conflagration, and becoming ashes under the feet of the righteous." They have gone backward so far in their Judaizing and materializing as to take Saturday for the sacred day. Their religion "is wholly materialistic," and "heaven is reduced to a scene of material delights. These people have their camp-meetings, continuing them for days or weeks; and the fervor with which they sing, pray, exhort, and preach, about the trees, brooks, animals, and various delectations of their material heaven, and of the conflagration and resurrection with which it is to be introduced, is most inspiring and seductive to an imaginative auditory."

All this is a legitimate result, and will only show itself more openly and abundantly as it spreads, if it does spread, among the masses.

"By their fruit ye shall know them." Men of practical sense and clear intelligence — the common mind — will judge of such influences as these. They may be puzzled on questions of interpretation; possibly they may, by artful sophistry, become befogged on some very plain passages of the Bible: but they can read the significance of such facts as have been presented in this chapter. When religionists openly assail certain documents or statements of fact as too horrible to be believed, nay, so incredible that men are justified in discarding the Bible if they be found there; when they openly range themselves in this discussion on the side of the Universalist and the infidel, not only employing their favorite arguments, but expressing sympathy with them as much-abused classes of individuals, and even siding with them as having clearly the best of the argument as against orthodoxy; when a great body of them push their interpretation down to the grossest form of materialism, deny to man any other spirit than the breath of the body, declare that he differs from the brute only in having a superior organization, and that he dies, and turns to dust, just like the brute,—plain men can read the fruit and the character of such a system.

And, if such be the tendencies so speedily developed, what shall be the results in due time? Hitherto the doctrine has been advocated chiefly by men of Christian education and evangelical sympathies,—men who will never lose the power of those early influences. Let it pass slowly but surely into other hands; let it pervade any considerable body of men and women, removed from all surrounding restraints; and we venture to say, sustained by the history of Epicureanism and of French Revolutionism, as well as by the apostolic warning (1 Cor. xv. 32) and the whole drift of corrupt humanity, that there will at last be found in that community such a fountain of materialism and sensualism as will carry large numbers, if not the mass, down to the habits of the beasts whose destinies they claim: "Let us eat and drink; for to-morrow we die."

NOTES.

NOTE A.—Page 84.

EXTRACTS ON LIFE AND DEATH.

"Life and death," remarks Umbreit, "are set over against one another in the Old Testament as well as the New Testament: the one as including all good that can befall us; the other, all evil," p. 246; *Alford*, ii. p. 304.

Olshausen says (ii. 313), "The creature contemplated as in isolation from God is in θάνατος, *death*, and only has life in connection with God, the fountain of life." Again: more fully (p. 360), "With a deeply spiritual meaning, the Scripture, in general, ascribes true being to the creature only in connection with the origin of that being: where sin dissolves that connection, there death (θανατος) steps in (Gen. iii. 3); and hence he who lives in a state of sin is called dead (νεκρός). Accordingly, perdition (ἀπώλεια) is to be taken as the antithesis to life (ζωή), and equivalent to death. It does not denote an annihilation of substance; but the true idea of life (that of the spirit) requires consciousness, and that not of the senses merely, but a spiritual consciousness. This is wanting where there is a deprivation of spiritual life generally, and the animal or carnal man (ἄνθρωπος ψυχικός or σαρκικός) only vegetates; such a condition, therefore, is called the absence of life, or death. Now, the design of the advent of the Logos in the flesh was to pour life again into dead humanity from a living fountain, to restore the connection which has been destroyed. ... Without re-union to the fountain of life through faith, man remains in death."—*Philo de Profugis*, iv. 258; Ζωὴ μὲν αἰώνιος ἡ πρὸς τὸ ὂν καταφυγή, θάνατος δ' ὁ ἀπὸ τούτου δρασμός.; *Ols.* ii. 360.

Tholuck.—John iii. 36: "Here, indeed, eternal life is regarded as a present thing, as in v. 24, xvii. 3, then in its consummation as something future: that, nevertheless, the οὐκ ὄψεται presupposes an οὐχ ὁρᾷ, may be readily inferred from the antithesis μένει ἡ ὀργή. The condition of man without faith is a condition of ὀργή (Eph. ii. 9), and the correlative of it is misery, the θάνατος." Again, on Rom. v. 12: "The Scripture usage lays hold of the notions, life and death, in their innermost depths. Life is the unrestrained self-unfolding of a being according to its indwelling idea; where it takes place, there is harmony, and, on the subjective side, self-satisfaction, blessedness. Accordingly, also, biblical usage in reference to life and death includes next the notion of well-feeling and happiness (3 M. xviii. 5; 5 M. xxx. 15; Jer. xxi. 8; Prov. xi. 19; Sir. 15, 17, and in New Testament mostly with ethical reference, Matt. viii. 22; Luke x. 28, xv. 32; John v. 24; 1 John iii. 14; Jas. i. 15, etc.) But especially ζωή is emphatically used to designate self-satisfaction or bliss in the other world (Matt. vii. 14, xviii. 9; John iii. 36; Acts xi. 18, and here Rom. v. 18); and θάνατος to designate future misery,— the life that does not deserve the name (Rom. i. 32; 2 Cor. ii. 16, vii. 10; Jas. i. 15, v. 20). The life hereafter, attaining to the perfect self-development, is the ὄντως ζωή (1 Tim. vi. 19); and the completed death is, in the Apocalypse, named, with an emphasis already found in the Targums, the ὁ δεύτερος θάνατος. Even the word ἀποθανεῖν, Paul uses as a designation of the loss of the true life caused by the sins, in this world as well as in the future " (Rom. vii. 10, viii. 12).

Similarly, Alford. Thus on John vi. 51: "The death of the body is not reckoned as death, any more than the life of the body is reckoned as life." On John xi. 25, 26, he paraphrases: "Faith in me is the source of life, both here and hereafter; and those who have it have life, so that they shall never die; physical death being overlooked and disregarded, in comparison with that which is really and only *death*." Again, on 1 John v. 12: "The 'having the life' is the actually possessing it, not indeed in its most glorious development, but in all its reality and vitality." On 1 John iii. 15, "'Abideth in death,' in that realm of death in which all men are by nature. . . . The words have no reference to *future* death any further than as he who is and abides in death can but end in death." Lücke speaks to the same effect in briefer terms.

Meyer uses similar statements. Thus on John iii. 36: "Hath eternal life "— he *hath* eternal life, namely, the Messianic ζωή which in its true development is already a *present* possession of believers. At the Parousia it is completed and glorified."

De Wette (John v. 24) remarks on "hath eternal life," "has, possesses, not shall have. 'Shall not come into condemnation' is the same as 'shall not see death' (viii. 51). 'Has passed,' even in the act of believing; this perfect is to be held fast as such, as in iii. 18; 1 John iii. 14. 'From death,' from spiritual death."

These extracts might be extended almost indefinitely. The agreement of respectable expositors is unanimous. To miss this deep meaning of the Scripture terms is not to see the light of noon-day.

NOTE B.—Page 198.

Phil. i. 21-24.

Mr. Hudson makes some four or even five different and incompatible attempts on the passage. 1. He says that "the passage should be compared with the context. Paul had just said that Christ would be 'magnified in his body, whether by life or by death.' When he then adds, 'To live is Christ, and to die is gain,' he may signify the gain to the cause of Christ by the martyrdom which in his prison he now awaited." To which we answer (1) The passage given as "the context" is but one subordinate clause of the context. The full drift of the context is given above. (2) The Greek does not fairly admit the signification, "gain to the cause of Christ." The position of ἐμοὶ γὰρ (*for to me*) is such, that it stands related alike to both parts of the sentence; and its special emphasis confines the gain personally to the apostle—for *to me* to die is gain. So, very clearly, ver. 23. But Mr. Hudson abandons this for a second suggestion, that, 2, Paul may signify "his own greater reward in the resurrection." But the possibility of his referring merely to the distant resurrection is cut off by the subsequent alternative discussed already,—the interference of the joy he longed for with his further stay in the flesh. Not satisfied here, Mr. Hudson suggests, 3, "Moreover, such were his present afflictions, that any form of death would be a welcome release." But (1) the motive which Paul actually proceeds to unfold is not the desire to escape present trial, but the longing for Christ's presence; and (2) it is a libel on Paul to attribute to him as his governing motive, or as a burning desire, the *idea of shrinking* away from the trials of life. Precisely the contrary. For while he was always joyful in the thought of his crown (2 Tim. iv. 8), the eternal weight of glory (2 Cor. iv. 17), and the presence of Christ (2 Cor. v. 8), yet the thought of shrinking away from his trials is nowhere to be found. "We glory in tribulations" (Rom. v. 3). "None of these things move me" (Acts xx. 24). "I take pleasure in infirmities, in reproaches, in necessities, in persecutions, in distresses, for Christ's sake" (2 Cor. xii. 10). Not choosing to rest on either of these positions, Mr. Hudson abandons them for a fourth, which itself splits in two in the utterance. 4. "But there are some reasons for supposing that the phrase here rendered 'to depart' (εἰς τὸ ἀναλῦσαι) may signify 'to return,' or 'the release,' with special allusion to the coming-back of the dead from *hades*, of which the early Christians made so much." Without following this writer in all the weaknesses of his subsequent argument,* we may say, (1) that this attempt to refer the phrase to such a supposed well-known event as "the release," is equally weak as disingenuous, unless it can be shown (*a*) that such event, is well known to the *New Testament writers*, and (*b*) that this term is sometimes used by them to describe it; for neither of which can one particle of evidence be adduced. (2) The writer gives two entirely different translations, both of which he would use at the same time; neither of which will help him. Of these translations, (*a*) if we attempt to use the meaning "release," the verb ἀναλῦσαι is in that sense always active, requiring an object, and should here be translated "having a desire for releasing" some one else. But if we take it in a passive sense, "a desire for the release," i.e. *being released*, the verb should be passive, ἀναλυθῆναι. Furthermore it would still signify death, being released from this life; for it is of this life the apostle is speaking, not of *hades*. If (*b*) we take the meaning to "return" (which is undoubtedly one phase of departure which the word sometimes though not commonly designates), we render no aid to the doctrine of unconsciousness at death, but simply make the apostle assert the pre-existence of the soul in heaven; inasmuch as he is speaking only of two states or situations,—being in the flesh and being with Christ. If he is made to call his departure from this life to heaven a "return," of course he was in heaven before he came into the flesh.

Such are some of the unsatisfied and incompatible evasions by which it is attempted to break the plain meaning of this passage. We have been willing to follow them somewhat in detail, that the reader may see whether this is or is not handling the word of God deceitfully.

The whole case is simple: both the common meaning of the word, its scriptural usage, and the clear requisitions of the context. The word translated "depart" (ἀναλῦσαι) is a transitive verb, and means radically to loose, to unloose, 1, any thing connected, tangled, or knotted; hence to unbind fetters or free a captive; 2, any thing bound or made fast, or fixed; hence to dissolve or decompose, and hence also (as a naval or military term) to loose anchor, or break up camp,† and thus very com-

---

* E.g. The erroneous assertion that the Hebrew שׁוּב "always signifies to return," the attempt to magnify a manuscript variation in the Septuagint of Josh. xvii. 8, above the received and settled text.

† Like the Hebrew נסע, to pull up [tent-pins]; hence to depart generally (and the English break up, break away, cut loose, etc.).

monly *to depart* (the departure may or may not be a "return"); 3, something difficult, as to solve a problem. And the derived noun ἀνάλυσις in like manner means a loosing; 1, a loosing of the connected parts of a whole, decomposition, dissection, destruction; 2, a *breaking-up* or *departure*; 3, solution of a problem or difficulty.

In classic Greek, the meaning "departure" is one of the common meanings.

In the New Testament, the verb and noun occur but three times. (1) In 2 Tim. iv. 6, where it most clearly means departure: "I am now ready to be offered, and the time of my departure (ἀνάλυσις) is at hand;" uttered shortly before the apostle's decease. (2) In Luke xii. 36, where, though translated "return," it apparently means simply to "depart" or "break up" from the wedding (though in order to return, see Robinson's Lex.), as the actual return is expressed by the words immediately following, "that when he *cometh* and knocketh," etc. (3) In the present passage, where it stands in contrast with the preceding "live in the flesh," and the following, "abide in the flesh," and immediately connected with the phrase, "and be with the Lord," and means as translated, "to depart."

The Septuagint furnishes but twelve instances occurring in the Apocrypha (of which Mr. Hudson quotes but six), and among these "depart" is a leading meaning, e.g., Judith xiii. 1; 1 Esdras vii. 3 (twice); Mac. xii. 7. In several other instances, the same meaning is appropriate, although, as the departure actually was a return, there is no objection to using that word; e.g., Tobit ii. 9; Wis. ii. 1. In Mac. viii. 25, it reads literally, "Pursuing them for a considerable time, they broke up [the pursuit], being restrained by the hour; for it was [the day] before the Sabbath." In 2 Mac. ix. 1, "Antiochus broke up [or departed] in a disorderly manner from Persia." Ch. xv. 28: "And having come from the battle, and *departing* [or perhaps dispersing] with joy, they learned," etc. In three remaining passages, the meaning is different. In Wis. xvi. 14, it means probably to release;* in Sir. iii. 15 (in the passive voice), "thy sins shall be *forgiven*"(i. e. unloosed). In the passage before us, the connection before and after holds us inevitably to the

---

* In Wis. v. 12, the usage is peculiar, where we have not the active, but the passive voice: "As when an arrow is shot at a mark, the air, being cut, immediately (εἰς ἑαυτὸν ἀνελύθη) is let loose upon itself," or better, "is dissolved into itself." To translate here simply "returns," overlooks the passive voice of the verb and the poetic force of the expression. These are all the instances of the Septuagint, which the reader can examine at his leisure. They show sufficiently the real meaning of the word.

present translation. It is one of a series of contrasted phrases, parallel to and explanatory of each other. It is (in ver. 20) "life" or "death;" ver. 21, "to live" or "to die;" ver. 22, "to live in the flesh;" ver. 22, 23, the strait betwixt the two, "to depart, and to be with Christ," or "to abide in the flesh;" and ver. 25, the assurance that "I shall abide and continue with you all." The reader of the original will also observe a connection which is not and can not easily be given in the translation. The two verbs ἀναλῦσαι and εἶναι are both gathered under one article so as to make them parts of the same transaction; literally "having a desire for the [act of] departing and being with Christ."

The language and connection abundantly indicate the received translation, and the received view of this passage. And the forced and contradictory explanations of those who impugn it speak for themselves.

NOTE C. — Page 223

HADES.

Many unsupported assertions have been made on the meaning and uses of this word in the New Testament. A sort of heathen mythology has been forced upon the sacred writers. Even in Robinson's New Testament Lexicon, *hades* is first defined according to the Greek mythology, and the writer proceeds: "The Hebrew *sheol* (שְׁאוֹל) signified, in like manner, the under-world, and was held to be a vast subterranean palace, full of thickest darkness, where dwelt the shades of the dead; but no distinction of place is indicated in the *sheol* of the Old Testament between the righteous and the wicked. For the Hebrew שְׁאוֹל, the Seventy have almost everywhere put ᾅδης; and, in accordance with this usage, the idea of *sheol* is found among the later Jews, more developed, and assimilated to the Greek *hades*. The souls of the righteous and the wicked were held to be separated; the former inhabiting the region of the blessed, the inferior paradise, or Eden of the Rabbins; while lower down was the abyss called *gehenna* or *tartarus*, in which the souls of the wicked are in torment. In the New Testament, ᾅδης is represented as a dreary prison with gates and bars; also the keys of *hades*," etc.

The reader will perceive that this statement is shaped mainly in accordance with the views of heathen and Rabbins. Common as it has become, we believe it to be unwarranted and unscriptural. The gates and keys of *hades* are no more to be taken literally than the "keys of the kingdom of heaven." As to any vast subterranean place, the common abode of good and evil "shades," or partitioned off into a higher and lower place, paradise and *gehenna*, — the interpretation seems to us worthy of the Rabbins to whom it refers for authority. The reader will find an article containing some good suggestions on the subject in the "Bibliotheca Sacra," vol. xiii. pp. 155, seq., by Prof. N. H. Griffin.

We will barely indicate what seems to us the true view. The etymology of the Hebrew שְׁאוֹל is doubtful: that of *hades* (ᾅδης, *a* privative, and ἰδεῖν, the unseen, invisible) corresponds apparently to the general idea indicated in the New Testament; the vague notion, not uncommon with us, of the invisible world. This is the radical notion of *sheol* or *hades* in both the Old Testament and the New, with one additional aspect, presently to be indicated. Still, according to the special conception connected with it in the speaker's thought, it may have a modifying color, as the mere state of the dead, or even the grave, as the land of silence to us, as the place of rest for the suffering good, or, especially, of terror to the evil-doers.

Accordingly, inasmuch as the whole race are sinners, and as death, the separation of soul and body, is the fruit of sin; so this one additional notion seems throughout the Bible to cling to *hades*, the invisible world or spirit-land, — that it is a place of terror to the natural man, and even to the regenerate man, except as that terror is overcome by Christ. It is sometimes personified as one of the great enemies of the race, and of Christ's ransomed and but partly sanctified followers. Here, then, we find the full but simple Scripture idea of *sheol* and *hades*: it is the state of the dead or the *invisible world* in general, but viewed *as a foe or object of terror* to man, even to the regenerate man partly sanctified. Though not in itself designating absolutely any thing more than the state after death, and sometimes even looking no farther than the grave, its coloring is that of aversion, and not of desire. It is the designation of a region of dread. Accordingly, it is so used uniformly, we think, in the Old Testament, and still more distinctly in the New. At the same time, we find, as we might expect, a much greater definiteness in the New Testament notion; so that, as Fairbairn has shown (" Hermeneutical Manual," p. 292, etc., Edinburgh ed.), the *sheol* of the older Scriptures is not the equivalent of the later *hades*.

In the New Testament, with whatever varieties of usage, *hades* always denotes that which is an object of dread; something evil, the antithesis of heaven, the enemy of Christ and his kingdom, the terror of man, and also of the regenerate, imperfect believer; a terror overcome only by Christ. Thus, Matt. xi. 23; Luke x. 15: "Thou, Capernaum, which art exalted unto heaven, shalt be brought down to hell" (*hades*). Here it is the opposite of heaven, and involves a terrific threat. Again, Matt.

xvi. 18: "On this rock, I will build my church; and the gates of hell shall not prevail against it." Here (apparently as the gathering-place of the wicked) it sums up the whole host of the enemies of Christ's kingdom. In the passage under discussion (Luke xvi. 18), it is the place of torment. In Acts ii. 27, 31, quoted from the Old Testament, "Thou wilt not leave my soul in hell" (*hades*), if it indicates somewhat more vaguely the state of the dead, it is still as an antagonist to Christ and his work. (Abandon, or give over *to hades*, is the form of the Hebrew original, Ps. xvi. 10.) In 1 Cor. xv. 55, "O death, where is thy sting? O grave,* where is thy victory?" it is the enemy and terror of fallen man. In Rev. i. 18: "I am he that liveth, and was dead; and behold I am alive for evermore, amen, and have the keys of death and hell" (*hades*); the same idea of victory over this terror to his children is somewhat clear. In Rev. vi. 8, where death rides on the pale horse, and hell (*hades*) followed with him, *hades*, though personified, is still the most terrible of foes. And finally, in the passage (Rev. xx. 13, 14) where "death and hell" (*hades*) delivered up the dead in them, and then "death and hell," and "whosoever was not found written in the book of life," were cast into the lake of fire, no difficulties of interpretation can hide the fact that *hades* is personified as one of the chief foes of Christ's kingdom. These are all the passages in the New Testament in which *hades* occurs, and they fully sustain our position.

NOTE D. — Page 241.

DANIEL XII. 2.

The method of Mr. Hudson with this passage is characteristic, and deserves a moment's attention as a specimen of his procedures. It will illustrate his way of marshaling a series of objections on which he dares not insist; of grasping at all possible stray help, and of straining his authorities. It is as follows: —

"It is thought by good critics that the prophet here speaks only of the resurrection of the righteous, called the 'first resurrection' in Rev. xx. 5; and that the passage should read, 'these [who awake] to everlasting life, and those [who do not awake] to shame and everlasting contempt.' This would agree with the Syriac version: 'some to death, and the eternal contempt of their companions.'

---

* But in the corrected text of Lachmann and Tischendorf, sustained by most of the older manuscripts ᾅδη is here displaced by θάνατε.

"But we are willing to take the passage as making no distinction between the first and the second resurrection. We need, then, only to correct the frequent dislocation by which the 'shame' as well as the 'contempt' is made everlasting. Though even on this we need not insist; for the word 'shame' can not refer to the feelings of the lost. The Hebrew (דְרָאוֹן) is used only here and in Isa. lxvi. 24 (Eng. 'an abhorring') where, says Dr. Wintle, it denotes 'a kind of spectacle, show, or nausea,' and is translated 'nausea' by Buxtorf in his concordance. The allusion seems to be to the putrefaction of death. The 'contempt,' if it expresses a feeling of the righteous, is farther described in such passages as Mal. iv. 3; Matt. xiii. 40–43; 2 Pet. ii. 9–12; Ps. xcii. 7; on which last passage Hengstenberg remarks perhaps too carelessly, 'The annihilation of the wicked comes into notice as the basis of the deliverance of the righteous, which is the proper theme of the psalm.'"

On this we remark, 1. Who these "*good* critics" are Mr. Hudson does not inform us. We think the best of them will be found to be Prof. Bush; the same good critic who learned to find *no* resurrection of the body at all in the Bible.

2. The attempted reading simply (1) interpolates something in the passage of which not a hint is found in the original. The reader will see that the prophet says not a word of any class " who do not awake : " he only declares that many *shall awake*, and divides *the awakened* into two classes; (2) makes the passage comprise two unfinished clauses,—clauses that contain no assertion, thus: many "shall awake; those who awake to everlasting life, and those who do not awake to shame and everlasting contempt"—what of them? The reader will perceive that nothing is asserted of them, there is no declaration, unless by interpolating more words, such as "are ordained unto," or the like; so as to read "those who do not awake [are ordained unto] shame and everlasting contempt." This double interpolation is certainly a laborious way of evading a very straightforward declaration.

3. The Syriac version does not "agree" with this procedure; for the Syriac version includes both classes among *the awakened*, as the reader will see by careful attention even to the quotation. The speciousness of Mr. Hudson's statement rests wholly on the reader's understanding the word *death* (*interitum*) in the unwarranted sense of annihilation.

4. It is hardly safe to "insist" that the shame is not, as well as the contempt, everlasting. "Shame," no doubt, means substantially reproach or disgrace (rather than the feelings of the lost). But the strict translation would change the connecting "and" into "to,"—"some to disgrace, to contempt everlasting." The second clause is thus a fuller

unfolding of the first, and no violence is therefore done by understanding the passage in nearly the common mode. It is a disgrace or shame, an abhorrence, which is everlasting.

5. Mr. Hudson seems to say that the *word* translated "contempt" (and not the *application* of it in Isa. lxvi. 24) is an allusion "to the putrefaction of death." The structure of his sentences justifies and requires that mode of understanding him. But the reader should be advised, that the *word* contains no such reference whatever : it means by general consent, "an abhorrence," or an object of abhorrence.

6. It is a worthy climax of this piece of exegetical legerdemain when Hengstenberg is cited so as to leave the impression (not removed by the phrase, "perhaps too carelessly") that he teaches Mr. Hudson's doctrine. We think no man will venture openly to claim Hengstenberg as an annihilationist. Undoubtedly he uses the word "annihilation" (*vernichtung*) in a popular way, as we use it in reference to a party or an army thoroughly routed and overwhelmed. The use made by Mr. Hudson of this passage is a good illustration of the methods of his system.

NOTE E. — Page 258.

REV. XX. 10.

The author of "Debt and Grace," in his subsequent work, "Christ our Life,"* finds it necessary to make a more earnest attempt on Rev. xx. 10. He opens with the cool announcement : "We think the argument for the eternal misery of all finally impenitent men and women is reduced to this single passage." The reader, of course, is prepared to find that a writer who concedes to his adversaries only such a standing-point as this solitary text will easily see that this text also teaches an "utter and irreparable destruction," i.e. annihilation. In the outset, however, he admits that the passage is against him. "Let us inquire *whether the passage shall annul* all the apparent reasons we have discovered for immortality through Christ alone, and, seated on a throne of symbols *shall overrule* the obvious sense of hundreds of other passages ; or may it be fairly interpreted in accordance with those reasons and that obvious sense ?" i.e. with the sense which has been exposed and refuted in the preceding pages of this volume.

The process consists in turning away from that portion of the verse which is *perfectly full and explicit*, and endeavoring to put such a con-

---

* P. 145, *seq.*

struction on certain other more indefinite phrases as may break down the meaning of the more express. We can not follow all the windings of the effort. Mr. Hudson, as usual, is too wary to trust to the individual strength of his arguments; and he accumulates a large number of suggestions, such as they are, some of which, as usual, he would be willing to waive. This constitutes one chief difficulty of following or answering him.

1. His first point is, that the "lake of fire and brimstone" must of necessity mean "a proper destruction" [annihilation], notwithstanding the explicit statement of the verse itself that it is the place of torment for ever and ever. He even appeals to Rev. xiv. 10, as an instance of "fire and brimstone" denoting "destruction," in defiance of the plainest assertion of the verse, "He shall be *tormented* with fire and brimstone," and the explanation following, "and the smoke of their *torment* ascendeth up for ever and ever, and they *have no rest day nor night.*" He also appeals to Rev. xxi. 8, "Shall *have their part* in the lake which burneth with fire and brimstone," as though it were for him rather than against him. Paying no attention to the statement (Rev. xix. 20), "these both were *cast alive* into a lake of fire burning with brimstone," and the most positive designation of the flames of hell (Luke xvi. 24) as the means of protracted torment, not of extinction, he innocently asks, "Why should the same terms be used just once denoting torment without destruction?"

2. He says that "we have just seen that four symbolical powers are cast into the same lake of fire, and come to an end. Two of them are by name associated with Satan. All that is said of him is said of them." Hence he must come to an end. We answer, 1. The fact is not conceded. The long array of quotations adduced by Mr. Hudson in support of his view is vitiated by his inveterate habit of interpreting "destruction," etc., in such quotations in the sense of annihilation; also by his artfully assuming that the "annihilation of their *power*" (quoted from S. Scott and DeWette), and their "eternal removal" (Düsterdieck), is the annihilation of them. Some of the parties quoted, however, agree with him. But the point is not conceded by us. See Note O. 2. If a symbolical power, an abstraction, itself dissolves, passes away, when its function is finally arrested, how lame the inference that an actual concrete existence thus ceases to be! and, furthermore, when we are definitely informed that his confinement in the place of punishment (the abyss) leaves his activity unimpaired.

3. It is positively alleged that Satan is not immortal. Two texts are cited: "The seed of the woman shall" *crush* "the serpent's head,"

where the same word is also used of the woman's heel (Gen. iii. 15), the same Hebrew word which the living Job employs where he says, "He *breaketh* me with a tempest" (Job. ix. 17); and the wholly irrelevant passage in Dan. vii. 11. In this same connection, the author of " Christ our Life," somewhat directly contradicts the author of "Debt and Grace." The latter had said (p. 215), " the words in Heb. ii. 14, and 1 John iii. 8, express indeed the dispossession of Satan *rather than his final destruction*. The former says (p. 146), " The dispossession of the adversary, and the destroying of his works (Heb. ii. 14; 1 John iii. 8), indicate *any thing rather than the perpetuity* of that which Satanic malice would most desire."

4. The author endeavors to connect with this passage verse 9 of the same chapter, where a "large class of the ungodly [on earth] is said to be *devoured* by fire coming down out of heaven." Here Prof. Stuart is quoted as saying that it "denotes utter excision." Now we will pause just to ask, whether, by this citation, Mr. Hudson means to make the impression that Stuart held that the Bible teaches the *annihilation* of any portion of the wicked ? If not, why does he quote him in this connection ? If he does, can he be ignorant that he is making the grossest of misrepresentations ? After a similar citation from Daubuz (" utterly destroyed them "), and a similarly ambiguous one from the Targum of Jonathan, through Dr. Gill, Mr. Hudson comes to the conclusion, that " the *whole force of the passage,* compared with ver. 14, 15, goes to involve Satan in the same doom," i.e. annihilation. This is what it is to be " fairly interpreted ! "

Thus far, however, the process is like that of a skillful juggler, who, by side feints, diverts attention from the real fact. It has consisted in keeping out of sight the actual statement in question, "tormented day and night for ever and ever." Now it becomes necessary to notice it. Accordingly, " not as his own view, but to meet the views of others," Mr. Hudson suggests, that the whole transaction in question may not be a part of the final judgment, but may so long precede it, that the phrase, " for ever and ever " may apply to the interval ! Not satisfied with this, he tries again.

5. " If the phrase [for ever and ever] were insisted on as denoting an absolute eternity, it might denote eternity of effect." No, it can not; it expressly describes eternity of continuous process — "tormented day and night for ever and ever." Still unsatisfied, he tries yet once more.

6. " But if the phrase ' day and night ' be taken to denote the continuation of torment, and this absolutely for ever and ever, here are two things assumed which cannot be proven. 1. That the 'ages of ages'

must be God's own future eternity. 2. That the phrase 'day and night' does not limit the import of the following phrase."

To which we answer 1. (*a*) The man who denies that the strongest expression for absolute eternity has its legitimate meaning, is the man who must make good his own assertion. (*b*) The phrase *is* the phrase which in this same book of Revelation is used *ten times* of God's own [and Christ's] future eternity," glory and praise (i. 6, 18; iv. 9, 10; v. 13, 14; vii. 12; x. 6; xi. 15; xv. 7), — once of the future glory of the righteous (xxii. 5), and three other times only (of which this is one); and in each of those three remaining cases it is used of the punishment of transgressors (xiv. 11; xix. 3; xx. 10). It requires, therefore, a good degree of hardihood to deny, that, in the present instance, the phrase denotes an absolute eternity. 2. That the phrase "day and night," while it does "qualify," does not "limit" the following phrase, is evident (*a*) from the common meaning of the phrase in the Scriptures, which is *incessantly* or *constantly*, as already shown page 256, and as appears xii. 10; and (*b*) from the fact, that, in this book of Revelation, the same phrase is applied to the worship of heaven (iv. 8.)

Apparently aware that these positions of his are untenable, Mr. Hudson resorts to the usual course of seeming to waive them for a final attempt to break down the settled, constant meaning of the word "torment" (βασανίζω). As the question is vital to him, and a failure here is total, it may be well to give his argument in full.

" Yet even granting these assumptions [in regard to the meaning of 'for ever and ever'] the dramatic use of the word 'torment,' specially suitable to the symbolic character of the book, is too well supported by other passages to allow its literal sense against all other Scripture. See Job x. 21, 22, as cited above, and Ezek. xxxii. 24, 25, 30, where, in the Septuagint, this very word βάσανος is applied to the state of death. So in Wis. iii. 1 : 'The souls of the just are in the hands of God, and torment may not touch them;' where the context shows that the 'torment' is death. And Ecclus. xxi. 10, 11 : 'The congregation of sinners is like tow heaped together, and the end of them is a flame of fire. The way of sinners is made plain with stones; and in their end is hell and darkness and pains.' See also the extended drama in Isa. xiv. 9–20." *

Now let the reader turn back from this chaos, and ask what is the simple point at issue. This: Is the "*word* '*torment*'" (βασανίζω) and its correlates used in Scripture to denote a non-existent and unconscious condition; so that to be "tormented for ever and ever" can properly or

---

* Christ our Life, p. 148.

fairly mean to be deprived of all existence and feeling for ever and ever?

Let the reader also notice two preliminary points of confusion (to use a mild term) introduced by the author. 1. He speaks of the "dramatic use of the word 'torment,'" as the antithesis to "the literal sense." There is no such use of a *word*, except of certain terms like stage, act, scene, employed sometimes to designate certain matters connected with the drama, and thus having a dramatic *use*. No man will claim "torment" as being one of these terms. There is such a thing as dramatic composition,—a composition, poem, or play "accommodated to action :" to speak of a dramatic use of a *word*, except as above indicated, is to talk nonsense. The question is, has a word its primary or secondary, its literal or figurative (or pregnant), its ordinary or an extraordinary *sense:* in other words, does "torment" mean torment, or does it mean something else? 2. The author also says that this "dramatic use of the word 'torment' is too well supported by other passages to allow its literal sense against all other Scripture." Against all other Scripture! What is it that all other Scripture proves, — the "dramatic use of this word," or in general the unconscious state of the wicked after death? Probably the latter; but, in either case, the assumption is worthy of attention.

Now let us see what foundation Mr. Hudson finds in Scripture for his denial of the established meaning of the word "torment" ($\beta\alpha\sigma\alpha\nu i\zeta\omega$ and its derivatives). 1. He does not venture to cite a passage from the New Testament, although the verb ($\beta\alpha\sigma\alpha\nu i\zeta\omega$, torment) occurs eleven times besides the present passage; the noun ($\beta\acute{\alpha}\sigma\alpha\nu o\varsigma$, torment), three times; another derivative noun ($\beta\alpha\sigma\alpha\nu\iota\sigma\mu\acute{o}\varsigma$, torment or tormenting), five times; and the word "tormentor" ($\beta\alpha\sigma\alpha\nu\iota\sigma\tau\acute{\eta}\varsigma$) once. The New Testament usage, which is sufficiently abundant, gives him not a shadow of support. 2. In default of any aid from the New Testament, the author turns to the Septuagint version of the Old Testament and Apocrypha (completed two or three hundred years previously).

Mr. Hudson makes a show of citing four passages (two of them from the Apocrypha) to invalidate the established and received meaning of $\beta\acute{\alpha}\sigma\alpha\nu o\varsigma$, "torment." Only two of these passages cited, however, contain the word. Job x. 21, 22, does not contain it in any form; neither does Ecclesiasticus xxi. 10, 11. According to the common edition of the Septuagint* and King James's version, the close of verse 10 is as follows: "At the end thereof [of the way] is the pit of hell." The text as given by Mr. Hudson, however, would not even indicate a different

---

* Van Ess: Leipsic, 1855.

meaning of the word "torment,"—"In their end is hell, darkness, and pains." The citations, then, are reduced to two passages. One of these occurs Ezek. xxxii. 24 (repeated in ver. 25, 30), where the Septuagint differs from our version, reading (instead of "They have borne their shame with them that go down to the pit"), "They received their 'torment,' or suffering (βάσανον) with them that go down to the pit." There can be little doubt that the word was employed by the Septuagint translators in the ordinary sense of suffering or injury, as the Hebrew verb (כלם from which the noun כלמה shame) sometimes bears the general sense of injure, either in word or deed, like the Arabic word of the same form, which means *to wound*. Instead of Mr. Hudson's statement, that here the word βάσανος is applied to "the state of death," the only assertion which the text or context warrants is, that it is applied to the *experience of the dead or the dying;* and there is no reason whatever in the case to press the word aside from its usual meaning, as intended by the Septuagint translators, of suffering. The second and remaining instance cited is equally futile : " Wis. iii. 1, ' The souls of the just are in the hand of God, and torment may not touch them ; ' where the context shows that the torment is death." The context shows no such thing. It clearly means great suffering or "misery," in opposition to the actual happiness of the blessed, as the reader may see by reading the next few verses for himself. 2. "In the sight of the unwise they seemed to die, and their departure is taken for *misery*, " 3. "And their going from us to be utter destruction ; *but they are in peace.*" 4. "For though they be *punished in the sight of men* [a seeming suffering], yet is their hope full of immortality." 5. "And, having been *a little chastised*, they shall be greatly rewarded." 8. "They shall judge the nations, and have dominion over the people ; and their Lord shall reign forever," etc.

Mr. Hudson thus cites two cases to disprove the established meaning of βάσανος, which both fail him. If he had been more successful in finding isolated instances of a diverse meaning, how could it affect the meaning of the word in an instance where a continuous and protracted process is so clearly indicated ? — "tormented day and night for ever and ever." What methods will a Universalist and an annihilationist not resort to ?

NOTE F. — Page 288.

UNQUENCHABLE FIRE.

Blain, Hastings, and Hudson endeavor to derive much help from the passage in Eusebius containing the phrase πυρὶ ἀσβέστῳ. In his Ecclesiastical History, book vi. chap. 41, there occur the following sentences (Cruse's Translation): "Of these, the one immediately denied; but the other, named Cronion, surnamed Eunus, and the aged Julian himself, having confessed the Lord, were carried on camels throughout the whole city, a very large one you know; and in this elevation were scourged, and finally consumed in an immense fire (πυρὶ ἀσβέστῳ), surrounded by the thronging crowds of spectators. . . . After these, Epimachus and Alexander, who had continued for a long time in prison, enduring innumerable sufferings from the scourges and scrapers, were also destroyed in an immense fire, πυρὶ ἀσβέστῳ."

These three writers make very great account of this case, all of them committing the mistake of ascribing to Eusebius a term which he only quotes from Dionysius, bishop of Alexandria. Says Mr. Hudson, "How can our opponents hope for our conviction in this matter while they offer no explanation of Eusebius's use of the phrase in question, and do not even notice it? Thus not only Mr. Landis, but Prof. Hovey, who argues from the passage (Mark ix. 42, etc.), Dr. Post, Dr. Long, Prof. Barrows. Are not these writers aware of the passage in Eusebius? Let them show that he used the passage ignorantly or improperly, and we shall be so far better instructed. Do the words of Eusebius show a *usus loquendi*, or do they not?"

The answer is very easy. The words of Dionysius do not show a *usus loquendi*. The simple fact which appears throughout these quotations from Dionysius is, that he had a habit of making very free use of Scripture phraseology, both by direct quotation and by allusion; sometimes very "improperly." His adoption of Scripture phraseology is more abudant than his numerous direct citations, and often is strained to meet the case.

To show his frequent imitations of Scripture phraseology would require a careful examination of the Greek original. As instances, we find in a few lines (on page 245, Schwegler's edition), the phrases ἀπέδωκε τὸ πνεῦμα, ἀμέμπτως, λυθῇ (be forgiven), ἀπολύσατε (absolve); (on page 249), ἀναπαυσαμένου (deceased), ἀγαλλιῶνται, φιλαδελφία, δοξάζοντες, καθ᾽ ὑπερβολήν. In the opening of his narrative, we meet the apostolic phrase, "I speak before God, and he knows I lie not;" and in the immediate sequel, we are reminded of the Scripture by such phrases as the following, many of them quite noticeable: ἀναζήτησιν, ὑδοποιήσαντος, εὗρε τὸν οἶκον ἔρημον (Matt. xxiii. 38), οἰκονομίας, γάμους (in the plural), ἐπέστησαν (came suddenly upon), οἶδεν ὁ θεὸς (2 Cor. xi. 12, 31), γυμνὸς εν τῷ λινῷ ἐσθήματι (Mark xiv. 51), κοινωνοί μου καὶ μέτοχοι, δεισιδαιμονίαν, θρησκείαν, πιστὴν γυναῖκα, βδελυττομένην, ὁμοθυμαδὸν, ὡς ἐι δυνατὸν σκανδαλίσαι καὶ τοὺς ἐκλεκτούς, δισκόλως σωθήσονται, δεσμῶν καὶ φυλακῆς (Heb. xi. 36, etc.).

Clear instances of his misapplication or strained use of Scripture phraseology are the following: When the persecuting officer Frumentarius simply searches for him in the wrong places, Dionysius says, "He was *smitten with blindness*, not being able to find the house; for he could not believe that I would remain at home when persecuted."—Book vi. chapter 40. He justifies himself for adhering to certain decisions of previous bishops concerning heretics, by quoting "for thou shalt not remove, as it is said, the landmarks of thy neighbor, which thy fathers have placed."—Book vii. chapter 7. See his exaggerated use of Scripture allusions in his description of the state of things during a sedition at Alexandria: "It would be more easy for any one, I would not say to go beyond the limits of the province, but even to travel from east to west, than to go from Alexandria to Alexandria. For the very heart of the city is more desolate and impassable than that vast and trackless desert which the Israelites traversed in two generations; and our smooth and tranquil harbors have become like that sea which opened and arose like walls on both sides, enabled them to drive through, and in whose highway the Egyptians were overwhelmed. For often they appear like the Red Sea from the frequent slaughters committed in them; but the river which washes the city has sometimes appeared more dry than the parched desert, and more exhausting than that in which Israel was so overcome with thirst on their journey, that they exclaimed against Moses, and the water flowed for them from the broken rock, by the power of Him who alone doeth wondrous works. Sometimes, also, it has so overflowed, that it has inundated all the country round; the roads and fields seeming to threaten that flood of waters which happened in the days of Noah. It also flows always polluted with blood and slaughter, and the constant drowning of men, such as it formerly was when, before Pharaoh, it was changed into blood and putrid matter."—Book vii. chap. 21. Again, in the next chapter (22), in describing a pestilence which followed the sedition, he writes: "For as it is written respecting the first-born of Egypt, thus now also a great lamentation has arisen; for there is not a house in which there is not one dead."

Surely, a writer who uses Scripture in this loose way is but a poor reliance to prove the meaning of a Scripture phrase as against the Scripture usage itself. Such an appeal only betrays the weakness of the cause. Dionysius simply misuses the Scripture phrase.

Mr. Hudson is equally unfortunate in some of his other references, which he would seem not to have examined personally. He refers us in both his books to the phrase ἀσβέστη φλόξ, as found in the Iliad xiii. 169, 564. We do not find it in either passage; though we find the word ἀσβέστη in the first, but not in the second. The phrase does occur in xvii. 89, where Hector, darting about in his resplendent armor, is said to be "like the inextinguishable flame of Vulcan," — the flames which the Vulcan (Hephestus) of the mythology keeps perpetually burning beneath Mount Etna. It is also found in xvi. 123, and means strictly "inextinguishable flame;" the fire being personified as a power that is never wearied out like fighting warriors: "They cast tireless fire into the swift ship, its inextinguishable flame immediately pours along," etc. It would not have been to the purpose of Mr. Hudson to state the fact, that the word *asbestos* occurs quite often in the Iliad and Odyssey, and that the only meanings assigned to it in Crusius' Homeric Lexicon are "inextinguishable," "incessant," "unintermitted," "endless."

Again: he refers to Philo, i. 389 and ii. 254. Neither passage helps him: one of them is as strongly against him as language can be. It reads thus: "The law says, 'A fire shall be kept burning on the altar for ever unextinguished, πῦρ διὰ παντὸς ἄσβεστον; with great reason and propriety, I think; for since the graces of God are everlasting and unceasing and uninterrupted, which we now enjoy day and night, and since the symbol of gratitude is the sacred flame, it is fitting that it should be kindled, and that it should remain unextinguished for ever, ἀεὶ ἄσβεστος" (ii. 254). The other passage (i. 389) contains only the word ἄσβεστος in the hyperbolical and paradoxical statement, that the artificer (δημιουργὸς) of pleasure "takes the most shameful pains through life to corrupt the incorruptible, and to extinguish the remaining inextinguishable lights of nature." Here the paradox is evident; and the same petty principle that would take away from ἄσβεστα its meaning of "inextinguishable" would take from ἄφθαρτα its meaning "incorruptible."

A passage from Cicero is given as parallel, containing the phrase *ignis aeternus*, which means strictly the "perpetual fire." Cicero says (pro Fonteio, c. 17), "Take heed lest that perpetual fire kept by the nightly toils and vigils of Fonteio be said to be extinguished by the tears of your priestess."

The Anthology is quoted: "A fire is soon put out; but a woman is an inextinguishable fire "— where the words have their meaning as usual, only there is an extravagance in the declaration. It is the hyperbolic way of putting it, as Scott, on the other hand, calls woman "a ministering angel."

Has Mr. Hudson ever heard of the "fallacy of references"? To what purpose are citations so irrelevant? And, supposing there can be found occasional instances of improper or strained use of the word ἄσβεστος, what force have they against its proper and stated meaning, and that, too, in passages where the reiteration and the connection prove that it is deliberately and thoughtfully employed?

We have been willing to follow the futile efforts of this writer thus far. We will only add, that *a single passage of Hippolytus*, who lived a hundred years earlier than Eusebius, being in public life before the close of the second century, *most decisively settles the meaning* of πῦρ ἄσβεστος, as well as some related points. In speaking of the Pharisees, Hippolytus says (book ix. chap. 28), "These also hold the resurrection of the flesh, the immortality of the soul, a judgment to come, and a conflagration; and that the just will be incorruptible (ἀφθάρτους), but the unjust will be punished for ever in unquenchable fire (ἀδίκους δὲ εἰσαεὶ κολασθήσεσθαι ἐν πυρὶ ἀσβέστῳ)." Language could not be more explicit if written on purpose to cut off all cavil.

NOTE G. — Page 290.

THE MEANING OF κόλασις.

The verb κολάζω, and the derivative noun κόλασις, when applied to the treatment of offenders, convey the broad but simple notion of punishment, or the infliction of harm and suffering, in whatever way, upon body or mind, by blows, words, or outward condition. This is the signification which a careful analysis of the classic and the Alexandrian Greek alike sustains.

The word is said by lexicographers to have designated at first a pruning of trees, — examples being cited only from Theophrastus. (So also, *pain* and *punish*, according to them, came through the Latin from the Greek ποίνη, *quit-money;* and *vengeance* from *vindico, vim-dico*, to *assert a claim* in law).

From this primitive meaning, some annihilationists have endeavored to draw the signification "cutting-off," "excision," that is, annihilation. Two difficulties lie in the way; (1) In no instance does the word seem to have acquired that meaning; (2) it could not easily acquire it, since, as Mr. Hudson well remarks, "in pruning, the tree is not 'cut off,' only the branches."

The meaning of *restraint* is alleged as one of its significations, occasionally occurring. Here, however, this meaning will not help the cause of annihilation; nor, indeed, is this meaning sustained in connection with the treatment of offenders, in regard to whom it constantly signifies, as Mr. Hudson seems to admit, "punishment."

Is there a difference between κόλασις and τιμωρία? So says Aristotle (Rhet. i. 10, 17): the former is for the improvement of the offender, the latter for the vindication of law and justice. But this distinction evidently disappeared from common usage. It certainly is not kept up even in classic Greek, and does not appear in the Septuagint. The word κόλασις is often made synonymous with τιμωρία, often includes it, as we shall incidentally show. Nor would the distinction avail any thing for annihilationism.

Mr. Hudson accepts the meaning "punishment," as he must; but he adds, "The word by no means determines the *kind* of punishment." Certainly not the method, which may be various; but the *nature* of punishment, as infliction of pain, suffering, or harm, is constantly implied, and often directly expressed.

Thus, to take a specimen of classic Greek, the writer of which was born in apostolic times, Plutarch *De sera numinis vindicta*, we find that (1) κολάζω and its derivatives are the prevalent terms that express the sufferings of the wicked, occurring some forty or fifty times or more; (2) κόλασις is continually used interchangeably with τιμωρία, often in the same sentence (sections 9, 10, 11, 19, 24, 25); (3) its meaning is unfolded in such phrases as "undergoing terrible sufferings, and shameful and painful inflictions of vengeance τιμωρίας" (sect. 25), "bearing his own cross" (sect. 9), "having many fears, and hard experiences, and incessant cares and troubles," (ib.) being exercised "with sufferings and fears and apprehensions and anxieties (sect. 10), "shameful and distressing" (sect. 18), taking place through both "the person and condition" (sect. 24), and many other allusions to various forms of suffering; and (4) it is deliberately argued (sect. 11), that, if death were the end of suffering, it would be the end of punishment, τιμωρία; which is not the case.

If we turn back to the Septuagint, we find the same idea of inflicted suffering in whatever form. Thus, 1 Esdr. viii. 24 (a passage confounded by Mr. Hudson with Ezra vii. 26), the disobedient are to be punished, κολασθήσονται, "whether by death or other infliction, τιμωρίᾳ, or penalty of money, or imprisonment." In repeated instances, κολάζω is interchanged with βασανίζω. Thus Wis. xvi. 1 : " Therefore they were punished (ἐκολάσθησαν) worthily, and by the multitude of beasts tormented " (ἐβασανίσθησαν). The writer follows with the specification of various bodily and mental tortures. In Wis. xix. 4, κόλασιν is interchanged with βασάνοις; apparently iii. 1–4 ; clearly xi. 9, 10. In other passages, the word includes bodily and mental sufferings, such as thirst, tortures and terrors from wild beasts (Wis. iii. 11), injuries inflicted on enemies (1 Mac. vii. 7), and the woes visited upon the house of Israel for disobedience (Ezek. xviii. 30, "so iniquity shall not be your ruin," κόλασιν; see also xliv. 12). This last thought is taken up by the Septuagint in such wise, that when the Hebrews term their idols stumblingblocks (מִכְשׁוֹל), as the cause of sin and woe (*Rosenmüller*), the Septuagint translates by κόλασις (Ezek. xiv. 3, 4, 7).

The reader who may wish to examine all the passages in which the word occurs will find the following : Ezek. xiv. 3, 4, 7 ; xviii. 30 ; xliii. 12 ; xliv. 12 ; 1 Esdr. viii. 24 ; Wis. Sol. iii. 4 ; xi. 5, 9, 14, 17 ; xii. 15, 27 ; xiv. 10 ; xvi. 1, 2, 9, 24 ; xviii. 11, 22 ; xix. 4 ; 1 Mac. vii. 7 ; 2 Mac. vi. 14 ; iv. 38 ; 3 Mac. i. 3 ; vi. 3.

But, says Mr. Hudson, "The word by no means determines the *kind* of punishment. It may be torment, or it may put an end to torment (Wis. xix. 4). It may be banishment, confiscation of goods, or imprisonment (3 Esdr. vii. 27). In most of the passages, it is death. In one (Wis. iii. 1–4), it is the loss of immortality, or utter destruction, which seems also to be regarded as a 'torment;' and in another the destruction of an idol made of wood, in token of God's displeasure, is called punishment (Wis. xiv. 8–10). To say nothing of these remarkable instances, those in which the punishment designated is death show that the word does not necessarily denote torment." *

Here is the old juggle upon end, destruction, death,—all which are assumed to be extinction. The passage, Wis. xix. 4, does not pronounce the κόλασις to be a termination of torment, but its consummation or goal, "the fulfilling" of what "was wanting to their torments." The passage, Wis. iii. 1–4, does not declare the κόλασις to be "loss of immortality, or utter destruction," i.e. extinction. It simply says, that, in the eyes of men, the death of the pious seemed to be a calamity or misery (κάκωσις), and ruin (σύντριμμα) ; whereas they are "in peace," and "*no torment shall touch them.*" And both the passages thus cited seem clearly to imply that death itself only continues and completes the sufferings or "torments" of the wicked.

* Debt and Grace, p. 191.

If we turn to the apostolic fathers, the same notion of suffering inflicted seems always to attach itself to the word κόλασις. The word, we believe, does not occur in the epistle of Barnabas, but we have the phrase ὁδὸς᾽ θανάτου αἰωνίου μετὰ τιμωρίας, the path of eternal death with vengeance (sect. xx., ed. Dressel).

Clement (2d ep. ad Corinth, sect. vi.) makes αἰωνίου κολάσεως the antithesis of ἀνάπαυσιν, rest, and (sect. viii.) declares that none can deliver those appointed to be cast into the furnace of fire, and that, "after we have departed from this world, no longer can we then confess or repent." When he unfolds the future destiny of the righteous and the disobedient (sect. x., xi.), he declares that peace shall follow the one, while the other shall be wretched, ταλαίπωροι; and that men do not know "what torment (βάσανον) the pleasure of this world has, and what delight the coming promise."

Ignatius (ad Romanos, sect. v.) enumerates as the *sufferings* (κολάσεις) inflicted by the devil, "fire and the cross, conflicts with wild beasts, lacerations, fractures, dislocations of bones, amputation of limbs, and contusions of the whole body." It is the only instance in which we have found the word in his letters.

In the "Martyrium Ignatii" (written probably by his surviving companions), there occurs (sect. vii.) the phrase, "immortal (or deathless) death," θανάτῳ ἀθανάτῳ. In the "Martyrium Polycarpi," we are told that the martyred followers of Christ, "despising the torments of this world (βασάνων), by one hour's endurance escaped the eternal punishment, τὴν αἰώνιον κόλασιν. And the fire of their fierce tormentors seemed cool to them; for they had before their eyes the fire that is eternal, and never extinguished. . . . In like manner they endured terrible sufferings (κολάσεις), being condemned to wild beasts, and bound upon spiny shellfish (*murices*), and buffeted with various other tortures (βασάνοις), that, if possible, the tyrant might, by incessant suffering (κολάσεως), bring them to a denial of Christ." And again (sect. xi.): Polycarp is represented as replying, "You threaten me with the fire that burns for a season, and is soon extinguished; for you are ignorant of the fire of the future judgment, and of eternal punishment (κολάσεως), reserved for the wicked.

It is very evident that the writers of the classic, the Alexandrian, and patristic Greek were ignorant of any κόλασις that excluded the idea of suffering.

NOTE H.—Page 297.

GEHENNA.

After all that has been written upon the Greek word γεέννα (the later Jewish גֵּיהִנָּם), there exists a very common misconception regarding it,— the supposition that this composite word in the time of Christ had two meanings, a primary and usual meaning as the name of a valley south of Jerusalem, and an unusual and secondary or figurative meaning, denoting the place of future punishment. Thus Mr. Barnes, on Matt. v. 22: "The word *gehenna*, commonly translated 'hell,' is made up of two Hebrew words, and signifies the Valley of Hinnom. . . . It was called 'the *gehenna* of fire;' and was the image which *our Saviour* often employed to denote the future punishment of the wicked." And even Lange writes, "Originally גֵּי הִנֹּם, the Valley of Hinnom . . . King Josiah converted it into a place of abomination where dead bodies were thrown out and burnt (2 Kings xxiii. 10, 14). Hence *it served as a symbol* of condemnation, and of the abode of lost spirits."

From the statement of Mr. Barnes, the reader might infer that this use of the term to denote hell was a peculiarity of our Saviour; and from that of Lange, that it was not the proper meaning of the word, but rather a poetic conception.

But, first, this word was abundantly employed *by the Jews* to denote the place of future punishment. Says Lightfoot (Horæ Hebr. Works, vol. ii. p. 141), "The Jews do very usually express hell, or the place of the damned, by the word גֵּיהִנָּם, which might be shown by infinite examples." To the same effect Winer, RWB, vol. i. p. 492; Gesenius's Thesaurus, p. 281, etc. Even Alger ("Doctrine of a Future Life," p. 328) is obliged to write thus: "In some of the Targums or Chaldee paraphrases of the Hebrew Scriptures, especially in the Targum of Jonathan Ben Uzziel, we meet repeated applications of the word *gehenna* to signify a punishment by fire in the future state. *This is a fact about which there can be no question.* And to the documents showing such a usage of the word, the best scholars are pretty well agreed in assigning a date as early as the days of Christ. The evidence afforded by these Targums, together with the marked application of the term by Jesus himself, and the similar general use of it immediately after, both by Christians and Jews, render it not improbable that *gehenna* was known to the cotemporaries of the Saviour as the metaphorical name of hell." The word in this sense belongs, then, to the Targums as much as to the New Testament; is actually found in the Talmud as well as in the Church fathers; and was employed by the Rabbins no less than by the Saviour.

And, secondly, evidence is entirely wanting, so far as we can ascertain, that, at the time of Christ, the one word γέεννα, גֵּיהִנֹּם, was ever used in any other sense than to denote the place of future punishment. The change that had passed upon it was greater than that which transferred παράδεισος, from designating a garden (Gen. ii. 8, seq.) or a park (Neh. ii. 8), to signify heaven (Luke xxiii. 43) : for in the latter case the word remained unchanged in form, and its old meaning can still be found in Josephus (Antiq., vii. 14, 4 ; viii. 7, 3) ; but in the former case a change passes upon the form of the words, and the old meaning ceases to appear.

The Greek form γέεννα is not found in the Septuagint: the nearest and only approach to it is γαιέννα in Josh. xviii. 16. Twice it is γὲ Βενεννόμ (2 Chron. xxviii. 3 ; xxxiii. 6). In Jer. xix. 2, 6, the Hebrew is translated τὸ πολυάνδριον υἱοῦ Ἐννὸμ, and πολυάνδριον υἱῶν τῶν τέκνων αὐτῶν (the sepulcher of the son of Hinnom, the sepulcher of the sons of their children) ; and in all other passages, φάραγξ Ἐννὸμ Valley of Hinnom (Josh. xv. 8, twice) or more commonly φάραγξ υἱοῦ Ἐννὸμ Valley of the son of Hinnom (2 Kings xviii. 10; Jer. vii. 31, 32; xxxii. 35). And the Hebrew to which it corresponds is *the phrase* גֵּיא בֶן־הִנֹּם or גֵּי, Valley of the son of Hinnom (Jer. vii. 32 ; xix. 2, 6 ; 2 Chron. xxviii. 3; xxxiii. 6 ; Josh. xv. 8; xviii. 16, twice) ; גֵּי בְּנֵי הִנֹּם Valley of the sons of Hinnom (2 Kings xxiii. 10), and in two instances גֵּי הִנֹּם Valley of Hinnom (Neh. xi. 30 ; Josh. xv. 8).

Thus it appears from the date of Joshua to that of Chronicles to have been customary with the Jews to designate the locality in question, not by a word but by a phrase, and with the Septuagint translators to represent that Hebrew phrase by a variety of phrases, but in no instance by the precise word γέεννα, though in one case nearly approximating to it. The phrase or the word does not appear in the Apocrypha. But we learn from the later portions of the Old Testament that the locality itself had been invested with associations of the utmost abhorrence ; and, *some hundreds of years later*, a single word appears unquestionably derived from that phrase, yet differing from it in form, and employed by Targumist, Rabbin, the great Redeemer, and the Christian fathers alike, to designate the place of future punishment, with no cited instance in which it clearly bears any other meaning. We find Jerome designating the valley by the full phrase *vallis filiorum Ennom* (Hier. in Jer. vii. 22), and Eusebius in the "Onomasticon," φάραγξ τῶν υἱῶν Ἐννώμ, while the Arabs from the twelfth century to the present time call it by the full name, *Wady* (or valley) *Jehennam.*

We may accordingly accept the statement of Gesenius as a fair history of the word. He first describes the original locality itself under its full title, as "a valley on the south and east of Jerusalem, through which ran the southern boundary of the tribe of Benjamin, and the northern of Judah, famous for its human sacrifices offered to Moloch (2 Kings xxiii. 10; Jer. vii. 32; xix. 2, 6); also called Tophet, and by special distinction הַגַּיְא (the valley, Jer. ii. 23), Sept. ἐν τῷ πολυανδρίῳ, i.e. in the place of sepulchers; for such was the Valley of Hinnom. After these horrid sacrifices were abolished, the name of this valley, *contracted and changed* (Chald. גֵּיהִנָּם, Gr. in New Test. γεέννα), *began to be employed concerning hell and its torments,* — in my judgment, as though the chief abode of idolatry, i.e. of evil demons" (Thesaurus p. 280, 281). It is, therefore, in strict accordance with the facts of the case that Passow, in defining γεέννα, simply says, "A word borrowed from the Hebrew, *hell* (New Test. Ch. Fathers, Orac. Sib.")." Winer also states the case substantially in the same manner. After describing the locality from which the name was derived as a place "where, at various early periods, the ungodly Israelites offered their children to Moloch," he adds, "therefore was this place abhorred as profane, and, among the later Jews, with reference to the fires of Moloch, it served as a symbol of hell, the place of everlasting condemnation, which, therefore, was called γεέννα Chaldee גֵּיהִנָּם."

It has been often asserted that fires were kept constantly burning in the Valley of Hinnom to consume the filth and offal that were cast there. But Dr. Robinson denies that there is "evidence of any other fires having kept up in the valley than the original fires of Moloch (New Test. Lexicon, γεέννα, Bib. Res., vol. i. 404). Still more destitute of foundation is the assertion by Barnes and others, that "this valley was called *the gehenna of fire.*" Few terms have been the subject of more loose statements than this word γεέννα.

I am happy to confirm these statements by the full concurrence of my friend, Prof. E. P. Barrows of Andover. He writes, —

"*First*, That the Chaldee word גֵּיהִנָּם, the Greek γεέννα, represents, so far as mere derivation is concerned, the Hebrew גֵּי הִנֹּם (Josh. xv. 8), which is a compendium for the full expression גֵּי בֶן־הִנֹּם, that occurs in the same verse. A connecting link between the two occurs in Jonathan's Targum, Isa. lxvi. 24, in the form גֵּיהִנָּם.

"*Secondly*, That, in our Lord's day, the Chaldee גֵּיהִנָּם, and the Greek γεέννα, had come in well-established theological usage — probably long before the beginning of the Christian era — to signify hell, i.e. the *place of torment for the wicked*; and that this was the *only* sense of the word. The

Targum of Jonathan, which employs the word גֵּיהִנָּם (Isa. lxvi. 24) to denote the place of punishment of the wicked, uses the words בַּר חִנָּם חֵילָת as the equivalent of גֵּיא בֶן־הִנֹּם (Jer. xix. 2; xxxii. 35; Josh. xv. 8; 2 Kings xxiii. 10); and for גֵּי הִנֹּם (Josh. xv. 8) he uses, in like manner, חִנָּם חֵילָת. I have not access to the Targum on Chronicles, and therefore can not speak of 2 Chron. xxviii. 3; xxxiii. 6.

"How the word came to be thus employed is a question about which there is room for different opinions. . . . But, theory as to the manner of transfer aside, the transfer itself is certain. And it had become as complete in our Lord's day, as that of the word *pagan*, that is "villager," is in our day. As well might one say, that, when we use the word "pagan" we mean the inhabitant of a village, as when the New Testament, u conformity with all we know of the usage of the age, uses the word γέεννα, it refers to the pretended fires kept burning in the valley south of Jerusalem. I know of no passage in the Rabbinical writings where the word גֵּיהִנָּם means any thing else but the place where the wicked are punished. They tell us in one of their legends, puerile enough it is true, but pertinent to the point in question, that גֵּיהִנָּם was made on the *second* day, which is the reason why it is not said of that day, 'God saw that it was good.'—See in Buxtorf's Lexicon. But we know that the Valley of the son of Hinnom was made on the *third* day, when the dry land was separated from the water."

NOTE I.— Page 188.

FUTURE RETRIBUTION IN THE BOOK OF ENOCH.

We have not thought it necessary to encumber our text with extracts from this remarkable book; but, as Mr. Hudson has endeavored to confuse its clear testimony, the subject deserves a note.

The so-called Book of Enoch was alluded to by several of the Christian fathers of the second century (Irenæus, Clement of Alexandria, Origen, Tertullian), and was quoted in considerable fragments by Syncellus of the eighth century; but it was unknown as a whole until 1773, when Bruce, the traveler, brought from Abyssinia three copies of it in the Ethiopic language. It is known to have previously existed in Greek, and is thought by some, including Dillmann, to have come from a Hebrew (or Aramean) original.

The Ethiopian version was first translated into English, quite defectively, by Rev. R. Laurence (afterwards Archbishop of Cashel), in the year 1821; but was far more carefully translated into German, and more adequately edited by Dr. A. Dillmann in 1853. There were intermediate editions by Gfrörer and Hofmann, founded on the translation of Laurence; but Dillmann's edition is the only adequate one.

In the earlier discussions, on the basis of an imperfect edition, and from considerations connected with the quotation in Jude, several writers (Stuart, Lücke, Nitzsch, Weisse) regarded it as the work of a Christian writer, composed soon after the destruction of Jerusalem. Lücke, however, retracted his opinion, and adopted the now prevalent view, advocated by Davidson, Dillmann, Westcott, Köstlin, Ewald, that the book was written by a Jew some considerable time before the Christian era. Hilgenfeld adopts the same view as to the body of the work, which he assigns to the beginning of the first century before Christ; but he supposes interpolations by some Christian writer, not including the passages that bear on our argument. Of the other writers above mentioned, Ewald refers the composition of the ground-work to the period between B.C. 144 and B.C. 120, and the final form of the book to the first half of the century before Christ. Lücke refers the main part of it to the beginning of the Maccabæan struggle, and the remainder to the time of the rise of Herod the Great; Dillmann to the time of John Hyrcanus, B.C. 110; and Köstlin to the period between 110 and 64 B.C. This now general agreement as to the early date and Jewish origin of the book is quite noticeable.

Mr. Hudson firmly maintains the Jewish origin of the book, but endeavors to break the force of its testimony on the subject of future punishment (Debt and Grace, pp. 216-218).

Dillmann, in his elaborate edition of the work, makes, among others, the following statements: "The doctrine of the condition after death, the resurrection, and future retribution, holds a very prominent place in the author's system. Throughout his book, he often recurs to the subject, and gives very expanded statements concerning it, speaking more expressly and particularly than we read in any other author before the time of Christ. In chap. xxii., he enters upon a detailed description of Sheol; informs us in what part of the earth it is situated, and how it is so arranged that here, immediately after death, a first and preliminary retribution for the evil and the good can take place at once. He copiously describes Gehenna, the place of punishment for the theocratic sinners, in chaps. xxvi., xxvii., liv., lvi., xc.; and always names, as the means of punishment, fire and darkness, yet without indicating how the two can be supposed together. He describes also the hell of the fallen angels and the disobedient powers of nature; the lake of fire beyond the limits of heaven and earth, in empty space (Tartarus), chaps.

xviii., xix., xxi., xc. He delineates the resurrection of the dead, chaps. li., lxi.; and minutely describes the Messianic judgment upon the living and the dead, Jew and Heathen, the earthly and the heavenly, (chaps. xlvii., liii.–lvi., lxi.–lxiii., lxix., xc.), chiefly after the method of Daniel. . . . God, appearing with all the holy angels, and the Messiah, discriminate upon the deeds of men; and first the fallen angels, then the haughty heathen rulers who have oppressed the people, and all apostate Israelites, go to their eternal place of punishment, while on the other side, the church of the righteous is brought to its manifestation." (Einleitung, 19–21).

Such is the general drift of teaching on this subject, according to Dillmann's analysis. Now for a few specimens. First, the *immediate* doom of sinners. Chap. xxii. describes (as a communication from Raphael to Enoch) "a place in the west, under a great high mountain," a place "capacious and smooth, deep and dark," where "the spirits, the souls of the dead, are destined to be collected;" in which, however, there is to be a separation among the spirits. "And thus are the souls of the righteous separated: there is a water-fountain, and above it light.* Even so is there a like division made for sinners, when they die and are buried on earth, without being overtaken by judgment in their lifetime. Here will their souls be separated in this great suffering, until the great day of judgment and punishment and torment comes for the blasphemers, to eternity, and the vengeance on their souls; and here they are confined till eternity. And since it is before the eternity [i.e. the final doom: Dillmann], therefore is this separation † for the souls of those who make outcry and complaint of their overthrow, because they were destroyed in the day of sinners: so has it been done for the souls of men who were not righteous, but sinners ripened in guilt,— they shall be with the wicked, and like them, but their souls shall not be put to death in the day of judgment, nor shall they come out from hence." There is no ambiguity here. Again (chap. xxvii.): "This cursed valley is for those who shall be cursed to eternity. Here must be gathered all those who utter with their mouths unseemly words against God, and speak irreverently of his glory; here shall they be collected, and here shall be the place of their punishment. And in the last time, an example will be made of a righteous judgment upon them before the saints, to eternity always. Thereupon will they who found mercy praise the Lord of glory, the eternal King." Again, with singular similarity to

---

* We follow Dillmann where he deviates from Laurence.
† An additional or second division for the wicked. — See Dillmann.

the Saviour's phrase, the severity of their doom is thus described (chap. xxxviii.): "When the light of the righteous, and of the elect who dwell on the earth, shall shine forth, where shall then be the dwelling of sinners, and the abode of those who have denied the Lord of spirits? It would have been better for them had they never been born."

The fate and the abode of the fallen angels and their partners in guilt is thus described (chap. xxi.): "And from thence I passed on to another place, still more terrible than the other, and saw something dreadful. A great fire was there, that flamed and blazed; and it had divisions. It was bounded by an absolute abyss, and great pillars of fire dropped down therein. Its extent and greatness I could not discern, nor could I discover its origin. Then said I, 'How terrible is this place! and what torture to look upon it!' Then answered me Uriel, one of the holy angels who was with me,— he answered, and said unto me, 'Enoch, why art thou alarmed and amazed at this terrible place, at sight of this place of suffering?' And he said unto me, 'This place is the prison of the angels, and here will they be kept imprisoned to eternity.'" To a similar fiery abode (chaps. xviii., xix.,) are condemned the disobedient stars, "bound," and "rolling over the fire;" here too are the angels who cohabited with women, and the women their companions. The same place is described (chap. xc.) as "the place of punishment," "a place full of fire, flaming, and full of pillars of fire," "fiery deeps," into which were cast the stars, the unfaithful shepherds, and the blinded sheep.

The resurrection is asserted (chap. li.) thus: "In those days shall the earth give back that which was intrusted to it, and the kingdom of the dead shall give back what was intrusted to it, and destruction shall give up what it owes. And he will select the righteous and the holy from among them; for the day of their salvation has come." Again, chap. lxi. 5: "And these measures shall reveal all that was hidden in the depths of the earth; and those who perished throughout the deserts, and those that were devoured by the fish of the sea and by the beasts, shall return, and trust upon the day of the Elect [the Messiah]; since none shall perish in the presence of the Lord of spirits, nor shall any be capable of perishing." So also the resurrection of the righteous is affirmed in chaps. xci., xcii., c.

Among the scenes of judgment, we are told (chap. lxii.), "In that day shall all the kings, the princes, the exalted, and those who possess the earth, stand up and see, and know that He is sitting on the throne of his glory. . . . Trouble shall come upon them as upon a woman in travail. One portion of them shall look upon another. They shall be astonished, and shall humble their countenances, and trouble shall seize them, when they see this Son of the woman sitting on the throne of his glory. . . . And all the mighty kings, and the exalted, and those who rule over the earth, shall fall down on their faces before him, and shall worship him. They shall fix their hopes on this Son of man, shall pray to him, and beseech him for mercy. Then shall the Lord of spirits hasten to expel them from his presence. Their faces shall be full of confusion, and darkness shall cover their faces. And the angels of punishment shall take them to inflict retribution upon 'them, because they oppressed his children and elect."

The final portion of the wicked is thus set forth (chap. ciii.) : " Woe to you, sinners, when you die in your sins, and they who are like you say, respecting you, ' Blessed are these sinners, they have lived out their whole period, and now they die in happiness and in wealth. Distress and slaughter they knew not while alive; in honor they die; nor ever in their lifetime did judgment overtake them.' Know you not that into the kingdom of the dead your souls shall go down, and they shall fare ill, and great shall be your misery? And into darkness, and into sorrows, and into burning flame, will your spirit go at the great judgment; and the great judgment shall be for all generations to eternity. Woe unto you; for you have no peace!"

The book closes (chap. cviii.) with the contrasted destinies of the righteous and the wicked. "Another writing which Enoch wrote for his son Methuselah, and for those who come after him, and who will have kept the law in the last days. You who have done so, and now wait in those days till the evil-doers shall have made an end, and the power of evil shall have reached an end, wait until sin pass away; for their name shall be blotted out from the books of the holy, and they shall cry out and lament in a waste, desert place, and shall burn in fire where there is no earth. Then I perceived, as it were, a cloud which I could not clearly discern; for from its depth I could not look up to it. And the flame of its fire I saw burn bright; and it whirled like a glittering mountain, and was agitated from side to side. Then I inquired of one of the holy angels who were with me, and said, ' What is that glittering object? for it is not heaven, but the flame of a burning fire, and the sound of outcry and weeping and lamentations and extreme suffering.' And he said to me, 'That place which thou seest, — into it shall be brought the spirits of the sinners and blasphemers, and of those who do evil and prevent all that God spoke by the mouth of the prophets concerning future things. . . . And I' [says God] ' will bring forth into splendid light those who loved my holy name; and I will place each on a throne of glory,— his own glory. And they shall shine ages without number.' For righteous is the judgment of God : to the true he will give truth in the habitations of uprightness; and they shall see how those who were born in darkness into darkness shall be cast, while the righteous shine. And the sinners shall cry out, and shall see them as they shine; and also they shall go thither, where days and times are prescribed for them."

These extracts might be greatly increased; but, as they are decisive, we refrain. Nor do we care to examine in detail Mr. Hudson's faint attempts to confuse the testimony. In the presence of these distinct and varied declarations that the wicked enter upon a state of conscious suffering at death, that they and the fallen angels are doomed to eternal suffering cotemporaneous with the blessedness of the righteous, it is of no avail for him to remark that " the book is as silent respecting immortality, as the Scriptures themselves,"— a proposition which we have no occasion to dispute; or that " some of the expressions may denote eternity of effect," — for a sufficient number and variety of them cannot be so evaded; or that " the style of the book is highly dramatic,"— the feeblest of all rejoinders to its accumulated testimony. To say that " the expression, 'their souls shall not be annihilated in the day of judgment,' does not necessarily imply that they will *never* be annihilated," is certainly a very narrow foothold in itself, and disappears before the express statements concerning their subsequent fate of woe. The perpetual juggle on the words "perish," "consumed," "slain," "destroyed," is extinguished by the explanations of the context in many instances, which puts words into the mouths, and suffering into the souls, of these slain and perished persons. Thus one of Mr. Hudson's quotations — " our spirits have been consumed, lessened, and diminished"— is uttered by the victims themselves, who immediately add, in still intenser forms, "*we have perished*, have been tormented and destroyed " (chap. ciii.). Another of his quotations, — " Their names shall be blotted out from the holy book; their seed shall be destroyed, and their souls slain"— is *immediately* followed by a statement which he does not see fit to quote: " They shall cry out and lament in the invisible waste ; and in the fire shall they burn" (cv. Laurence, cviii. Dillmann). The word " slain " here, as Dillmann shows, signifies " the eternal death, the wearing-away of the spirit in everlasting pain." Others of his few quotations admit of the same explanation, while some of them (e.g. ch. xc.) evidently refer only to the removal of the wicked from the earth. The Book of Enoch is a difficult text-book for annihilationists.

As this book gives the Jewish opinions one or two centuries before

Christ, we also subjoin the testimony of Hippolytus in the second century after Christ. In describing the Jewish sects, he speaks first of the Essenes. "They strongly hold the doctrine of the resurrection; for they profess that the flesh also will be raised, and will become immortal, as the soul is already immortal; this [soul], they say, having departed to a light and airy place, which the Greeks hearing of called islands of the blessed, remains there till the judgment. . . . And they say there will be a judgment, and a conflagration of the universe; and the wicked will be punished for ever." (Lib. ix. 27.) His statement concerning the doctrine of the Pharisees may be found on page 377 of his volume, and is very express in regard to the eternal *duration* of the punishment. His testimony concerning the Sadducees conforms to that of the Scriptures and of Josephus; and he adds that the sect prevailed largely in Samaria. To this sect alone, he ascribes the entire denial of immortality and of retribution. "They deny a resurrection of the flesh, and think that the soul does not continue to exist; that it has life only, and for this purpose only was never made; but the notion of the resurrection is fulfilled in our leaving children on the earth when we die. But after death they hope to experience neither good nor evil; for there will be a dissolution both of soul and body; and man, like other animals, departs into non-existence." (Lib. ix. 29.)

www.ingramcontent.com/pod-product-compliance
Lightning Source LLC
Chambersburg PA
CBHW031413230426
43668CB00007B/298